"THIS IS NEW YORK,
HONEY!"

A Homage to Manhattan, with Love and Rage

"THIS IS NEW YORK, HONEY!"

A Homage to Manhattan, with Love and Rage

Michele Landsberg

CANADIAN CATALOGUING IN PUBLICATION
DATA
Landsberg, Michele, 1939–
This is New York, honey

ISBN 0-7710-4654-5

1. New York (N.Y.) – Description – 1981-
2. New York (N.Y.) – Social conditions.   I. Title.

F128.55.L3 1989   974.7'10443   C89–
095120–9

Design by T. M. Craan

Printed and bound in the U.S.A.

McClelland & Stewart Inc.
The Canadian Publishers
481 University Avenue
Toronto, Ontario
M5G 2E9

CONTENTS

For Stephen
It goes without saying

Acknowledgements:

With keen gratitude to my editor, David Kilgour, and to all the friends, colleagues, and acquaintances who helped me in their different but uniformly generous ways to discover New York, among them: Linsey Abrams, Maria Antonia Alonso, Esther and Bob Broner, Julie Bruck, Mary Carmen and Carmen Martinez, Ellen Charney, Phyllis Chesler, Liz diLauro, Edith Isaac-Rose, Beverly Jablons, Bea Kreloff, Dorothea Lang, Anne Lewison and Paul Ratnofsky, Jimmy McFadyen, Betsy and Phil Pochoda, Letty Cottin Pogrebin, Lilly Rivlin, and Ann Volkes.

A Note to the Reader

Columns previously published in the *Globe and Mail* are indicated with vertical lines in the margins.

INTRODUCTION

■

"Only in New York!" It's a mantra, a boast, a consolation. Shaking their heads in mock exasperation, New Yorkers exchange the ritual phrase at the scene of fights, accidents, impromptu street theatre, or any eruption of Manhattan-style absurdity.

Tourists take up the chant. In 1987, the Whitney museum filled several rooms with a life-size three-dimensional comic book by artist Red Grooms. "Manhattan Ruckus" was a bright, knowing, cock-eyed celebration of the city's garish excitements and lurid shocks. Good-humoured crowds unwittingly recreated the life outside the museum as they crushed in to walk through jaunty papier-mâché buildings, teeter over rickety bridges, and, best of all, stand in a rocking, roaring, graffiti-smeared replica of a subway car, with its papier-mâché inhabitants leering and lolling with the sway of the car. "Only in New York!" In another room, a Red Grooms western ranch scene drew polite and passing glances. The real thrill was to become a participant in an artwork of one's own New York experience.

Critics warn that New York is in danger of losing its soul, becoming a theme park for tourists. And it's true that New York devours itself. A world centre of the arts, and happy recipient of more than $2.5 billion a year spent by tourists drawn by its musical, graphic, and theatrical splendours, it devotes far less to its arts than any other city: only a fraction of one per cent of its municipal budget.

But no matter; New York spawned unimaginable wealth when other cities were sleepy towns, and therefore has an inexhaustible legacy of museums, music, architecture, history, literature, and paintings to keep its legend alive.

New York mythologizes itself. In our minds, wherever on this continent we grew up, New York had the weight and

■

heft of a place more real than real. Fragments of song rattle around in our heads: East side, west side . . . . the sunny side of the street . . . *don't be late* for the Harlem strutters' ball.

The richest city on earth, New York is our universal icon of the glittering possibilities and horrifying underside of urban life. Its largest single export is waste paper. Garbage barges from New York dispiritedly wander the high seas. Medical garbage washes onto its beaches; sunbathers, escaping the city's heat and menace, find AIDS-tainted needles and blood vials in the sand: memento mori. And every month, two or three dead babies turn up in garbage bags and bins in the bleakest slums, a reminder of the city's profligate disregard of individual lives.

How can anyone love so monstrous a city? Ask any of its ninety thousand hopeful new immigrants every year; ask any of its inhabitants, who could leave if they wished, but can't bear to cut themselves off from the centre of vitality and power. The "New" in "New York" is real; like a giant machine, the city creates the newest songs, books, fashions, ideas, slang, monsters, and master-minds that will be tomorrow's news in Halifax or Hong Kong. The newness is a constant stimulant, an addictive drug. Banished to anywhere else, New Yorkers feel deprived, diminished by not being part of the newest and latest.

When my husband, Stephen Lewis, was appointed Canada's ambassador to the United Nations in the fall of 1984, the news came in a phone call. I overheard his half of the conversation. "Yes, Mr. Prime Minister. . . . The United Nations? Well . . ." I was hopping around the room in an agony of suspense, breathing, "New York? New York! Oh, do it!"

He did it, and we were transported overnight to everyone's dream of New York: an enormous apartment in the centre of Manhattan, ready and furnished, with household staff standing by, car and driver at the door. Living in unaccustomed luxury had to affect my view of New York, of course, just as a tourist, revelling in holiday freedom and hotel room service, sometimes sees a foreign place in glossier colours than it deserves. But I also worked in New York;

roamed the streets; made friends; lined up for postage stamps and movie tickets; took the subway everywhere; lived more in my sneakers than in my Mrs. Ambassador dresses.

Besides, my fascination with the city predated my sudden stroke of luck. Every city in the world has its appeal, but none draws me like New York. Of course, city love, like sexual attraction, is deeply personal and idiosyncratic. To say that I love New York is not to deride the loyalty others have for Vancouver or Montreal; comparing cities is as fruitless as comparing husbands. And no love is uncomplicated. I set out to write a book, incorporating some of the columns I originally wrote for the *Globe and Mail*, which would be a light-hearted record of my life in New York. Mysterious things happened as I sat at my computer in Toronto. I relived my Manhattan delights, but I also lived again my frustration over racism, poverty, and runaway development; happiness and outrage are as commingled in this book as they are in me.

This isn't meant to be a travel book, though the pleasures of exploring the city are important, and are described in some detail. And I've included a short but, I hope, practical selection of recommended New York guidebooks at the end. On the whole, though, I've tried to reflect the shocks, raptures, preoccupations, and perplexities of a newcomer to the metropolis. My reactions are necessarily personal; there are eight million versions of New York, and this one is mine.

This book also reflects the unreasoning attachment anyone might feel to any great city, especially an attachment formed in childhood, when the intoxicating promise of city life is inseparable from the excited hopes of twentieth-century youth.

My first trip anywhere outside southern Ontario was to New York; I was a schoolchild when my parents, my brother, and I came for a visit during Christmas holidays. Toronto was such a quiet town, then, criss-crossed with hydro wires and bound in by strict convention, that Torontonians actually thought of Buffalo as an excitingly wicked hot spot.

Grand Central Station was my first cathedral. From dark to dark we came on the CNR: from the thrilling and unaccustomed pre-dawn blackness of our front porch in Toronto, where we puffed "smoke" into the icy air and stamped our galoshes in excruciating impatience to be gone; then rattling down all day through the frozen fields, restless and finally groggy on the rough upholstered seats of the train; decanted at last, sleepy and overawed, into the echoing, vaulted dimness of Grand Central Station. The immense space muffled our voices and footsteps; waiting by the clock for our relatives to meet us, I clutched my mother's hand and lolled my head back. More than a hundred feet above, a tangle of starry constellations wove and blurred in the huge indoor dusk.

Far behind me, Toronto's Union Station, the only palace of my childhood, instantly shrivelled and drooped like a pricked balloon.

We stayed with my Aunt Ann and Uncle Ben in their little box of an apartment in the Bronx. Everything in New York was astonishing. It was 1948, I was nine years old, and I knew nothing about New York from movies, songs, or books. Uncle Ben, a taxi driver, proudly showed us the sights. We drove down the Bowery to see the bums sleeping in doorways.

"But do they sleep there all night?" Ungraspable. The grown-ups laboured to explain, amused by my horror. "But where are their wives?" Finally they grew too bored to explain any more about drunkenness and falling through the bottom of the known world. We drove down Wall Street, rubber-necking, said my uncle, and I rolled this new word around in my mouth, savouring its rude slanginess. We zoomed to the top of the Empire State Building; the wind up there on the observation deck stopped my breath in my throat and blinded me to the city below; it was the exhilaration of terror.

At the Automat, I dropped a nickel in the slot, opened the little door, and took out a piece of apple pie. For the first time, I saw food uncomplicated by love, labour, or gratitude; it was a miracle of the future, a vision of effortless, impersonal, automated abundance, and I swallowed it marvelling.

At Times Square, awash in light, waterfalls and rivers of light, news running around buildings in light, we stared in rapture at a giant woman, her head flung back, a Camel tilted in her fingers, giant rings of smoke puffing from her mouth more miraculously than water struck from a rock.

We went to Radio City Music Hall in the subway, which no one had thought to explain to me in advance. I had known only the sedate Toronto streetcars, rocking along at a matronly pace, cosy with the familiar smell of wet wood floors and steaming mittens. Now, thundering and rocketing through pitch-dark tunnels under New York, dizzy with speed and amazement, I clung to a pole and abruptly threw up.

There was not even time to register the disgrace; in a moment we were ascending majestic staircases, sitting in splendour, gasping at the machine perfection of the Rockettes. They showed a movie, *Slaughter on Tenth Avenue*: Apache dancers, erotic and violent in disturbing combination; a man loved a woman and stabbed her. And even before I could absorb this latest astonishing revelation of previously unsuspected adult mysteries, we were rushed from there in a river of people and were suddenly sitting in the Latin Quarter, a real night-club with a live radio show in progress, and before I could consult the matinée menu, I was being whisked between the packed tables to the stage to participate in the broadcast. It was a story-telling contest with four or five of us children winkled out of the audience; one boy started a story, and each of us had to carry forward the narration. I was last, and it was easy; stories were what I knew about, and I could see the eyes of the frantically cheerful announcer signalling me that it was time to wrap up, so on one gulp of breath I drew all the story's loose ends together in a gabble of a finale, and the audience's applause made me the fifty-dollar grand-prize winner. And no sooner was I flushed and triumphant in my seat again, glowing under the beamed approval of my mother and my Aunt Sue, than they were calling my number for the door prize: a necklace and a bracelet with a tiny heart of blue on gold.

My Aunt Ann, at home in the Bronx, heard our elevator arrive like a chariot clattering home with the spoils. At the end of a long corridor, she threw open her door and screamed, "I heard you on the radio!"

All down the long hall, doors banged open and neighbours leaned out, exchanging the news; I sailed forward to my aunt's welcoming embrace like a returned warrior through the crowd's hurrahs.

On New Year's Eve, left alone with my aunt and uncle's newest amazement, a small and blurry black and white television set, my brother and I peered at the screen until our eyes ached, vainly parsing the crowds in Times Square to glimpse our relatives. And then, silly and wild with the collective merriment (who could imagine that grown-ups would be so uninhibited in public? Never in Canada!), we prised open the window and leaned into the sad and dreary air shaft and called "Happy New Year!" to the walls.

Subways, smoking billboards, sexy dancers, machine dancers, television, skyscrapers, fame and prizes sprinkled over me as lightly, effortlessly as confetti. . .

I didn't get a chance to visit New York again until I was eighteen. It had never crossed my mind that I could go back to this miraculous city. It was a mirage of the glittering future, and I a one-time space voyager.

The years of New York's terrible slide towards bankruptcy, in the 1970s, finished off that envious Canadian dictum: "It's a wonderful place to visit, but I wouldn't want to live there!" Now, no one even talked of visiting. New York's eclipse meant that a nagging little toothache of comparison was soothed. Toronto and Vancouver basked in self-congratulation; from New York's civic shipwreck, fragments of bleak news washed up on our shores and were eagerly pounced on, images of a city looting its way through blackouts and heat waves; the sullen background glare of slums burning; filth in the gutters, prowlers on the streets, armed guards in the schools, ruin and debauchery; frightened New Yorkers huddling behind their curtains while Kitty Genovese was stalked and murdered in the streets below.

And even when New York rebounded in the eighties, it was still tourist New York we admired. Broadway, the

Empire State Building, Bloomingdale's. Like many other Canadian visitors, my husband and I went for the opera, the theatre, the Metropolitan Museum, the Sunday shuffle past the famous stores on Fifth Avenue.

When I moved there, I gradually discovered a whole new reality: the special quality of life in a great metropolis lies not just in the cultural peaks and splendours, but also in the smallest daily transactions. I learned that new adventures, insights, and pleasures awaited me every time I stepped out my door and onto the New York streets. Any willing explorer can follow me there; to walk in New York is the beginning.

CHAPTER I
·
If You Walk . . . .

A week after I moved to Manhattan in the sultry summer of 1985, I stepped out my front door one morning and was struck by a dizzy joy, a lightning conviction that I belonged here, that I should have been born here, that being born in Toronto had been a terrible mistake, and that by sheer dazzling random luck I had been floated effortlessly and unsuspecting to what I now saw was my promised land.

Sunlight touched the feathery little trees along 62nd Street, the air held the moist, fresh promise of big-city summer mornings, and even the pavement beneath my feet sparkled subtly . . . a trick, I later learned, of mica mixed in the concrete.

Given that American politics outraged every political fibre of my being (and all my fibres are political), that I was revolted by the 1980s glut of heartless wealth, and that I feared sudden heat-stroke death in the steamy tropical New York summers, my falling in love was a surprise.

Nevertheless, for the next three years, I opened my eyes every morning with the tingling anticipation of a child waking on her birthday, and I never left New York, even for a holiday or family visit at home in Canada, without a long backward look at the Manhattan skyline and a sense of acute deprivation.

What could account for the infatuation? When I left Toronto, my ears rang with the parting admonitions of friends and acquaintances: "Watch out for muggers!" "Don't go in Central Park!" "Whatever you do, don't take the subway!" The fearfulness of megalopolitan life was dinned into me. And yet, I knew from frequent weekend trips that New York offered unparallelled riches of opera, galleries, museums, shops, concerts, and theatre. Menace and cultural splendours – the two polar extremes best known to the visitor.

What I couldn't know until I lived there was that walking the streets, the simplest and most mundane of all activities, could be intoxicating and addictive and one of the things I would love most. The streets of New York are superabundant with life, colour, action, and anecdote; they're like a river of stories you can dip into and out of for as much humour, poignancy, or drama as your soul requires at the moment. I know that had I moved to Manhattan to take a job as a Woolworth's clerk, the crowded streets would probably not have enchanted me as they did. But writing is a solitary task. To plunge from my silent, eight-by-nine-foot writing cupboard into the tidal surge of the streets was like an instant charge of electricity.

Already, that morning soon after my arrival, I was savouring the unique diversity of the crowds. Traffic poured down Park Avenue; on the corner, the tough-looking limousine drivers had set out their folding chairs and basked in the sun while their bosses enjoyed a "power breakfast" at the Regency Hotel down the block. Here came the dog walker, coolly in control – and ready to glare at any intrusive would-be patters or cluckers – of an élite little convoy of Afghans, Lhasa apsos, and Yorkshire terriers. Grocery delivery boys rattled past on their wheeled carts; early shoppers headed for Madison Avenue; Sal, the plump and loose-lipped homeless man on our block, still slept on the stairs of the doughty Colonial Club across the street; crisp professionals quick-walked with their briefcases; the doormen emerged all along the street to squint up at the blue sky and exchange pleasantries; a blind man, a giggle of teenagers, a musician with a guitar case . . .

Like millions of iron filings, people stream to magnetic New York, and their mere presence in one place is a million-fold mutual confirmation: to be there is to have arrived somewhere central and magnificent. So much haste, ambition, and urgency pour through the streets that you can't but feel a vicarious intensity.

And there's an extra intoxicant of defiant liberty. You are here; you have shaken off the constraints and narrowness of your home town, and you are startled to find yourself besotted by the sheer din and press of the crowds. You realize that people everywhere else are congratulating themselves on their lovely trees and fresh air, and you know that generations of city planners and pontificators have pronounced their disgust at so much concrete, congestion, and filth, and with a burst of inward and rebellious joy, you feel exactly what Walt Whitman wrote: "Keep your splendid, silent sun/Keep your woods, O Nature . . . /Give me faces and streets . . . . give me the streets of Manhattan!"

Of course, Whitman was exulting over erotic possibilities in the city of "interminable eyes . . . comrades and lovers by the thousands." But you don't have to be a sexual adventurer to feel in your veins the pulse of the possible. The city, humming that morning with sunlight, heat, and possibility, took me in, swallowed me up democratically with the millions of others; in a week, anonymous and alive, I felt both freer and more at home than I'd ever felt on the politely neutral sidewalks of my native Toronto.

New York is surely the world's most accessible great city. Other capitals have their mesmerizing beauties and charms, but none other in my experience enfolds you so nonchalantly. My aunt has lived for nearly fifty years in Paris, and is still considered a foreigner; stay in London for a week and snide clerks, while relieving you of your coin, will let you know how contemptibly outlandish you are.

Relentlessly mercantile New York, on the other hand, does not bother to place you – at least not while you are on the street. Partly this cheerful indifference is due to the chaotically diverse nature of the people and the sheer variety of activity, legitimate and illegitimate, that fills its streets around the clock. New York has always been America's port of entry for tides of unprivileged immigrants; the earliest visitors to New Amsterdam were already complaining about the city's foreign "riff-raff" of Jews and blacks, and energetic riff-raff has been pouring in undeterred ever since – Irish, Italian, Jewish, Chinese, Vietnamese, Korean, Haitian, Puerto Rican, Arab and Israeli, Afghani and Indian, legal and illegal, filling the streets with a polychrome vitality that triumphs over neighbourhood homogeneity. Gloriously, liberatingly, New York shrugs; its distinctive tone is a tolerance, a positive relish, for difference and eccentricity.

Physically, the place invites you. Thanks to the grid system, much maligned by urban commentators ("rumoured to have been based on a mason's seive," sniffed one writer), and thanks to the numbered streets, the newcomer quickly feels confident. Manhattan is so small – twenty-three square miles – and so crowded that virtually everywhere is downtown, and uses overlap tumultuously. You are never more than a doorstep away from the life of the city.

As a weekend visitor, I had spent my time in theatres, museums, or concert halls. Though I was stunned to observe the throngs on the sidewalks, I never took time to join them for longer than it took me to get to my destination. But once I was living there, I quickly discovered that I was as drawn to the street as I was to more celebrated sites. I would set out for a shop or a gallery and end up finding excuses to prolong my walk. The glory of this street life is that it's as open to a twenty-four-hour tourist as it is to an *habitué*.

William Whyte, the amiable scholar of cities, says that urbanites are naturally drawn to crowds. A downtown corner that clocks fewer than a thousand pedestrians an hour marks a dead, defeated city centre; he has actually surveyed my home turf – the corner of Lexington and 59th – and measured the flow at five thousand an hour.

Elsewhere, cities sprawl and meander; green suburbs for the middle class and wealthy are tucked into the centre, a luxury of privacy and peace that comes at the cost of walkability and interest. No Canadian city, in fact, has Manhattan's intense urbanity of brownstones, mansions, tenements, apartment buildings, and town houses lining the streets, cheek by jowl with busy avenues of shops. Luckily, Manhattan has not an inch to spare for strip plazas, vast supermarkets, and surface parking lots. Where the street has been spared the depredations of developers, you walk between harmonious rows of five-storey brownstones, each narrow enough that you are continually amused by the variety of little stores with their goods displayed intimately at your elbow. The scale fits the human body, surrounds you, nudges your attention with infinite pleasing or startling details.

Wherever modern developers have muscled their way in, here or elsewhere, stores are sure to be set back at a glassy distance or at fancy angles, above or below street level or removed entirely to a mall, with windswept, littered, empty space going to waste. Walking, you feel unanchored.

Where the old still stands, the feeling is European and adult. In most parts of Manhattan, movies, bookstores, small groceries, restaurants, bars, and even theatres and galleries are within a few minutes' walk, so you can spontaneously slip out the door after dinner and stroll down the block to the show. Morning, noon, and night, the city lures you out of doors with its public vivacity. In more suburban cities, people go home to their families, close the door, and stay in.

Urban experts are always deploring the way bulldozers long ago levelled Manhattan's topography and built up every inch in monotonous short blocks. To me, it's a boon. The regular rhythm of short blocks means that new possibilities open at corners every two hundred feet; you can zig and zag and change your route on the spur of the moment as fresh streetscapes invite your exploration. And level ground – no hills to pant up – is bliss to the pedestrian.

Within a few days you will have adopted the New York walk. Rapidly, skilfully, you negotiate the jammed sidewalks at twice your home-town pace; triumphant as an athlete at the end of a well-played game, you conquer the congestion. Half a block ahead, you calculate the swerve you will need to skirt the sidewalk bazaar of the Senegalese pedlar at the corner; you've measured the crowd and planned your quick crossing to the other side of the street; you've figured out that gridlock at the stop-light will let you cut daringly through the stalled traffic without losing a single beat to the pedestrian red light. You pass, cut in, advance on a surge of skill and adrenalin; just getting to the corner store to buy a bunch of flowers can have the drama of a sailboat race.

■

And there's another reason for the exhilaration a new-comer feels on the streets. People in New York have a wry self-awareness as denizens of an impossible place: corrupt, overcrowded, dangerous, filthy, and irresistibly, crazily exciting. People are aware of themselves as *New Yorkers*, a special breed; they write letters to the papers describing nutty street and subway incidents; they read about their familiar landmarks, streets, restaurants, and fellow citizens in novels, hear them celebrated in songs, poems, plays, movies; they see themselves as players on a stage, and the whole soaring and glorifying architecture of the place confirms them in their specialness. Look up at the mosaics and murals in the Fuller Building, the Equitable, the Woolworth Building, in banks or public housing, high schools or even some subway entrances, and you will see the workers who built the place immortalized.

New York, centre of publishing, communications, and the arts, celebrates itself constantly. Every street name has resonance; whether we listened to the Metropolitan Opera on our radios in Toronto or read Whitman and Wharton in Manitoba, we are all surrogate citizens, and those who arrive here, like those to the city born, consciously live up to it.

Watch the police hold back a surge of St. Patrick's Day celebrants or an unruly mob of demonstrators outside an embassy, and note their seen-it-all unruffleability. Their seemingly infinite tolerance for the mad, the excited, the dishevelled, and the merely drunk is calming; whatever is going on, they've seen far worse.

The sense of being a player in an important drama is probably essential to enjoying life in a crowded, tense, rushed, and often abrasive metropolis. It's also a great alibi. Nothing sums up the New York attitude so pungently as an anecdote I read in a newspaper. A rain-sodden student, after vainly trying to hail a cab during a thunderstorm, finally succeeded in flagging one down, only to have an elegantly clothed older woman leap ruthlessly in ahead of her. "This is New York, honey!" sneered the older woman (read: "This is

New *Yawk*, honey!"). Outraged, the student snatched the door open, socked the usurper, and snarled right back, "Yeah, this is New York, honey!"

I relished this story, not as an example of New Yorkers' rudeness, but of their instinctive claim to an archetypal urban character that can be used as an automatic justification for any outrageousness.

On the street, the feeling of ordinary life being part of a larger narrative is bracing. You may be a stranger, but you are never at a loss for a fellow observer to share an ironic appreciation of the passing show. On Park Avenue, a trim-suited businessman hurrying north past the Seagram's Building as I rush south is consciously practising pedestrian flair, slicing through the crowds as I am; suddenly, a black man on a skateboard, singing loudly, wearing a winged purple helmet, crimson backpack, brilliant yellow gloves, and skin-tight spandex pants, blazes south on a finely calculated diagonal between us. The businessman and I exchange amused glances at this flashing incongruity and skill, the nonchalantly satirical comment of the skateboard on our own self-important hurry, and we laugh out loud together.

Because every neighbourhood is so freckled with diversity, the ceaseless crowds are never monotonous. In shopping malls anywhere – like Toronto's Eaton Centre, for example, which ravaged Yonge Street by moving the shops indoors – the crowds are made up of citizens reduced to the single dull function of shopping. Except for the teenage idlers, people seem tense or listlessly exhausted, politely avoiding eye contact and taking no interest in each other.

But on Manhattan streets, the crowds are enlivened by sheer diversity of purpose. Many are there to con you or sell you something: three-card monte dealers, setting up shop with a cardboard box, a tattered deck of cards, keen sleight-of-hand skills, and a couple of confederates disguised as eagerly betting members of the crowd, are acting out an elaborate comedy. Wherever someone is trying to sell, trick, preach, or perform, a small crowd eddies around, and lively conversations ensue. New Yorkers are voluble, gregarious, and love to be in the know, offer directions, or comment sagely on the passing scene.

And something is always happening. In New York at midnight, a block from my sedate front door, I encounter secret servicemen, with walkie-talkie wires attached to their ears and bulges under their suit jackets, buying fresh-squeezed orange juice from the Korean grocer; they are bodyguards for a foreign dignitary staying at the Regency, taking a coffee break in the middle of their shift. Jostling between them are a muttering bag lady, a restaurant owner stepping from his white limousine to collect the night's receipts while late diners are still eating at tables open to the sidewalk, a couple in tuxedo and evening gown carrying an armful of orchids returning from a publicity party at Bloomingdale's (the rented spotlights are still criss-crossing the night sky above the store from the flat-bed trucks double-parked on Lexington) and a crowd of movie-goers walking home from the half-dozen cinemas on Third Avenue.

The family of aproned grocers rearranging the apples in the sidewalk display, the Haitian cab driver leaning on his car to drink a take-out coffee, the newsie slinging bundles of the *New York Times* off the back of a truck, the cashmere-clad man walking his Yorkie, and I, a journalist just finished writing to deadline, are like a chorus of observers; several of us exchange sad smiles and civically disgusted raised eyebrows as we note two homeless people rummaging hopefully in the garbage outside the croissant bakery.

At midnight, in my midtown neighbourhood in Toronto, all will be darkness and silent houses; the stores will be closed; the streets empty; a single car accelerating around the corner will rouse irritated sleepers from their peace.

Here, the drama of diversity is still playing to its cease-lessly changing audience. This is my third errand today on foot, and each time I have walked through a dozen vignettes whose import has been noted and shared by alert strangers.

Only a week after arriving, I had fallen in love with the streets of New York, the crowded, jostling, hot, filthy, infinitely exciting and promising streets that would infallibly, for the next three years, greet me every day and night with that same exhilarating jump of my heart, that surge of anticipation and pure, unreasoning, helpless happiness.

Across the glassy surface of the ornamental lake, shimmering like a Monet painting with the reflected pink of blossoming trees, a tiny row-boat advances with tiny musical splashings of the oars. A mechanical man is rowing; with each stroke he leans stiffly forward and bends his elbows, and his sweater rides up at the back. He is a marvel of miniature realism. Sailboats swoop past him in long parabolas: two sloops, a cutter, and even a rosy-sailed schooner, five feet tall.

You can't walk a block in Manhattan without being amused, startled, or fascinated. I stumbled onto this scene of hallucinatory tranquillity in Central Park, just out of earshot of the hoot and roar of New York traffic. The boats are radio-operated by elderly hobbyists, who proudly explained that the sailboats are propelled only by the breeze, with the shorebound skippers manipulating sheets and tillers by remote-control device; the row-boat is moved solely by the little clockwork dipping of its oars.

"Where can I get one?" asked a woman in a track suit.

"You want the whole schmear?" a boat handler replied.

"I'm the producer of *A Long Day's Journey Into Night*," the woman explained parenthetically to me as I lent her a pencil to write down the address of a hobby store. "It opens on Broadway tonight, and here I am relaxing. Isn't that ridiculous?"

New York, the neophyte soon learns, is not the dark, dirty, and dangerous canyon of popular imagination. New York is beautiful, and New York is a walker's heaven.

You may be maddened by the surging pedestrian crowds or the gridlocked, blaring traffic ("Don't even

THINK of honking. Fine: $50" says a futile new sign above the cacophony), but you can't be bored. After living here for two and a half seasons, I am still astonished and galvanized by the amount of sunshine, the energy on the streets, and the variegated beauty of the buildings.

You walk nearly everywhere, because Manhattan is tiny, and it's faster on foot, and because the streetscapes are so crammed with interest. It must be because New York was densely built up by the early part of this century, when wealth was still exuberant and decoration was not yet a naughty word.

In my Upper East Side neighbourhood, the streets actually seem furnished. Curly wrought iron is lavished everywhere, in gates, banisters, window grilles, and the tender curve of a romantic balcony. The town houses rise straight from the pavement, with their front doors up or down a few steps and each with some small delight for the eye: a sculptured goddess over the door, a miniature tulip garden or a window surrounded by stone rabbits and frogs. Although a chaste Palladian villa may crowd incongruously up against a frothy French château, the whole effect is humane and harmonious, perhaps because the façades line the sidewalk like an unbroken living-room wall or a theatrical set.

Nearly every block in Manhattan, opulent or poor, offers this visual feast of architectural variety. It's fashionable to sneer at the "tourist trap" of Greenwich Village, for example, but behind its main streets packed with gawking out-of-towners or youthful revellers lie intimate little streets, hidden courtyards of 150-year-old houses, and an atmosphere of gaslight and cobblestones.

Wall Street skyscrapers differ delectably in style, too, with their grimacing gargoyles or art-deco graces. In Soho, entire streets of elaborate cast-iron buildings mimic a *mélange* of historic styles. And even the run-down districts, seedy and patched like a rained-on collage, still bear faint traces of vanished elegance.

Most neighbourhoods still boast a village-like kaleidoscope of small-scale commerce: the shoemaker, the French bakery, the all-night grocery spilling a dazzle of flowers and fruits onto the sidewalk; delivery boys on bicycles or skateboards. And there are the street-corner vendors, almost Dickensian in their ubiquity and quick-wittedness. They may not cry "Cherry ripe!" any more, but they have their sardonic modern version. "*Bon appetit*," a panhandler leers to affluent customers entering a David's Cookies store, and reaps a handsome hatful of guilt money. A grinning seller of "gold" watches hooks customers with a sly appeal to the larcenous: "Get 'em while they're hot!"

There's a store, it seems, to serve every quirk of the immense population. Near our apartment, a boutique specializes in matching jewellery for dog owners and their pets; another, Tender Buttons (name stolen from Gertrude Stein), sells nothing but exotic and antique buttons. My favourite so far is a Harlem sign I glimpsed from a bus: Heav'n-li Heavy, Styles for the Corpulent Woman.

Because private space is so scarce, New Yorkers tend to live more of their lives in public. People eat, smoke, talk, sing, barter, and argue on the streets; push-cart vendors sell everything from shashlik to thick soups, hot knishes, and gourmet ice cream. You can wolf down your meal while crossing streets against the red light, or plunk down with the rest of the crowd on church steps, benches, fountain rims, or even on a monumental sculpture – which the crowd casually uses as a swing – hanging on chains at the corner of Third Avenue and 49th Street.

No wonder so many well-dressed women here wear sneakers with their tailored suits. If you live in Manhattan, you have to walk. And when the newcomer slows down, after the first dazed weeks of museum blitzing and gallery gulping, he or she is sure to learn that walking in New York, anywhere, anytime, is one of the city's great unadvertised pleasures.

"But isn't it dangerous?" Yes. Danger, though, is not a depressant; human beings adjust to a certain level of possible menace and go right on functioning. When I spent a year in Israel at the age of eighteen, my mother read every newspaper account of Middle East "incidents" with an immediate sense of my peril; meanwhile, I was drinking in sunshine, antiquities, hard field labour, a new language. . . . Danger was a random possibility that hardly impinged on my consciousness.

In New York, the walker quickly learns that a resolute pace is the first line of defence. You do not walk down deserted side streets at night; you stick with the crowds, walk where there are lights and people, hold your elbow over your purse at all times, cross the street promptly when you spot a band of suspicious loungers ahead of you. All these precautions become second nature, and all are pretty well worthless if you happen to be in the wrong place at the wrong time.

The tallest man I know, who is also convincingly massive and moustached, was mugged in Times Square at two o'clock on a sunlit weekday. A quick shove in the small of the back from a running teenager, a lurch sideways as he staggered off balance for a fraction of a moment, and his wallet was gone in the hands of a second teenager, already vanished in the crowd by the time he was steady on his feet again.

A *New York Newsday* columnist described how he was threatened in a subway stairwell by a knife-wielding mugger on the Upper East Side. The reporter decided to run for it rather than hand over his wallet, and in a desperate flight along busy streets, chased by the enraged and armed thief, he, the victim, was mistaken by the passers-by for a criminal. Who else would be frantically fleeing through the crowds?

Inventive New York crooks devise seasonal specialties and even take national characteristics into account. At the height of tourist season in 1987, the *New York Times* reported that every day, at Kennedy Airport, twenty-five to thirty Japanese visitors were falling prey to "the ketchup and mustard scam." At fast-food counters, a pair of young men would squirt the bewildered tourist with squeeze bottles of condiments and then, politely offering to clean the victim off, would rifle his or her pockets. Easy to picture the polite tourist holding still to be fleeced.

And at Christmas, when department stores are crammed to the doors with frustrated shoppers, beware of the dapper salesman who materializes out of the crowd, helps you to select a gift with professional knowledge of the merchandise, offers gallantly to take your credit card to the cash desk for you, and then disappears. Permanently.

Canadians love New York anyway; more than two million of them visit the state each year, and of those who come to Manhattan, some may be mugged, but most seem to find that the threat wakes them up and gives a certain edge to their pleasures. Hardly anyone can resist having a look at the famed squalor of 42nd Street, even knowing that more than two thousand robberies a year take place in the blocks around Times Square.

42nd Street west of Sixth Avenue is one of the most crowded streets in New York. Most of the people there are not pure of heart. The walker, wading through an aura of stinking poverty, filth, disease, and criminality, will be offered every form of vice. At night, the pleasure-seeking crowds, the lights and the noise and the impromptu entertainments tend to drown out the squalor. In daylight, though, the sheer rage, misery, or vacancy on people's faces may shock you with revulsion or even despair. You cannot help but feel like a mark . . . or experience a kind of skin-crawling shame at walking whole and untouched past the people of the lower depths, who, if they note your presence, may shoot you a red-rimmed glare of contempt.

This, too, is part of living in the city, and one of the reasons I have walked many times (unscathed) from one end of 42nd Street to the other. Like jiggling a kaleidoscope, it seems to settle the earthy simplicity of the Greek bakery at one end, and the UN's idealistic aspiration at the other, into a new and comprehensible pattern.

■

From the squalid to the sublime, the homey to the dazzling, 42nd Street is the visitor's most direct and rewarding route through the heart, soul, and innards of New
York City.

Dazed tourists often spend their daylight sight-seeing
hours shuffling up and down Fifth Avenue amidst the
consumer hordes. But 42nd Street, river to river, is a
better bet, a perfect microcosm of the city.

Start your stroll a few blocks north on Ninth Avenue
at 45th Street, where sunlight floods the amiably shabby
avenue and the shopkeepers are small-town friendly. At
the tiny Greek pastry shop, Poseidon, the baker comes
out of the back room with floury arms. "Just one *flogera*?
You gonna eat it now? Wait, I'll get you one hot from the
oven." A perfect pre-trek breakfast: meltingly crisp phyl-
lo pastry wrapped around a not-too-sweet custard,
washed down with a SoHo lemon spritzer.

From Ninth Avenue east along 42nd to Broadway, it's
mostly Grunj City. The Port Authority bus terminal
spews the wretched masses onto the street to mingle with
the commuters, outreach workers, prostitutes, baffled
tourists, and drug pedlars. Welfare hotels moulder next to
porn cinemas. Look above the garish signs for ghostly
evidence of the theatres they once were. But don't be
tempted to see even a first-run movie along this stretch:
the patrons tend to talk (curse, laugh, shout) at full volume. Just last week, a maddened movie-goer shot and
killed a persistently yapping seventeen-year-old.

Maybe the preponderance of blacks and Hispanics on
these blocks accounts for the eagerness of the mayor and
the big developers to level Times Square and replace its
ramshackle, seamy, polyglot energy with bland office
towers. Memories and landmarks radiate all around the
Square: Shubert Alley, the Ziegfeld Follies, the Great
White Way, Diamond Jim Brady, New Year's Eve – see
this once-cheerful hub before it's gone forever.

Between Sixth and Fifth, Bryant Park occupies the
whole south side of the block with its formal green space

where a Crystal Palace once stood. Renovations are under way – restaurants at the back of the library, new entrances to open the park to the surrounding streets – in order to wrest this public space back from the junkies.

The Grace Building, one of New York's most foolishly ugly, swoops down like a glassy ski-jump on the north side. Compare it to the attractive 1931 office building nearby at 11 West 42nd, with its stone carvings and chandeliered arcade.

You could take days to explore the *beaux arts* splendours of the New York Public Library at the corner of Fifth. So spend at least a few minutes to marvel at the soaring, all-marble entrance hall, peek into the richly coffered and panelled exhibition rooms, and see the immense third-floor public reading rooms. High shafts of sunlight fall onto the scholarly wooden tables with their intimate brass lamps, where generations of aspiring intellectuals studied and scribbled . . . and still do.

Do good and buy your souvenirs in the library's tempting little gift shop. Afterwards, sit on the broad library steps to admire the ceaseless parade of humanity, not to mention the stony rumps of the celebrated library lions.

A block east, grab an espresso and chat with strangers in the airy sculpture court of the Philip Morris building, with its pocket-sized branch of the Whitney Museum. Cross the street, wedge through the crowds, the shoe-shine men, and the vendors of stolen books, and enter Grand Central Terminal. Every heart is gladdened by this breathtaking cathedral space, dim and shadowy at its 125-foot height, and lit by dusty sunlight from the beautiful west windows. I love the clock kiosk and the ticket windows for their railroad-era brass details; if you're a like-minded nostalgic, or just plain hungry, follow the signs downstairs to the Oyster Bar and eat sumptuously in the clattering, elbows-on-table camaraderie under the wonderful tiled vaulting. (A house specialty, and my favourite, is the seafood "pan roast"; despite its name,

■

this is a sort of creamy, paprika-spiked chowder plump with fresh seafood.)

The Bowery Savings Bank across the street from Grand Central flaunts the power of New York money. Stupendously lavish, marbled and pillared and bronzed and tiled, it still has elegant art-deco banking tables where you can write out cheques with an art-deco ball-point.

Art deco, in fact, rules the block. The Chanin Building at Third Avenue swirls with exuberant leaves and flowers, and across the street, at the very last Horn and Hardart Automat, nostalgia lovers can still get awful apple pie by dropping a token into the slot and opening the little glass door. When I was nine, the Automat thrilled me with technological wonder. Today, it's quiet, faded, and quaint. Last time I tried to get apple pie, a Puerto Rican worker, briefly glimpsed in the kitchen behind the glass cases, had to move the little turntable by hand. It's a cafeteria for old people now, where coffee still comes from a dolphin-spouted urn and a disabled penny-for-your-weight machine idles by the wash-room doors.

On the north-east corner is the town's favourite skyscraper, the Chrysler Building. Stylized radiator ornaments and hubcaps sprout from the facade, and at night its crowning semicircles glitter with lights. The lobby is a bower of African marble in tawny caramel and deep, rippling russets. The inlaid elevator doors and interiors are almost crazily beautiful. The signs, the ceilings, and even the bronze letter slots in this lobby are art-deco wonders.

Farther along 42nd Street, absorb the misty hush of the tiered indoor forest in the Ford Foundation building. And don't miss the Daily News lobby with its huge, slowly turning globe, its front-page posters, outdated world maps (so long, Ceylon and Sumatra), and floor inlaid with brass mileage markers. (What did they know, in 1930, when they immortalized "Baie Comeau, 647 miles" along with Rome and Honolulu?)

Wander east through Tudor City, a graceful apartment cluster with its own gardens, *faux* Tudor little post office and stores.

Soon you will reach the East River, where the United Nations stands behind its row of snapping flags. From its wide, peaceful gardens, you can stare across the river at the famous Pepsi-Cola neon sign and ruminate on New York's jumble of the grand and the grotty, the crassly commercial and the lofty of spirit. On one long street, you've sampled it all.

Of course, New York's public wonders did not come into being through the prudent foresight of its politicians. Quite the contrary. New York's government has always been staggeringly corrupt, frequently vicious, and reliably numbskull. To the great good fortune of its inhabitants, however, the city has never been short of gargantuan private wealth, an ardently city-loving bourgeoisie, and individual genius. Occasionally, private vision and public venality came together in fruitful embrace.

Central Park, the city's great boon for walkers, sprang from one of those unlikely couplings. Frederick Law Olmsted, America's first (hence, self-taught) landscape architect, a self-described social democrat and a tireless reformer, was an abolitionist and an environmentalist before he became a great urban planner. His colleague in the design and engineering of Central Park was Calvert Vaux, the architect to whom we also owe the Metropolitan Museum of Art and the Museum of Natural History.

Olmsted's bitter account (in a pamphlet called "The Spoils of the Park") of his twenty-four-year struggle to build and then safeguard the park is all you ever need to read about municipal corruption in New York; the system works exactly the same way today. Politicians initiate grandiose projects in order to gain electoral advantage and, above all, to provide jobs and graft for the constituents who will work to put them back in office. At every step of the project, anyone who puts the public good above secret graft will be hounded, harassed, blackmailed, and vilified (with the co-operation of some newspapers with close ties to the political machine or some of its beneficiaries), and, usually, driven off at last.

Olmsted and Vaux began work in 1858. A municipal politician had proposed a park on the East River; another, seeking to top this popular idea, came up with a plan for a "central park" smack in the middle of the city. For at least part of that time, during the late 1860s and early 1870s, Olmsted and Vaux had to contend with a municipal government rotten with the corruption of "Boss" Tweed, a politician-racketeer-extortionist of stupefying greed and gall, who, with other officials known as the Tweed Ring, looted the city treasury to the tune of at least $75 million.

But corruption, favouritism, and influence-peddling had already begun to flourish before Boss Tweed reached his heights of infamy. When Olmsted showed up for work on his first day as superintendent, he found a ragtag army of derelicts already on the payroll. A resentful engineer led him on a strenuous tour of inspection through bogs and swamps "steeped in the overflow and mush of pigsties and bone-boiling yards" of which "the stench was sickening." Gangs of lolling labourers laughed good-humouredly at the suggestion that he would be supervising their "work." On the third day, a foreman looked up from reading his newspaper when the persistent Olmsted returned and sneered, "Hello, Fred; get around pretty often, don't you?"

Through their twenty-four years of work on the park, Olmsted and Vaux fought against overwhelming odds. "I once received in six days more than seven thousand letters of advice as to appointments, nearly all from men in office," wrote Olmsted. He was threatened by mobs of surly Democrats bearing letters entitling them to jobs; his house was broken into, his honesty publicly impugned, and his work constantly subverted by greedy developers and opportunists who tried to build everything from speedways to "merchandise halls" in the park.

■

Later, "practical" appointees to park management tried to spruce up Olmsted's visionary landscaping. "In the interest of that good taste which delights in a house painted white with green blinds, whitewashed cherry-trees [and] plaster statuettes on stumps . . . ," park employees cleared Olmsted's carefully planted hillside perennials, swept the leaf-mould from crevices where it had been placed to nurture plant growth, and hacked away the natural vines, mosses, and lichens of which Olmsted was so proud, and which, he wrote with savage gloom, they no doubt considered of "low, depraved and unpractical taste."

Miraculously, Olmsted and Vaux, with the help of an indignant public, managed to save the park as we know it now.

> Putting it simply and strongly, if [the visitor] doesn't here, in his thought, keep patting the Park on the back, he is guilty not alone of a failure of natural tenderness, but of a real deviation from social morality.
>
> – Henry James

Or, as more recent boosters would say, "You gotta have Park!" Because Central Park is not merely a bosky 840 acres of wooded loveliness, quietly exhaling oxygen in the midst of the continent's greatest city, but also a dazzling social experiment, the first of its kind in North America. To see the park in full spring flower, pink magnolias blurring into clouds of cherry blossoms, with every colour of New Yorker in Easter finery surging amiably about amidst balloons, flowers, pencil portraitists, impromptu jazz bands, puppeteers, chamber orchestras, carousels, and chess players, is to believe again in the possibility of city life.

One recent rainy day, I climbed the stairs to the top of the old Arsenal at the Fifth Avenue side of the park, sloshed across the roof, and entered the romantic round turret office of Ethan Carr, park historian. He is an earnest young man with a button-down look and passionate ideals. "It was a great democratic undertaking," he says. "The bourgeoisie feared that the park would be a haven for ruffians and [a] blot on the city; instead, it was an enormous popular success from the beginning."

There was, of course, a time of blots and ruffians. The giant "be-ins" of the 1960s trampled the grass to bare hard-pan, and the devastating municipal bankruptcy of the 1970s doomed the park to erosion and desolation. But lo, the winter is past: the flora are being replanted and the follies, fountains, and pavilions renovated. The atmosphere is no longer one of danger, but of civil gaiety.

The park is my backyard, as it is for thirteen million other visitors every year. On sunny afternoons, I find a soft patch of grass to read, bask, and listen to Mozart played by my favourite park musician . . . Philip, "the People's Violinist," in ruffled shirt, tuxedo, and beatific smile. At the park's south end, I might pause by the tempura wagon to pick up a snack, or browse through open-air bookstalls. Or I might head north, drifting past quiet banks of forsythia, daffodils, and azalea, to lunch finally at the Loeb Boathouse (chilli in a delicious pastry basket).

Central Park feels inexhaustibly immense, thanks to the genius of Frederick Law Olmsted and Calvert Vaux. Four roads, all of them cleverly sunk out of sight and sound, carry traffic across its width. Winding walks lead pedestrians across quaint cast-iron bridges, while horse carriages pass on another level. Any casual stroll will take you (by careful design) from shady groves to sunny vistas, from open meadows to rocky pools. And the great Mall – with three hundred of the last stately elms in America – is a grand procession climaxing in a spacious Victorian view.

Everyone who works for the park breathes Mr. Olmsted's name in reverence. "He was like a painter; he knew the bark colours of every tree in winter, and how each would look next to a stand of dry grasses," said Pamela Robins, a Canadian who is the city's chief horticulturalist. "Every inch is planned: when one tree is turning into a puff of pink, another puff of yellow is just beyond."

Olmsted was a romantic. He stocked the famous Sheep Meadow (now a radio-free zone for kite flying and grass sprawling) with real sheep, because of the "richly picturesque flakiness of their wool." The Dairy, a Victorian cottage now splendidly restored as an information centre and gallery, once had cows and dairymaids to serve fresh milk to city children. And all twenty-two gates into the park are named with enthusiastic egalitarianism in honour of the city's diverse people: Farmers' Gate, Artists', Artisans', Girls', Boys', Engineers'.

Olmsted meant Central Park to be completely countrified, blotting out its urban surroundings. But the city crept up around it. Today, from deep within the park, the skyscrapers are visible on every side, although (a pleasing compromise) magically softened and distanced by the wavering line of fresh green.

And the park is intensely *used*. Little sub-communities have sprung up: the boccie players, the baseball fanatics, the kite fanciers, the break dancers all have their appointed sites and hours of gathering.

The roller-skaters punctually appear on Lilac Walk every weekend, making it reverberate to their motorcycle-sized boom boxes while hundreds gather to gape. They swoop, undulate, execute death-defying leaps, back bends, and speed manoeuvres. A muscled woman with a grey pony-tail and sleeveless T-shirt disco dances to her dreamy inner music; a giant black man with shaved head and kerchief knotted around his brow (he's a cop in real life, I'm told) practises exquisitely delicate pirouettes. Nearby, a Puerto Rican woman, whose goods are stored in a small fleet of bundle buggies, does a brisk regular weekend business in roast pork, rice, liquor from a bagged bottle, and, as a bystander explains, "other customer services," most of which can be inhaled.

■

"We got finesse, we got charisma, we burn holes in the earth, we're out beyond the galaxies, you dig?" a skater named Quincy informs me. "And all the regulars chip in for the radio batteries."

When Olmsted began work, there was nothing here but rocks, swamp, bone-boiling shacks, open sewers, and rambling pigs. And he was saddled by Boss Tweed with a thousand shiftless labourers recruited from local gangs like the Bowery Boys and the Dead Rabbit.

Today, the park is a leafy nirvana for bird-watchers and naturalists, a rustic refresher for the urban frazzled, a pleasure-ground where every age, race, and kind rubs elbows in genial coexistence.

It would be a failure of social morality, said Henry James, not to pat the place on the back; I pat it tenderly, gratefully, every day.

Central Park, of course, has its darker side. Decapitated chickens sometimes turn up behind the shrubbery in the northern, more deserted tracts, where voodoo practitioners have held their midnight rites. Horseback riders in the upper west zones have been occasionally mugged, and a guide on a bird-watching tour of the Ramble (a wild patch of forest where we saw crowned night herons and worm-eating warblers, among dozens of other species) warned darkly, "Never, never come into the Ramble alone." The park after nightfall is probably not a wise venture, unless you stick to the crowded, well-lit walkways around the perimeter.

(Just as I wrote this, I heard the news that a young woman had been brutally raped and nearly murdered by a rampaging gang of young boys. She had been jogging late at night, alone, in the dangerously deserted north end of the park. A hateful word, "wilding," came into the urban lexicon.)

All these undertones of menace and mystery, however, make one more grateful for the safety of the daytime park, where the most casual stroller shares in the feeling of sociability triumphing over the secretive lawlessness of the shadows.

■

The public life of the park is a marvel I had not tasted before, either in formal French gardens, where everyone stuck grimly to the paths, or in Canadian parks, which seem more strictly dedicated to nature. On a bright Sunday, Central Park is a carnival of impromptu events: play-school picnics, balloon artists, dozens of jam sessions, even professional marionette shows, particularly one regular near the model boat pond, whose miniature circus, complete with fire-eater and equestrienne, draws huge and appreciative audiences.

I once stopped for an hour to listen to a couple of old black singers belting out country blues to the accompaniment of an electric guitar. The performance was pleasure enough, but I noticed again the current of heightened enjoyment among the casual listeners, the smiles and comments exchanged. The stress of New York life is so great that these fortuitous shared moments seem to bring a keener, more conscious delight.

Eighteen million tourists visit Manhattan every year. If you are one of those who arrives in the summer, there will inevitably come a moment when you conclude that New York air is made of chicken soup. Steamy, stifling, viscous, unbreathable. And you'll be the limp noodle feebly stirring at the bottom of the bowl.

As a frequent noodler along these streets, unwilling to give up my urban pleasures even during the dog days, I'm willing to share my survival tactics. The trick is to keep a mental check-list of oases: little tide pools of tranquillity where the beat beat beat of the streets fades away, your brow smoothes, and your thoughts drift from focused to fluffy.

At the Metropolitan Museum of Art, for example, plan to take a break in the Astor Court, an exquisite Ming dynasty garden and house miraculously set down in the middle of the museum. Enter through a round "moon gate" (the plaque over the door says, in Chinese, "In search of quietude") and something intangible, something cool and silvery, instantly wafts around you.

■

The court, lovingly created with ancient techniques by Chinese craftsmen, is like poetry in stone, wood, and water. Wander the elegant walkways; admire the delicate lattice windows, the subdued glow of polished wood. Sit on the "moon-viewing" terrace to hear the hushed music of water bubbling up beside Cold Spring Pavilion. Invite your soul; this is one of the most perfect places in New York.

More roustabout and light-hearted are the Exxon and McGraw-Hill mini-parks, hidden away behind the office towers on Sixth Avenue. From the Canadian Consulate in the Exxon Building, walk a few yards west on 49th Street to arrive at the park entrance. You'll find flowers, croissants for sale, comfortable tables and chairs, a waterfall, and, best of all, a glass tunnel over which pours a continual torrent of water. Stand in the tunnel and feel your temperature drop deliciously.

If you are near Grand Central Terminal, stop at the corner of Park and 42nd Street to see the midtown branch of the Whitney Museum, right off the garden lobby of the Philip Morris building. The lobby itself is riotous with pop-art sculptures. Buy an espresso and relax on friendly terms with Lichtenstein, Calder, and Oldenburg.

Another branch of the Whitney (and another, enormous Lichtenstein) can be found at the Equitable Building on the other side of town; this is an especially airy oasis, where you can relax on an icy swoop of green marble bench, all silky curves, and contemplate a rustling reed garden in a square pool.

On my way home from the post office on a sweltering day, I always stop at St. Bartholomew's at the corner of Park and 50th. I tend to think of this church as St. Bart the Crooked; pleading a spurious poverty in a lengthy battle with the city for permission to build an office tower on one corner of its property, St. Bart's was actually revealed to have cooked its books. Still, I am grateful to it. Right at the corner, behind iron railings and often deserted, is a tiny slice of a water garden with elegant, curved,

■

wrought-iron benches. Just steps away from the traffic, I sit in perfect rural bliss, listening to the musical murmur of water running through miniature aqueducts and spilling from level to level. Dusty city sparrows, perkily bathing, are often the only other living beings.

Water is the lure at another favourite oasis. Coming home from the library, I slip into Paley Park, a vest-pocket park on 53rd just east of Fifth Avenue. Tucked between buildings and opening to the street, this little space has all the welcoming informality of a store-front. The back wall of the park is a sheet waterfall whose constant roar dims out the street noise; I buy a coffee from the discreet little kiosk, and, under a feathery canopy of tree-shade, read my library books with an extra sense of luxury.

A good friend first introduced me to a virtually unknown oasis: the tiny, secretive, and magical Erol Beker Chapel of the Good Shepherd, upstairs in St. Peter's church in the Citicorp Building at Lexington and 54th. You're likely to be blissfully alone here, in a small room that is really a pure white three-dimensional sculpture by Louise Nevelson. It's just like day-dreaming in a wind-carved snow-drift. Nevelson's abstract biblical symbols seem to float and hover on all four walls. Serenity flows from them into your wearied eyes, even if you make no effort to interpret them. Delightfully, this place makes no demands.

Farther east in midtown, I discovered the most beautiful of all the vest-pocket parks. Greenacre Park is sandwiched by buildings at 217 East 51st, between Second and Third avenues. On a meltingly hot day, I walked into the dappled shade, heard a brook flowing over rocks, and felt I'd found nirvana. Negative ions practically sparkle from a spectacular twenty-five-foot-high waterfall with five thousand gallons of water a minute to crash, tumble, roar, and otherwise make merry while obliterating the heat and noise of the city. One of the joys of this meticulously maintained park is that everyone who relaxes there seems conscious of sharing a civilized splendour with fellow citizens.

The hard-edged, acquisitive glitter of Madison Avenue is less amiable, but you can find respite from consumer frenzy by retreating to the lush bamboo garden in the IBM Building at 57th Street. Outside, a large, horizontal sculpture mimics the concrete slabs of Manhattan. It's set, mesmerizingly, over a rush of sliding water that reminds you Manhattan is an island. Inside, it's easy to strike up conversations with fellow enchantees who wander appreciatively amidst the dazzling flower displays. There's a coffee bar, a gardeners' shop, noon-hour concerts, and the free and excellent IBM art gallery.

In winter, this garden offers one of New York's more poignantly ironic sights. At the Christmas season, when brilliant banks of poinsettias nestle under the bamboos, glance in the plate-glass windows late at night, just before the garden closes, and see, at each one of the garden tables, a lone, homeless man, sitting asleep, shabby parcels bundled around his feet amidst the elegant floral beauties. The IBM security guards stand watch in admirable tolerance over this tableau of lonely misery.

In the late afternoon, take the Staten Island ferry. A mere twenty-five cents buys a forty-minute return trip on these sturdy boats. Gulls swoop, the engine thrums comfortably, and the sun gilds the Statue of Liberty as you lean on the rail. It will suddenly occur to you that New York is a splendid harbour, and you'll see why it became a great mercantile centre. As the ferry chugs farther out, the view widens. To your left is the broad sweep of the Hudson; to your right, the East River and its receding series of lovely bridges, beginning with the Brooklyn. And right in the middle, the skyscrapers crowd the tip of tiny Manhattan.

At this distance, and surrounded by the freshness of water, you may be surprised by a rush of tenderness for that familiar skyline, with all the energy and aspiration it represents. Manhattan, even in mid-summer, can still delight the visitor who is prudent enough to plan for spiritual refreshment at oases along the way.

There are hidden gardens all over Manhattan. A surprising number of them are public, and any tourist can track them down with a good street-by-street guide (see my suggested list at the end of this book) or by calling the city's Green Thumb organization of community gardens. Still, the very best are those you happen on serendipitously. On Hudson Street once, I pushed open a little rounded door in a stone wall and found myself in the country-like garden of St. Luke-in-the-fields church. Community volunteers had sculpted shrubbery into topiary and wound such cunning little paths through such a riot of flowers that you felt you could lose yourself for a sunny hour or two.

Another spring day, walking home down Fifth Avenue from a visit to an East Harlem public school, I was stunned by the sight of soaring, marvellously intricate wrought-iron gates opening into Central Park at 105th Street – gates, I later learned, that had been rescued from a demolished Vanderbilt mansion. This is the Conservatory Garden, the only formal flower garden in the park. I was just in the nick of the season to wander along under the pink clouds of the crab-apple allées, to admire the twenty thousand tulips blazing near the fountain where three stone women dance in the spray, and to wander up to the wisteria pergola, where I couldn't resist lingering to watch a Harlem wedding party being photographed. While the bride, groom, and relatives were at a pitch of romantic happiness, the little page boy in a white tuxedo and the bridesmaids lavish with lace were squirming, hopping, chasing each other, and being scolded for scuffing their shoes.

A little farther on, I found myself amidst wild flowers in a garden tucked away in a corner. This is the Secret Garden; you can't help but feel you are the only one to have found it. Gradually, it dawns on you that the Pan boy and the graceful girl sculpted in the reflecting pool are exactly like Mary and Dickon.

I sat on a bench to daydream for a while. As each little family group ambled in, the children would scamper forward to the pool while the adults stopped to read the bronze plaque set in the pavement: "To the Memory of Frances Hodgson Burnett." They'd pause, frown in an effort to remember, and then light up. Of course! *The Secret Garden*! Their eyes would instantly flash recognition to those already seated around the pool. Nobody said it aloud. But a delicate web of feeling wove through the air, drifting with the faint, cool scent of lilacs.

"New York is awful," grumbled a friend from Ottawa. "There aren't any trees."

"No kids in New York," complained a feature writer at the *Globe*.

Nerts to them both, I say. New York has plenty of tall greenery and little sprouts if you know where to look, which is not at midday in midtown, any more than it is in Toronto or Vancouver.

New York City, in fact, has seven hundred community gardens on public land (ninety-five of them in Manhattan alone), and countless others hidden away on rooftops and in courtyards. Secrecy and surprise grace them with an exotic magic all their own.

One day last week, in the simmering June heat, I glanced up from the pavement on 96th Street just west of Broadway and saw a thick fringe of pink roses dangling over the roof edge of a parking garage, roses ruffling and swaying in a roof level breeze. Beside the garage an iron gate stood open with a little sign: The Lotus Garden.

I climbed the inviting stairs and stepped into a sort of Eden, where I found Carrie Maher, head of the Garden People neighbourhood group, presiding over a sumptuous picnic. "We have our own climate up here," said Ms.

Maher, cheerfully snuffing the breeze and inviting me to share some Korean salads.

All around us, garden paths wound between beds of coral bells, columbines, bleeding hearts, ferns, and fever-few. Dazed bumblebees lurched about; a yellow and blue swallowtail butterfly waltzed around seven thousand square feet of paradise – half a block from Broadway – as though asphalt didn't exist.

Ms Maher, an energetic former comedy writer for theatre and television, is now a professional gardener. She met her partner and fiancé, Mark Greenwald, a former architect, when they both worked in a community garden. "I must have been hypnotized by an iris at a very early age," she muses.

The Lotus Garden, however, is not a professional duty but a local enthusiasm: Ms Maher was one of a community group that negotiated the public open space with developer William Zeckendorf, when he built the garage for a new condominium tower right on the site of a former neighbourhood garden.

"He gave us a $75,000 endowment, put lots of spig-ots on the walls, had his architects reinforce the garage roof, and trucked in three feet of specially mixed soil," Ms Maher told me. "We have gorgeous drainage."

Would-be gardeners from the neighbourhood were alerted by signs ("This bud's for you!") propped on the sidewalk on Broadway. About twenty-five of them dig and putter here regularly, many of them on their way to or from work.

"I can look down from my apartment window across the street and see briefcases lying in the dirt," said Ms. Maher.

One of the glories of the Lotus Garden is a lily pond, soon to be ennobled by a real lotus grown from seed by a Manchurian businessman in his Manhattan apartment. In the meantime, a resident frog named Mikey makes do with a sun-bath on a native lily-pad.

■

"Mikey knows me because I donated him and I'm in charge of feeding him," said local gardener Gillian Hageman, holding up a cunning little cage of sacrificial crickets. "I buy the crickets from a pet store."

Gillian, age six and a half, has coppery hair, amber eyes, and freckles so unabashedly adorable they would make Norman Rockwell blush. She comes to the garden nearly every day and has a calm, sun-washed kind of drawl. "I love all my plants, especially Dusty Miller, and I love the garden because it's so quiet."

Just then the quiet was broken by a phalanx of boisterous children from Spanish Harlem, shepherded by a woman called Joanne who had brought them over from St. John the Divine Cathedral where they have their own vegetable and flower garden in the cathedral close. They were on a sort of professional visit to check out the competition.

Juan, age seven, says, "I'm growing onions and artihohos."

"And letters," butts in Yahaira, a six-year-old sparkler, making up in enthusiasm for her vegetative inaccuracy. "And roses! The roses are growing. They started this small. Now they're growing pink! They're growing red!" She leaps up, pigtails flying, to show me how high they're growing.

The visitors approve of the Lotus Garden, because they get to use the hose.

By now, traffic and urban traumas have receded a thousand miles. I forget to rush, and spend two hours admiring the gooseberries, the currants, the fuzzy little peaches on the bough. One garden plot is planted in the shape of a happy face, with salvia lips. "A man who's a tango addict from Latin America planted this where his house-bound mother can see it from her window," Carrie Maher explains. "Last year, he planted 'I Love New York' in marigolds."

A Jamaican grandmother christened her flower pot "a permanent piece of Jamaica, like an embassy"; a Finnish agronomist's daughter planted a yucca that is now taller than she is. There is, by now, a permanent body of Lotus Garden lore, which includes the names of the enormous goldfish (Spot and BoomBoom) in the lily pond. Pam, a graphic designer, tells me that the garden has created a community. Spring is greeted with group excursions to plant nurseries; pot-luck lunches in the garden brighten the summer months, and, in winter, the gardeners meet to pore over catalogues.

Whereas a garden is a garden in Westmount or Willowdale, in New York, where it is invariably a piece of reclaimed real estate, wrested from concrete and developers, it comes closer to being an epiphany. "A garden," said Carrie Maher, "gives you the feeling of having your heart's desire."

CHAPTER 2

·

Liveable New York

A gawky young waitress scrubs her cloth over the counter top in a Rockefeller Center coffee shop and mutters, "New Year's Eve and I gotta work a ten-hour shift." A customer looks up from his coffee and gallantly offers to take her out dancing. "Hot stuff," she cracks sardonically with a snap of her cloth. "I can handle it."

When a Queens building contractor illegally rips out twenty-six roadside trees in Bayside, New York Parks Commissioner Henry J. Stern demands, and wins, a settlement for "arboricide" and proudly declaims to the newspapers, "The Bayside Twenty-Six shall not have died in vain."

A customer in a deli rebukes an aged waiter for bringing a dill pickle long after the customer has eaten his pastrami sandwich. "Wait, I'll bring you another half sandwich," the waiter shoots back.

In 1985, when the United Nations celebrated its fortieth anniversary and visiting dignitaries jammed the streets with their motorcades, traffic officials were in their quotable glory. Within hours, a new word had bobbed to the surface – "limolock," a variant of "gridlock." The city's traffic commissioner, gleefully ordering an illegally parked white Mercedes to be towed away, gloated that he was "an equal opportunity tower." A guard at the UN, watching the parade of foreign luminaries, told the *Times* that "we have bwanas to burn this week." And a traffic official, explaining why the city had towed away diplomatic cars belonging to Nicaragua and Madagascar, said, "They were naughty. Time and tide and fortieth anniversary wait for no man. We will schlepp them into the sunset."

If language is the mirror of the soul, then shine on, New York City. Judging by the zest with which Manhattanites express themselves, essayist Lionel Abel was absolutely right to call New York "the most vital of the great dying cities of the world." New Yorkers can't resist a smart retort, a brash exaggeration, or a fast quip. Working people in particular wear salty irreverence as a badge of honour and brandish the instant comeback as a weapon of democracy. Shocked visitors more accustomed to blandly neutral speech may interpret this as rudeness, but it's more often a case of ham on wry. When, for example, the city launched a tourism campaign to encourage greater politeness among New York vendors and clerks, the *Times*'s city columnist, William Geist, had a field day asking people in the street what they thought.

"This sounds like the greatest behavior modification effort since Mao took power in China," wisecracked a bystander. A hot-dog vendor said, "I have always considered courtesy to be a sign of weakness." And a cab driver, in a sardonic crescendo building to the ultimate brash punchline, confided that "people were not rude to him, that he was not rude to them, and that at the slightest hint of rudeness, he would sock them."

Edgy street banter only occasionally bears the hallmarks of elbows-out hostility. I once made the mistake of saying, to a street photographer who invited me to have my picture taken with a life-size cardboard cut-out of Ronald Reagan, "I'd rather die." Instantly, he swept an exaggerated bow and sneered, "Be my guest." More often, the quipster is self-consciously relishing the role of hard-boiled big-city survivor. ("This is New York, honey.") Even the crooks talk as though they're starring in a Damon Runyan version of their lives. A Mafia stool pigeon, confiding his fears to a reporter, said, "I'm dead without a doubt in a very severe manner."

All this linguistic impertinence, invention, and ironic flourish is part of the New York character – one part immigrant energy, one part street-smart hipster, and two parts burnishing of New Yorkers' egalitarian self-image. Rocco, one of the doormen in my building, saw me sailing out excitedly with an armful of flowers for a friend with a new baby. "How much did she weigh?" he asked me with intense interest. I didn't know. He threw out his arms in mock exas-

∎

52

peration. "But how ya gonna bet the numbah?" he cried. Echoes of Irish exaggeration, black slang, and Yiddish irony, borrowings from Broadway's glory days and gangster bravado, all promiscuously flavour the speech of New York's working people in defiance of protocol, middle-class norms, and suburban hypocrisies.

On St. Patrick's Day, the Puerto Rican proprietor of the corner coffee shop grins knowingly as he offers me a green bagel. The melting-pot language, too, is a way that New York has of thumbing its nose at conformity while bragging about its fertile cross-culturalism. Verbal dexterity, the cheapest and choicest instrument of generations of immigrants, shows up in the speed and delight with which New Yorkers bestow nicknames. An ovoid new office building, pink and publicly derided, instantly becomes the "Lipstick Building"; the lovely and seasonally changing flower-beds that run along the east-west axis of Rockefeller Center are dubbed the "Channel Gardens" because they lie between the French and British pavilions.

Old neighbourhoods emerging into new prosperity (or notoriety) are christened overnight: SoHo (south of Houston); TriBeCa (Triangle below Canal) and Alphabet City (the area including Avenues A, B, and C).

The naming of neighbourhoods, sometimes only a few square blocks in area, is a clue to the way people carve out a life and identity for themselves. Neighbourhoods are the life of the city. Strangers sometimes wonder how a city so immense in population, so overshadowed by gargantuan buildings, so seamed with violence and fear, can possibly be liveable. The mundane truth is that daily life in Manhattan can be as small-scaled and humane as life in a hamlet. Small stores, push-carts, news-stands, and coffee shops service every neighbourhood and form a smaller, agreeable daily world for the area residents, encouraging intense local loyalties. Some of my friends who live in the West Village solemnly swear that they never go above 14th Street; a friend who lives in Brooklyn laments that her Manhattan pals will never come "all the way out" (one subway stop from down-

■

town) to visit her in Brooklyn Heights; the more flamboyant Upper East Siders who give interviews to glossy magazines have been known to boast that they never set foot outside their own "silk stocking" zip code of 10021. You can be as fiercely parochial in the metropolis as the most obdurate villager . . . with the pleasant mitigation of big-city privacy. Those salty working-class New Yorkers who populate the stores and services of each neighbourhood will recognize you and greet you without knowing your name. There's a tingle of gratification in enjoying the sociability of a small-town main street while snugly keeping your identity and your life as private as you want them to be.

"But how," asks a reader at least once a month, "do you do your grocery shopping?"

Strange question, I thought. But of course; people are curious about the nuts and bolts of life in a city of eight million. A visitor, amidst skyscrapers, choked traffic, glittering boutiques, and outrageously expensive restaurants, might easily get the impression that there is nowhere to buy toilet paper.

On a scrubbed spring morning, stepping outside, I see it differently. It is almost as simple as living in a village.

Straight out the front door – no front yard or walk or dreary evergreen shrubs to distance me – I am in the thick of city life. Within two blocks of my apartment building I can get my clothes cleaned, pick up hot brioches for breakfast from a French baker, sit in an airy café for an espresso, post a letter, buy discs for my computer, dawdle through dozens of private art galleries (the great museums are a few blocks away), stock up on bagels and lox, pick up grapefruit spoons or teenagers' socks at ritzy Bloomingdale's or dirt-cheap Alexander's, or choose among three different supermarkets.

Tight for space, supermarkets here are small and slick. I can whip through in half an hour. At home, shopping was a marathon. Dazed in the acreage of a giant Loblaws,

■

54

I'd fall into a hypnotic trance in front of twelve different brands of olive oil. Even worse was the boring drudgery of lugging bags from store to cart to car to house.

Here, my own feet give me the same feeling of freedom and mobility that wheels gave me at home. Besides, all the supermarkets deliver promptly. (The delivery boys ride big tricycles with metal storage bins attached.) If I want, I can phone in my supermarket order, round the clock. By phone, I can also summon up "gourmet" diet dinners, fancy restaurant meals, videos, and even books.

Yes, books. There are four outstanding book stores within blocks of me. One of them is open till midnight and another – my personal Arcadia – will deliver within hours, neatly wrapped in flowered paper, any book for which I've developed an impatient passion.

But mostly I prefer to dash out myself. "There is never a better way of taking in life than walking in the street," wrote Henry James. Anonymous and happily gawking in the ceaseless flow of colourful strangers, I can wear my running shoes and the jacket with the torn pockets: New Yorkers are supremely tolerant of oddity. Merchants treat me with the same cheerful camaraderie as the diamond-decked lady next in line; the democratic ruthlessness of a mercantile city can be extraordinarily liberating.

Anonymous, but never lonely. Finishing a column at two in the morning, I head for my neighbourhood all-night news-stand, where the newsie knows which papers and magazines to hand me before I ask. On the way back, I drop in at my local Korean grocery, where flowers and fruit spill exuberantly across the sidewalk.

Sal, the homeless man who sits all night on a plastic milk crate, greets me by name. He watches the flowers for the grocer, and, in return, is fed from the grocer's hot-food deli counter. (The limo drivers at the Regency Hotel, Sal tells me, let him use their office to shower and shave. When he wants to sleep, he goes to one of ten first-run movie houses a five-minute walk away.)

Every corner, it seems, has a twenty-four-hour Korean grocery. Business is particularly brisk in the early evening, when working people, headed home, stop to fill plastic cartons with sliced fresh fruits and vegetables from the ubiquitous salad bar, or hot stews and vegetarian dishes from the steam table, all sold by the pound.

Rocketing rents, fuelled by untrammelled speculation, have seriously threatened this sense of neighbourhood amenity. The little mom-and-pop service shops – repairmen, cleaners, coffee shops, bakers – are being boutiqued out of existence in many areas. On the Upper West Side, long an island of shabby and elderly gentility, you can now buy Coca-Cola-brand clothes from a snazzy vending machine, but, residents complain bitterly, you can't get your toaster fixed any more. Still, enough remains to captivate anyone who grew up in a city dependent on cars.

The tension between the privacy of apartment life and the gregariousness of the streets is another peculiar Manhattan pleasure. For intimacy, I have my family, twelve floors above the ruckus; for banter, quips, and pungent observations, I have everyone who shares the crowded streets and subways with me.

Urbanologists have always deplored New York's chaotic squalor, but to me it is an even better place to live than to visit. I can walk to my local library and stop to read my books in a vest-pocket park on the way home – or, glorying in the sheer absence of public decorum, join the throngs who pause to sit unself-consciously on public steps, low walls, and balustrades, at the museum, the library, in front of churches – in a way I can't imagine in Toronto.

Yes, it is chronically dirty and congested, and, year by year, there are more mumbling and dishevelled beggars rattling their Styrofoam cups at you in subway entrances, on the buses, in doorways. But the streets are also carnivals, thoroughfares, bazaars, theatres. Ironically, because of the choked traffic, New York has become a city of pedestrians. Abandoning my car, like a hermit crab leaving its shell, I find that the boredom and alienation of doing errands have magically vanished.

How do I shop in NYC? The way I do everything here: with supreme ease, vivacity, and a sense of belonging to a larger life.

City dwellers, as Jonathan Raban says in *Soft City*, construct "their" city mentally, make invisible paths and clearings for themselves, lines of connection, pools of mutuality, and familiar landmarks that may be invisible or negligible to anyone else. Otherwise, in the huge, unknowable clamour and congestion, you can become unhitched from your surroundings, drift loose like those muttering bag ladies or apathetic isolates you see on park benches. And so "my neighbourhood" became not just the streets near where I lived, but expanded to include all my serendipities, my private haunts, and all the familiar landmarks of my friends' neighbourhoods, too.

Secret places, anomalies, and incongruities are particularly cherished by big-city dwellers, in part because you share them implicitly with a cabal of fellow discoverers. That's why new-comers often ask excitedly about Chumley's, a cosy tavern on Bedford Street in Greenwich Village. A hang-out for local writers since Prohibition days, Chumley's is hidden off a courtyard behind a small apartment building; you can't find it unless you know it's there. Apparently the owners never got around to putting up a sign after the era of illegality was over.

Mysterious places are a token of the city's bottomless depths of complexity; New Yorkers avidly collect such hide-aways, making them part of the private *terra cognita* that is their home. Of course, the more such places you can collect (the Turkish steam-bath, the off-beat museum, the perfect vantage-point for Fourth of July fireworks, the little-known source for 1920s sweater buttons or cut-rate roses), the more you are at home in the city.

Exploring Manhattan and staking a private claim to every part of it that delighted me with its different style, I was taking part in a time-honoured New York ritual.

■

Any summer night in the East Village, you may park yourself on a doorstep or in an outdoor café to watch the swirling masquerade: urban gypsies, vagrants, artists in artful tatters, vaguely rebellious kids in aggressive black, or bohemian kids expressing their *joie de vivre* in Juicy-Fruit plastic ornaments. Sauntering, schmoozing, or creating an uproar, here come the drunken frat boys, the glowering youths in Mohawks as elaborate as sculptures, the girls in Victorian nightgowns or nose rings. A black boy in an outsize overcoat has the back of his head shaved so that you can see, sculpted into his hair, a Keith Haring running-man figure captioned with the word FAST. This is the neighbourhood for youth; everyone (computer programmer, soap-opera actor, delivery boy, private-school girl) who wants to star in or be an audience to the theatre of the outrageous makes this a temporary neighbourhood.

Many of the crowd will be young people from the safely suburban outer boroughs of New Jersey or Long Island – the "bridge and tunnel" crowd, as some Manhattanites sneer – who flock to the city in their spare time to assume their real identities as dissidents, freaks, and artists of expressionist lifestyles.

The city is the place where you can lose and remake yourself, shake loose your Aunt Jo and Uncle Mo, drop one crowd and take up another in the space of a week. All the world's great cities offer this intoxicating freedom of rootlessness and possibility. But only New York started that way; only New York built itself from the beginning as a conglomeration of ethnic groups, each with its sense of entitlement to advancement and power.

The ancient cities of Europe, and their colonial outposts around the world, were the centres of their national culture and civilization. They had (and have) official academies to express, to monitor, to exemplify the purity and greatness of their splendid national language and art.

Raffish New York, new-world and polyglot from the start (by 1660, eighteen languages were spoken in New Amsterdam), could never be stuffed into such a starched shirt. New Yorkers rejoiced in their willy-nilly cosmopolitanism; though one ethnic group or another may dominate intellectual, artistic, financial, or social life for a while, New York has always gloried in its identity as a city of immigrants and upstarts.

Frederic Law Olmsted said it in 1870: "In Central Park, you may often see vast numbers of persons brought closely together, poor and rich, young and old, Jew and Gentile. I have seen a hundred thousand thus congregated . . ." and he rejoiced in their "glee in the prospect of coming together, all classes largely represented . . . each individual adding by his mere presence to the pleasures of all the others." By 1904, even the fastidious Anglophile Henry James enjoyed an evening of conversation and dinner on the Lower East Side, and was moved to predict that in New York there might arise "an ethnic synthesis" that could become "the very music of humanity."

Gleefully in my turn, I prowled the streets and parks of Manhattan, the mere presence of so many foreign others adding to my pleasure. No matter how clear and irrefutable the horrors of racism, it remains a characteristic of New Yorkers that they share that glee; a conscious pride in their own diversity is one of their defining qualities. Most big cities now boast a complete palette of races and languages, but nowhere else do people seem to derive so much satisfaction from that fact.

"All kinds here, all kinds!" an Ethiopian cab driver exulted to me, trying to explain his happiness at being in New York, and it was a feeling I saw constantly on people's faces when New York produced one of its dependable daily incongruities. On a lovely summer night at Damrosch Park (the outdoor band shell beside Lincoln Center), I sat on one of the benches near the back to hear Sweet Honey in the Rock, a powerful a cappella singing group of black women. The crowd was enjoying itself hugely. Puerto Rican kids were dancing in the aisles; an elderly group of Yiddish speakers in the back row could hardly contain their enthusiasm. When the group sang a hymn of praise and mourning for Steven

■

Biko, the murdered South African black activist, the whole motley audience roared its approval . . . approving the song, the sentiments, and its own multiracial tolerance.

New York draws the ambitious, true. But it's also a magnet for misfits: the creators, the arguers, the dreamers, the readers and writers and loners who never quite fit in their home towns and who come to New York determined to find a place more capacious of spirit. In many ways, New York does not disappoint.

Soon after I arrived, I picked up the *New York Times* and read an announcement: "Alternate side parking rules are suspended today because of Yom Kippur." I knew it was foolish to feel thrilled, but I couldn't help it. I'm a graduate of the University of Toronto, where, year after year, the authorities insisted that registration simply had to be held on Yom Kippur, the most solemn day of the Jewish year. No exceptions, no excuses. Adapt to *our* way or get lost . . . That, ironically, used to be the Canadian version of its self-proclaimed "cultural mosaic." New York, which trumpeted the melting pot instead (an idea I deplored in the abstract), democratically celebrates everyone.

At Christmas, the city is spangled with light; electric menorahs (the Channukah candelabra) are lit up in apartment lobbies and store windows, ecumenically sharing space with the wreaths and Christmas trees. You don't need excuses and exceptions here; you can be unembarrassedly what you are, and the city nonchalantly goes along with you.

My street was the marshalling ground for many of the national parades that regularly take over Fifth Avenue. A powerful stink of ammonia hung crudely before our swanky green awning for a week after the German parade: immense and gleaming Clydesdales and Belgians had stood along the curb, ready to pull spit-and-polish beer wagons, patient amidst the random belching of tubas and the belly rumbling of bass drums as the oompah band waited restlessly to begin.

Blue and white floats and excited children congregated for the Greek parade; the Irish jammed the entire city, and not just our street, for their annual display of civic power; Labour

Day poured rain on a sad and straggling march, testimony to the diminished ranks of the unionized working class.

Almost weekly, it seemed, a tight crowd of fiercely bearded, white-shirted Afghan men (no women) shouted angrily as they strode up Park Avenue on their way to demonstrate at the Soviet mission. Iranian dissidents commandeered the street corners with their insistent pleas, their clipboarded petitions, their striped dummy of a political prisoner sagging sideways on a chair like a dead body. Regularly, anti-government Polish activists plastered the lamp-posts with lengthy, unreadable screeds denouncing General Jaruzelski. Sometimes, the "ethnic synthesis" was even more inscrutable: in the 3:00 AM silence of Park Avenue, I was wakened by a rhythmic, sonorous chanting. Down on the street, marching swiftly and singing gloriously, was a double file of black men in robes, with a leader and a rear guard in business suits. Some secret black fraternity? I would never know. But I relished their mysterious harmony.

When I lived in Toronto, I read that Jesse Jackson had called New York "Hymietown." I felt angrily betrayed. But living in New York, walking along a busy downtown street, I suddenly thought with defiant joy: "Hymie! I'm a hymie in Hymietown!" I fantasized that one day I would meet Jesse Jackson – in New York, of course – and introduce myself with grave pride as "a hymie from Hymietown." In Manhattan, I was always as waggingly happy as a mutt among mongrels, my tongue hanging out with pleasure at every sign and signal of hybrid breeds.

Friends took me walking on the Lower East Side one broiling hot day (*Loisaida*, in Puerto Rican), promising me delights and surprises if I would just keep going as we limply trailed eastward on shimmering pavement. We crossed the FDR Drive (built on landfill consisting of rubble from blitzed London; Cockney FDR!) and arrived at the East River Park, a shabby and neglected strip of parched grass and trees bordering the river.

Caramba! The place was a living carnival; Puerto Rican children darted everywhere, licking homemade Sno-cones in neon colours bought from rickety carts; shirt-sleeved men sold beer from ice chests; Latin salsa jangled from radios where families sprawled on blankets, the music pierced by the occasional thwack of bat on ball from the dusty diamonds. On the river breeze was borne the rich, roasting smell of pork, and there, sure enough, a man of portly dignity tended a whole pig on a long shaft, which he turned slowly over an immense bed of coals. At the end of the shaft he had mounted the steering wheel of a car, which he handled with the casual flair of a captain at the helm.

For two dollars, he whacked off a piece of dripping, juicy meat for me; I ate it from a napkin as we strolled between the makeshift gambling booths and I marvelled at the peaceable family pleasures so close to the murky terrors of Alphabet City.

"Every Sunday," my friends said, beaming at me smugly, "Puerto Rican paradise."

Eating "ethnic," of course, is the classic way of establishing a warm, if fleeting, bond with New York's hundreds of intimate neighbourhoods and communities.

"What'll it be, sweethot?"

Ah, the music of my favourite Manhattan restaurants; the clink of crockery, the tingling spice of pastrami in the air, the cheerful camaraderie of the infra dig (or, as a friend of mine says, the infra money). Eating out in New York, you take the high road; I'll happily settle for the low.

Haute dining in New York is almost always a disappointment. No corn cakes with caviar, no sorrel sauce or sea urchin soup, can make up for the strain: you have to reserve weeks ahead, dress elegantly, wait in line despite your booking, sit at a table large enough for a saucer of sardines while trying not to smack your neighbour with the outsize menu, and, of course, the bill will be closely followed by post-traumatic shock syndrome.

Besides, price and pretension offer no guarantees. We took guests to the *dernier cri* in restaurants, a place so

■

exquisite that when the waiter brings the dessert of assorted caramel fantasies, he instructs you to eat them counter-clockwise, since they're arranged in ascending intensity of flavours. And then two of our party spent the rest of the night wondering if they would live long enough to find out what was wrong with the fish course they had both ordered.

Nope, give me down and dirty anytime. New York's coffee shops, for example, are one of the city's glories. You can find one on almost any business block, usually with counter and coffee urns straight out of the thirties and forties, most of them no wider than a subway car, and all of them clattering and steaming with busy *bonhomie*. Their names are opaque (Aristotle's and Book Review have no apparent philosophic or literary connections), their characters distinct, and each has its tough and funny counterpersons, wisecracking with the regulars and hollering their orders. "Sunrise on whiskey down!" they bellow for a fried egg on toasted rye.

If you're walking around New York, take a chance on small local caffés (that's not a typo; they're spelled in Italian here). Laden with new books from Three Lives Bookstore, I found a sunny spot in the Peacock Caffé on Greenwich Avenue; it's the kind of place where the tables wobble, you can make an espresso last two hours while you read, and in every dim corner, someone is earnestly writing a novel in longhand. On a cold day, slip into the Caffé Vivaldi on Jones Street to warm up with the crackling fire, classical music, and good sandwiches.

Time your restaurant visit just right and you can end up with unexpected perks. A friend and I walked across the Brooklyn Bridge, wandered chilled and famished around downtown Manhattan, and arrived at the cheap, unrenowned Skydive in the World Trade Center just in time for Friday happy hour: spectacular forty-fourth-floor views up the Hudson River, cosy booths, and a huge free buffet, including cold meats, Caesar salad, and spicy chicken wings. Or loaf over Sunday brunch at Sweet

■

Basil on Seventh Avenue South, and you'll have a coveted seat for a whole afternoon of mellow jazz trumpet by that wonderful old smoothie, Doc Cheatham.

Carefully chosen old restaurants are the perfect place to time travel. On Arthur Avenue, a street in Little Italy in the Bronx that seems untouched since the 1940s, my son and I ate sumptuously at Dominick's after a day of shopping (Parmesan reggiano, pepper bread, fresh roasted espresso) just before the New Year. The whole scene was straight out of the movies. Wood floors, hard-boiled waiters in not-so-white aprons, no menus, strangers sitting elbow-to-elbow at long tables. We were near the bar, where we could hear the Bronx-flavoured exchanges with Charlie, the presiding barkeep and cashier. "Cholly, gimme pitcha beer," or "Cholly. How are ya. A happy and a healthy, Cholly."

Ignore what anyone tells you about New York delis; the only real one left is the Carnegie, and it's succulently worth the wait, the shared tables, and the irreverent and often warring waiters.

If you hate the kind of yuppoid grazing spot that puts marigold petals in the crêpes, you'll love the wild mushrooms with whole roasted garlic cloves at the anti-nouvelle French bistro, Chez Louis, or the steamy clutter of the ancient Grand Dairy Restaurant on the Lower East Side. I was taken there by a friend whose father is the latke and matzah brei cook. All the waiters are old and seem to have bunions. "Ach, figure it out yourself," ours exclaimed, fumbling with the cutlery and then dumping the knives and forks down disgustedly. As we prepared to leave after our breakfast, he grouched, "Have a nice day, but hurry up. I got customers for this table."

For ultra cheap (ten dollars) and savoury curries, try Mitali on East 6th Street, Little India's restaurant row. But if you want to splurge, New York's favourite Indian restaurant (and mine) is Darbar, which is not only unfailingly excellent, but also both sophisticated and comfortable.

The guidebooks will tell you about the glamour spots, but they won't mention the corny delights of John's Italian, on East 12th, a time-honoured hang-out with great garlic bread (still!) and candles on the table. After dinner, stroll around the corner to DeRobertis pastry shop on First Avenue. Pass between the scented heaps of pastries to the ample booths at the back. Admire the ancient but handsome tiled floors and walls; local lore says they were installed by moonlighting tile men from nearby subway construction. Observe the sign that cautions you not to "lay across the seats." Order an espresso and a delicious puff pastry called "lulu" – welcome to the neighbourhood.

It could be argued, I suppose, that Manhattan's fabled social diversity has dwindled to a sort of gustatory dilettantism, a matter of consumer ethnicity. But I'd argue right back. There's more than taste-bud titillation and cheap sentiment at work. The little restaurants are not just doorways into local communities for the browsing outsider, they are also expressions of economic vitality. The neighbourhood restaurant is a leg up into the middle class for its proprietor; it draws money into the area, and acts as a hub of sociability for nearby residents and workers at small businesses.

The savour and tang of New York neighbourhoods arise from the rich jumble of their small-scale businesses, and the specialized services that spring up to supply them. (It's still fun to wander through the colourfully cluttered, though rapidly eroding, special districts: the wholesale-flower district, the button and findings district, the almost-vanished theatrical supply area near Times Square.) Jane Jacobs brilliantly describes the process in *The Death and Life of Great American Cities*. Creativity and enterprise, she says, need old buildings, where rents are marginal and the individual with a good idea can get a start or keep a toe-hold. It is the swarms of such small businesses that keep neighbourhoods percolating with activity, drawing fresh streams of customers, suppliers, and workers throughout the day and night.

Some of my most memorable encounters in New York have been with the practitioners of endangered crafts running their own little shops. Only a large and densely concentrated population can keep such specialized small services afloat. Already, we are accustomed to the homogenizing of smaller cities, with suburban malls and chain stores wiping out local businesses and dooming Main Street to abandonment and decay. Ironically, it is in big cities that you can still encounter the old-world style of small-scale artisanry. But here, too, the faint and foreboding aroma of nostalgia already clings to them.

Bruised memories and tattered hopes – who will mend them?

Irving Chais and Alice Zotta, that's who. They are two of a vanishing tribe of New York artisans who know how to fix things you care about.

I was lured to Irving's New York Doll Hospital (founded in 1900 by his grandparents) by its intriguingly cluttered second-floor window. In the narrow shop, between embankments of broken dolls and mountain ranges of their heaped clothes, a young woman was consulting Irving about a spotted black and yellow toy dog with a torn tummy. Irving wound its tail and it played "How Much Is That Doggie in the Window?"

"Adorable," murmured Irving, who later claimed to be ruthlessly unsentimental. The customer, meanwhile, stared around thunderstruck at "collector dolls," including an original, mint-condition Baby Pebbles for two hundred dollars.

"And just this morning I threw out Dick Tracy's granddaughter!" wailed the young woman.

"You threw out Honey Babe," Irv diagnosed with resigned sorrow. "Try not to think about it."

■

Stitching the spotted dog's stomach, Irving assured me that he's never lost a patient – not even the chewed, water-damaged, rotted, or crumbling ones, for whom he secretively pioneers techniques of reconstructive surgery.

Into the medieval jumble of the narrow old shop (doll torsos dangle from the rafters; rows of bisque heads stare from the shelves; little arms and legs sprout ghoulishly from the rummage), Irving's customers bring awkwardly wrapped bundles of emotion – love, yearning, and nostalgia – disguised as dolls.

"How could I quit?" he says, gesturing to a tower of boxes bearing tattered remnants from all over the United States.

Irving's most dramatic rescue involved three pathetic fragments of a doll's face. They were all that had survived in the pockets of a small girl who went through three Nazi concentration camps. As a middle-aged woman, she brought the fragments to Irving, who instantly recognized the make and style. He even had an original body in stock.

When the woman returned to see the miraculously rebuilt doll, she screamed: "Aimeleh! It's my Aimeleh!" Irving admits only that the woman cried.

Alice Zotta's work has less drama, perhaps, though equal artistry. When I first tracked her down to her cubby-hole in a midtown office tower, I was carrying my best new dress with two burn holes in it. It was reassuring to see women going in mournfully with bundles under their arms, and women coming out joyfully and fairly leaping onto the elevator.

Alice is a reweaver, an invisible mender, and one of the best (and cheapest) in the business. A tiny woman in a green jumper, she is almost invisible herself amidst the heaps of clothes she mends.

"Work? Don't ask. I have a French colonel who brings me things from Paris to mend." She answers the phone. "You see? That's from North Carolina."

■

Alice doesn't like to admit it ("Don't put it in; they'll think I'm crazy") but she loves her work so much that she arrives from her home in New Jersey at six o'clock every morning, seven days a week, and works fifteen hours a day. Even today, Columbus Day, "And he's my paisan!" she chortles. Her only recreation is to serve as a volunteer one night a week at the Hackensack Hospital.

Alice and her sister, Mary, learned the exacting work when they were thirteen years old, unpaid apprentices in the huge Marzotto factory in their home town near Vicenza. Now, in their cosy back room in Manhattan, they listen to Italian opera and peer through magnifying glasses.

"You have to thread the needle each time you weave one line. We take the threads from somewhere it doesn't show, in the hem. Gabardine is the worst. It's woven so tightly; fifty threads where other cloth has thirty. Moth holes, that's bad. You don't see but they chew around the edges and you got quicksand."

There is no pattern they cannot recreate exactly, using only their needles and threads. "You have to be patient; you have to love it," Mary says. "Sixteen is too old to start learning."

Alice works so hard that she never sees television, and therefore sometimes fails to recognize the celebrities who come desperately to her door.

"I've woven for Toscanini and President Kennedy. Lily Tomlin's pants I just did. Travolta came with a body-guard, and Perdue from the chickens. The old man with the cigar burns I didn't recognize till Mary told me it was George Burns." ("Perdue from the chickens" is a well-known poultry merchant.)

When Alice or Mary have mended something, it's impossible to detect the repair. They have invented, for example, a way of weaving in whole pieces of fabric for huge tears that no one else will touch.

"Sometimes people are almost hysterical when they see the results," Alice says, smiling.

■

Alice and her sister came to New York in their teens, alone. To get started, Alice says, "We rented a window by a tailor and sat there working in his shop."

Alice is "too soft" about prices. When custom tailors make an accidental snip in a thousand-dollar suit, they bring it to her and she feels so sorry for them she gives them a discount.

"Look," she says proudly, showing me a white silk dress with a pattern of red roses and green leaves. "Silk you can't weave. Can you see where I fixed the hole?" No, I can't. Even up close. One of the green leaves, it turns out, has been transplanted from the hem and sewn in with fairy-like stitches. Cost: thirty dollars.

When Alice and Irving retire, there will be no one to take their places. The money is good, but there are no young people with the patience to learn.

If you have a doll that's been too well-loved, with pushed-in eyes, maybe, and a torn silk dress, all I can say is get here fast.

If you spot an angry poster in shop windows as you walk by – a picture of Mayor Ed Koch's face circled and crossed through with the red prohibited symbol – you're seeing the last furiously impotent gesture by New York storekeepers as they're about to go under. Mayor Koch has, for three years, blocked a bill for commercial rent controls put forward by council member Ruth Messenger and supported by a majority of the City Council.

When a mayor, in league with mega-developers, heats up the speculative frenzy, more is lost than individual livelihoods. Gourmet food chains, upscale clothing stores, and bland office towers sweep in like blackboard erasers, wiping off the energetic human equation that was written and rewritten there before.

They call it "rent doom." Between four hundred and eight hundred small shops close down every month, according to the Coalition for Fair Business Rents, because of wildly spiralling rents. Bakeries, shoe repairers, pharmacies, cleaners . . . humble but essential services are swept aside by a tidal wave of Benettons, copy shops, and designer-cookie chain stores. Two blocks from our apartment, Joe's Shoe Repair did land-office business in a cluttered little shop evidently unchanged for at least forty years; there were still three tiny booths with swinging half-doors where customers could wait in modest sock-clad privacy while their shoes were repaired.

Joe vanished; so did the Phoenix Book Store, a wonderful old store-front near one of my favourite Greenwich Village cafés. I went there for some hard-to-find poetry and found the owner gloomily holding a closing sale. "Our rent went from $500 to $5,000 this month," he said. The *Village Voice* angrily documented other murders by greed: a Harlem supermarket's monthly rent jumped from $3,500 to $35,000; a florist who was one of Madison Avenue's original "Old New York" merchants saw his rent leap from $6,200 to $41,000.

Skilled workers are becoming as rare as rubies in the imperial city. For one thing, they have nowhere to live: a one-bedroom apartment costs $1,500 to $2,000 a month. Every time rents are cranked higher, the pressure squeezes out more and more ordinary workers and their small-scale establishments. Repair services based in the outer boroughs quickly adjust their prices to the assumed wealth of customers who can actually afford to live in Manhattan. Demand for scarce services, in turn, makes desperate householders willing victims to the bandit-style contractor who juggles six jobs at once. If a plumber tells you he's going out to buy a new length of pipe, don't expect to see him again for a week.

Two armed persons stood in my living room at midnight. "What's the secret code?" the woman said belligerently, her right hand hovering near her holster.

"Um . . . I forget," was my swift rejoinder.

Not only had I forgotten the secret code with which I'm supposed to signal the security company every

■

morning when I turn off our apartment's burglar alarm – I'd also forgotten to turn off the alarm, and had been going in and out all day, gaily tripping the buzzer in their offices. By midnight, the ever-alert security company decided to rush in the troops. From the time the alarm sounded, at dawn, till midnight, when the guards appeared, a genuine New York burglar would have already fenced the government silverware and be ordering margaritas on the beach at Acapulco.

Now these pistoleros summon me out of bed and all but accuse me of being a cat burglar.

"Of course," I finally confess. "I always break into people's apartments at night and put on their night-gowns."

"Okay, honey." The woman giggled. "I guess you got a point."

I tell you this because people love to hear New York horror stories. When you're far away from the imperial capital, it's delightful to contemplate the danger and delirium of life in Gotham City.

Once you're here, you discover that, while danger exists, it strikes so randomly there's no point worrying about it. You're just as likely to be killed by a falling beam from a construction site where corrupt unions have paid off corrupt safety inspectors as you are to be knifed by a cocaine-crazed mugger. A friend of mine who hates New York has had her car, her apartment, and even her front hall burglarized, vandalized, and scandalized. I, on the other hand, love New York and New York loves me – so far. I ride the subways and roam the streets, find twenty-dollar bills in the gutter just when I'm guiltily heading towards an impulse purchase, and have generally enjoyed the good luck of a happy sap who doesn't even know she's supposed to be scared and depressed.

Most of the mugging stories I hear from friends, in fact, have a mordantly funny side to them. A Canadian student is yanked into a dark alley and relieved (at gunpoint) of his cash and his Walkperson. As a thoughtful parting gesture, though, the mugger gives him his cab fare home and the tape from the little cassette player.

My personal horror stories are not about criminals but about the woes of domestic maintenance in a city where maintenance is becoming a lost art of the Incas.

A man arrives to install window blinds. He eyes the window, looks at the blind, and asks for a kitchen knife. "Too wide!" he says merrily, sawing at the wooden roller with the best bread knife. He leaves after putting up blinds that are an inch too narrow and that will thereafter crash to the floor whenever they're raised or lowered.

A plumber comes to discover why it's raining in Father Flaherty's bathroom on the floor below. When he finally departs, his work done, there's a crater in our bathroom floor similar to the Great Rift Valley. The expert tile men arrive. Solemnly, they pave around, down, and into the valley, leaving me with an elegantly tiled built-in catch basin, many assurances of the beauty and distinction of their craftsmanship, and a stupefying bill.

New York repair persons, like dentists, always tell you that the work you've had done previously was a ghastly and irreversible mistake. This softens you up for the bad news that they can't fix it, either, but that will be seventy-five dollars for the service call.

A hinge on our oven door is broken. Detachments of stove experts arrive, shake their heads gloomily, and depart ("That'll be seventy-five dollars for the service call"). Months pass; we learn to live with the crash of a detachable oven door and the threat of crushed toes. At last, defeated, we are driven to buying a new stove. We are charged for delivery, unhooking the old stove, installing the new one, and fifty dollars for the final favour of taking away the perfectly good hingeless one.

The TV goes fuzzy. A woman from Manhattan Cable detects trouble in the wiring in the apartment stairwell. She tinkers a while and tells us someone will come to complete the work. A week later, Manhattan Cable

■

72

returns. I explain where the cable needs fixing. "Oh, that's not my depahtment," says Repair Person A. Porcini. "Inside the apahtment, that's my depahtment. Anything in the hallways, that's another depahtment."

"So why did you come?" I feebly inquire of his departing back. "Have a nice day," he beams in reply.

I call a TV repair shop; the man who answers the phone tries to rent me his condo in Florida. "Very nicely furnished and near the beach," he says. It's a protracted struggle to focus his attention on picture tubes.

In the last throes of printing out a manuscript that is due that week, my computer printer develops spasmodic catalepsy. It starts, it shudders, it stops, it starts again, and faints dead away. At length, I find a computer repair person who says, "I'll be there tomorrow morning." A week goes by, marked by frantic phone calls, more false and cheery promises, a missed deadline, no repair person. I scream at my printer, cry, kick, and beg. It starts. Ten minutes later, the repairman stands in my doorway. "Great! It's working!" he observes keenly. As a special mercy, and in recognition of the fact that he does not have to cross the room actually to look at the machine, he charges me only the $145 minimum service fee.

Compared with the intricacies of domestic maintenance, a simple mugging sometimes seems like an appealingly straightforward disaster.

The housing crisis looms so large and so intractable on every New Yorker's horizon – even the well-housed are affected by the lack of affordable apartments for working people, as my story about bandit repairmen tries to point out – that when I was offered a chance to see a modestly brighter side of the story, I leaped at it.

Anne Lewison, a young Vancouver architect who lives and works in New York, led me forth one sunny January day to see "the unknown Lower East side." Fabled as a crowded immigrant slum at the turn of the century, and notoriously pocked with desolation even now, it is also, as I discovered, a home to some liveable working-class neighbourhoods.

We wandered along East Broadway, where a busy Chinese noodle factory had its door propped open to the sunshine; just above, carved in stone, was the name of the original inhabitant, a Yiddish newspaper. Farther east, and nearly at the southern tip of Manhattan, we came to a corner so obscure it's never mentioned in the guide books: the Two Bridges Urban Renewal Area, tucked between the Williamsburg Bridge to the north and the Manhattan Bridge immediately to the south.

Startled, I found myself in a quiet, red-brick enclave of publicly subsidized apartments built in the 1930s – grass, trees, a faded respectability, children trundling along the sidewalks on plastic trikes. Spanish, black, and Chinese families strolled and chatted. "In summer, they bring out card tables and play under the street lights," Lewison said.

The area may be far from utopian, but these solid buildings are an essential part of what made New York work as a great cosmopolitan city, and not just as a glittering Babylon for the rich.

When Lewison acted as my tour guide, she was still working for a firm (the Edelman Partnership) that was struggling to complete the last public-housing undertakings in Manhattan. President Reagan's relentless cutbacks soon put an end to these last few possibilities, and now Lewison works for an immense international firm.

One of Lewison's projects then was a Chinese senior citizens' apartment on Rutger's Slip, a short, empty street running up from the river, so lost from civic notice that it was officially "unmapped" (water and electricity cut off) some years ago. Lewison stood looking over the rubble-strewn empty lot for which she had scrupulously designed a building that included waist-high planters on the roof, so that elderly gardeners wouldn't have to bend. The lot remained empty for two more years, as the builders wrestled their way through the maze of regulations and straitened budgets. Today, at last, the building is up, and the senior gardeners are enjoying their roof.

A block away, we stopped for a rueful glance at two giant white slabs of apartment buildings, another Edelman project. In a book called *The Unsheltered Woman*, Judith Edelman documented the fourteen-year struggle to build this public housing. It started, in 1971, with a humane and enthusiastic design: street-level stores, playgrounds running down to the East River, spacious, low-rise apartments. Abruptly, then-President Richard Nixon cut off federal housing grants. The project was shelved. Then, unexpectedly, he offered special grants for pre-fab housing. The plans were hauled out and whittled down to suit ready-made concrete boxes. The pre-fab manufacturer went out of business. A new one was found; new plans had to accommodate the new style of boxes.

It reads uncannily like a script outline for Michael Frayn's Broadway hit *Benefactors*, which follows the painful erosion of an idealistic public-housing architect. Like Frayn's anti-hero, Judith Edelman had to watch her innovative buildings grow ever narrower, taller, meaner, on the drawing board. "Well, at least it's good housing with large windows," Lewison said, squinting up in the sunlight.

Almost in the shadow of these slabs we came to a pleasant cluster of three-storey red-brick row houses, also built by the Edelmans. Its genesis was typically loony. A federal grant was available, but only briefly. The city's multi-family-dwellings department couldn't rush through approval of the plans in time; the single-family department could. So single-family housing it is, intimate to the street, with prettily stepped gables.

We ambled through a vibrant Chinatown, past some of Lewison's favourite local signs: "Downstairs Studio: Two Flights Up" and "Dr. Lyons. Child. Adult. Orthodontia. Toothy Repair." We paused at a street stall to buy hot little Hong Kong egg cakes to eat from a paper bag while walking to Lewison's most bizarre assignment that year, a senior citizens' apartment house on the grounds of the monolithic court-house and men's jail known locally as the Tombs.

"We were asked to put anti-helicopter flag-poles on the roof to prevent prison breaks," she said, "but that would have interfered with the community room and garden. Now they're worried about a corner of our roof where the elevator bulkhead blocks the sight-lines of the prison's roof-top surveillance team. We have to fill in the space with a nasty variant of barbed wire called razor ribbon."

From the marble benches outside the Tombs, we surveyed the exhilarating jumble of architecture – from pale art deco to Victorian warehouse to scarlet-and-green Chinese pagoda – that rings the site. The romantically decrepit tenements are vanishing from the Lower East Side, and though Lewison lived in one and loved it, she doesn't mourn their passing. "Yes, they had their beautiful little cornices and carvings. But they were legislated out of existence by quite humane city rules about light, ventilation, and hygiene." Those rules make hassles – "This is low-income, high-headache housing we're building," she joked – but the precious living space that results is worth the headache.

Despite the bureaucratic maze, the smothering weight of three centuries' worth of accrued complications (Lewison was close-mouthed about protracted and ruinous negotiations with the powerful local Chinese Tongs), and the never-ending battle to wrest a little beauty out of starvation budgets, Lewison found it magical to be part of the peopling of Manhattan. "You have to hold on to the idea," she said, sighing over lost skirmishes for patterned brickwork and playgrounds, "that you are providing shelter."

Dogged idealism, however, has found little nourishment in Manhattan in recent years. Public housing has been thoroughly Koched, Trumped, and Bushed. In today's Manhattan, despite the successful example of earlier times, the sun rises and sets to gild the windows of ever more expensive office towers and condos. It was a little while later and a few miles farther up the East Side that I had occasion to experience the building boom for myself.

> The city seen from the Queensborough Bridge is always the city seen for the first time, in its first wild promise of all the mystery and the beauty in the world.
> – F. Scott Fitzgerald, *The Great Gatsby*

Every night for a year I've said good night to the city from my bedroom window where, beyond a pleasantly higgledy-piggledy roofscape, glittered the Queensborough Bridge. "Foolish to rhapsodize over a string of lights, the blaze of a power in which I have not the least part," the poet William Carlos Williams chided himself in a similar romantic moment. But that's just it: you can't help a little inward rhapsody, and you do feel somehow part of the city's immense vitality when you see from your window that sparkling swoop of lights over the East River.

Well, now I've had the quintessential Manhattan experience. They've stolen the Queensborough Bridge – my bridge. One night I noticed a strange dark bite out of its familiar shape; within two weeks, the bite grew into a huge gulp. The bridge had vanished behind an archly nouveau condo called the Uptown Memphis.

View snatching in this city is as common and unpunishable a crime as light bulb snatching. Still, it gives rise to surly thoughts. In a city so vertically crowded, where only the richest or the luckiest own any outdoor space, the view from an apartment window is one's *lebensraum*. You gaze over mighty avenues or hectic sidestreets and feel . . . connected.

New Yorkers fume, fret, throw farewell-to-the-view parties, or sue when their view is gobbled up. But such routine losses are the price you pay for hyper-density.

∎

"Satanic density," someone called it way back in the 1940s. Even farther back, in 1906, Maxim Gorky (who was miffed, anyway, because three different hotels threw the distinguished Russian author out into the street when they discovered that Mrs. Gorky was not Mrs.) saw New York as a giant, remorseless stomach grinding up and digesting its millions of denizens.

On a steaming hot day in August, you have to agree with Gorky's intestinal imagery. Plainly speaking, the city stinks. Waves of stench simmer up from the pavements, where drunks, vagrants, and Pekingese have left their marks, and where hundred-year-old sewers wearily exhale.

The city is so crowded that, when it rains, the avenues are jammed tight with umbrellas. Instant brolly-lock. To move forward at all, New Yorkers have learned to raise and lower their umbrellas as deftly as mariners working the rigging in a stiff gale. Even without rain, the constant pedestrian crowds can be exhausting. There are traffic jams and even collisions when a surge of cross-town bodies meets a surge of uptown bodies at a corner.

Like legendary Muscovites on the breadlines, New Yorkers queue for elevators, art galleries, soft drinks . . . and movies. You don't slip quietly into a popular movie on impulse; you buy your tickets in advance and line up for hours. There are compensations, of course. In the three-hour line-up for a new Woody Allen movie in a blizzard last winter, shivering strangers spelled each other off in the line, bought coffee for one another, and were genially amused by a tramp who shouted at them: "That's why Reagan got elected! Americans are crazy!"

Density means that some people pay more to park their cars mid-town than most Canadians pay to rent an apartment. Rampaging development squeezes out all those of underweening income. In one year alone, seventeen professional dance schools and four large rehearsal halls were demolished as real-estate moguls pushed out

■

the artists. A startled Brooklyn discovered that it had become a thriving creative centre almost overnight as artistic refugees from Manhattan fled across the river.

Despite all the horrors of sardine life in the city, few leave willingly. Gorky himself was baffled by this perversity. Unwittingly anticipating Tama Janowitz by nearly a century, he thought he had never seen "people so enslaved to life as in New York, and so tragicomically self-satisfied as in this huge phantasmagoria of stone, iron and glass."

True then, and still true. Why this insane contentment of New Yorkers? I think it has something to do with the pervasive sense of intensified life. Willy-nilly, you're part of it. The minute you step out of your door into the ceaseless press of the crowds, you have a walk-on part in the twenty-four-hour urban drama. In Toronto, Halifax, or Vancouver, you can stroll in a green dream in the heart of the city, alone as in any suburban cul-de-sac . . . and as stuck with yourself and your rootedness as a tree on a lawn. New York is a magnet because of its glorious double promise: you can cut free of your past, and yet, because everyone is an outsider, everyone instantly belongs. No other world capital confers *de facto* citizenship on newcomers so swiftly or generously.

The disappearance of my bridge, though, leads me to melancholy reflections. Perhaps this is the last of New York as a great city; the point of critical mass has been reached; the infrastructure is crumbling; all the people who made this a city of infinite possibility – the writers, arguers, creators – are being driven out by big-money real estate.

But others have reflected this way before me. "One would think that . . . the bankers and investors and business enterprisers who have been fostering this congestion . . . cancelling out, one by one, every sound reason for living here . . . must consider New York expendable."

Lewis Mumford said that in a fit of gloom. And that was in 1956.

■

All great cities come to us trailing clouds of clichés; snippets of news stories, movies, songs, and novels cling to their very names, and nothing gives us more instant satisfaction than confirming the truth of these preconceptions. Thus, at age nine, I enjoyed the feeling of shocked confirmation in which my family revelled as they told and retold the story of being charged a dollar for bread and butter with their meal in a New York restaurant. High prices, menace, muggers, and, for the past twenty years, the perils of subway travel, are all part of everyone's New York stock-in-trade.

For the first year I lived there, people from home would say automatically, on meeting me and hearing that I now lived in New York, "Oh, I hope you don't take the *subway*." If Manhattan itself is Canada's icon of urban life, the subway is the emblem of all that is dark, fraught with speed and danger, out of control. In fact, since I wrote this heartfelt tribute to underground travel, the subway system has steadily been gentrified to lure middle-class New Yorkers underground, perhaps in order to offset the millions of dollars lost to fare beaters. Stations are cleaner, and some have been renovated to restore their lovely old decorative tiles and wooden benches; I specially like the sedate beaver mosaics at Astor Place station (commemorating John Jacob Astor, whose fortune was built on lowly beaver fur), and the sprightly sloop at South Ferry. More and more cars are clean, well-lit, and even tolerably air-conditioned.

But even here, in the dank recesses of the earth, the gentrifying hand is obliterating the good with the bad. Transit Authority president David Gunn has targeted the beloved subway news-stands and kiosks as "unsightly." Within a year, the number of these little, cosily ramshackle outposts of light, colour, human presence, candy, and sustenance for printaholics, has been slashed from 171 to a mere 52. The wonderfully seedy stores in the Times Square Station are boarded up; even the buskers, jazz guitarists, and blues wailers seem fewer and farther between. In other words, that delicious multiplicity of use that gives you a daily lift, that bracing feeling you get from buying your evening paper as you zip through the station, or catching some tantalizingly dislocated snatch of Mozart or Ellington as you barrel past, all that is swept away, reduced to a dull efficiency.

Well before Bernie Goetz became a dubious national hero by trying to kill four black youths on the IRT at Christmas in 1984, the New York subway had become a hellish metaphor.

While the subways of Moscow, Montreal, London, and Paris are celebrated as distinctive symbols of urban living, the New York subway strikes fear into the hearts of everyone who doesn't live here, and even most of those who do. (A survey in the Bronx revealed that 23 per cent of adults and 33 per cent of youths carry weapons when they go underground, knives being the side-arm of choice.)

As a fairly regular rider of the Terror of the Deep, also known as the Beast by some transit cops, I have to say it's not nearly so bad as it's cracked up to be. True, it has a staggering crime rate, by Canadian standards – eleven homicides, twenty-eight rapes, and thirteen thousand felonies in 1985 – but all things are relative. There were, after all, two thousand murders above ground that year.

Like everything else in New York, the sheer scale of the thing is overwhelming: its size, speed, filth, even its corruption – one tunnel, still not open, has been under construction for twenty years. Three and a half million fares a day are deposited in turnstiles at 463 stations (and 118,000 more fare beaters jump over turnstiles or enter through exit gates); six thousand individually powered cars rattle along 687 miles of track at a top speed of forty miles an hour. Despite the fact that many of the cars are thirty years old and much of the equipment almost farcically outdated, close to 87 per cent of the trains arrive and depart on time.

The subway's terrible reputation is partly a subjective response to frightening surroundings. Nobody knows that better than I; on a visit to New York before I lived here, I took the subway for the first time to get back from the Brooklyn Museum. Flinching down a urine-soaked stairway to the murky depths, I asked directions from a stranger just as the train roared in.

"Don't get on the last ca-a-ar!" he screamed after me as I sprinted for the train. (The parlour car, as it's known, is the mobile headquarters for drug dealers.) I rode all the way to Manhattan in the heroic mood of one who has overcome great peril.

But the crime rate underground is in fact dropping, partly because of the four thousand transit police, at least one on every train after 8:00 PM. "Of course," conceded transit spokesman Bob Slovak, "an armed robbery in a train is a lot scarier, because there's nowhere to flee."

That thought does occur to me now and then as I joggle along in the stench, crowds, and graffiti grottiness. It's hard not to feel menaced in a car that resembles a moving coal bin, where the few working lights flicker wanly, and every possible surface (including emergency exit instructions) is a black smear of illiterate spray-painted scrawl.

(By 1989, every car on the east side lines, which are making a determined pitch for Wall Street commuters, is a model of sprightly newness. The cars with the hideously uncomfortable orange plastic seats, which don't fit anyone's derriere, are said to be Canadian made.)

The stations now have brightly lit "off-hours waiting areas" in sight of the ticket booth, where late travellers grimly bunch together. Around them stretch Piranesi vistas of vaulted gloom. Water drips from rusted overhead pipes to collect in rancid puddles on the stairways and between the tracks, scummed over with disintegrating candy wrappers and coffee cups. You imagine, though you rarely see, the rats.

The mad and the desperate are more visible. Beggars hiss at you on the stairways; sleepers bundled by the walls have the pallor of death, as though they haven't surfaced to the light in years . . . as indeed they may not have. Transit police call the homeless derelicts who live in abandoned tunnels "skells," a hideously evocative word. On the Grand Central Shuttle the other day, passengers practised stony avoidance as a trance-eyed man, whose denim jacket announced "Con-Chon-Thon for Lord Jesus, Master Dragon," treated us to a wheezing religious rap.

It wasn't always like this. In 1912, workers excavating for the new BMT were astonished to dig up the forgotten remains of the Beach Pneumatic Subway, the 1870 creation of Alfred Ely Beach. Any of us might have been amazed: that very first New York subway had a luxurious plush-seated car that ran a total of 312 feet under Broadway, propelled from behind by a huge fan. The carpeted – carpeted! – station was complete with paintings, a fountain, a grand piano, and Grecian statues holding up elegant globe lamps.

The current subway opened in 1904, and its first full day of operation earned the headline "Rush Hour Blockade." Rush hour is still traumatic. The police have thirty-seven German shepherds ("They're not dogs, they're wolves," leered Mayor Ed Koch) who, despite their limitations – they can't pursue thieves up escalators – have an impressive arrest record, being trained to "bite and hold, rather than devour a person's flesh" according to a reassuring officer. But rush hour is still the peak crime time.

I admit that it sounds, and frequently smells, awful. In summer, the heat, especially in stalled cars, is unbearable. The aging tracks are probably the world's noisiest. Still, improvements (rather like the work of Sisyphus) are ongoing. I have actually ridden on a gleaming new graffiti-free silver express to Brooklyn, in which a mellifluous conductor coaxingly announced, over a clear PA system, "Your local is waiting across the platform; step lively now to make your connection." The connection turned out to be a sinister, filthy shuttle in which restless teenagers passed ceaselessly from car to car, looking for easy marks.

■

Is this an indictment of the New York subway? No. Criss-crossing the city underground, I am always awed by the speed and convenience with which it transports its human freight, and I never fail to imagine the snarling, gridlocked traffic somewhere over my head. Part of New York's greatness is due to its huge, concentrated working population, and the city simply could not exist without the subway. Perhaps no city can be great without a subway.

Screeching, grinding, rattling, and roaring through the years, the subway still speaks hauntingly of the motto carved in stone at the City Hall station, a testament to that co-operative urban spirit: *Non nobis nati solum* – born not for ourselves alone.

Everywhere in Manhattan today, the lusty populism of that subway motto is at war with the narrow and crass élitism of the new rich. You could almost say that the roar and screech of the subway, anthem of New York's working people, is drowned by the collective purr of massed stretch limousines. All those distinctive democratic qualities that made New York liveable and whose echoes and reminders I cherish – the bustling life of neighbourhoods, of small industry and shops, of vigorously inventive street language; the tremendous underlying musculature of the subway, linking it all together and making it possible – are now at risk. New York is being smothered by the blight of limitless greed. To global money and its legions of manipulators, liveable New York is a pesky nuisance.

CHAPTER 3
·
Tom Wolfe's New York

If fate hadn't washed me up in Tom Wolfe's neighbourhood (on the same street, in fact), like a cuckoo in the nest of highest privilege, I might never have believed his fevered vision of *fin de siècle* life at the top. I might not have believed the fixation on status, the obsession with creamily perfect surfaces, the intense vacuity of the very rich, the perfumed airiness of their daily lives, and, above all, their paranoia.

To live in that bubble of wealth, that fragile shimmer of ease and safety surrounding the very rich in New York, is entrancing: you waft on the heady currents of flattery, power, sensual ease, *service*. But the price you pay, to judge by Tom Wolfe's *Bonfire of the Vanities*, is that thrill of pure icy horror along your veins when, every now and then, you sniff the cold, cloacal breath of menace gusting at you from the dark swamp. Every privileged class in history, I suppose, has had to repress its own fear of the poverty-stricken and potentially rebellious masses. Rarely, though, has a class of obscenely wealthy robber barons flaunted its riches so blithely under the very noses of the deprived and the hopeless – and this in the heart of a culture that constantly proclaims its classless-ness, opportunity, and democratic values.

Tom Wolfe is the perfect chronicler of the super-heated eighties in Manhattan, the time of "cataclysmic money," as Jane Jacobs presciently called it more than twenty years ago – money in such huge and sudden quantities that it churns up a society's value system, overturns the stable patterns of employment and the housing market, and subjects an entire city to uncontrollable upheaval.

In New York in the 1980s, money gushes like tap-water. Showered with financial preference by President Reagan and Mayor Ed Koch, the leverage artists, the arbitrageurs, and the mega-developers wallow in tax-free profits beyond the dreams of avarice. They loom through the waters like enormous predators, attended by fluttering schools of parasites: flower arrangers, real-estate agents, decorators, antique dealers, couturiers, gossip columnists – like those snouty little *ramoras* (shark suckers) clustering around sharks.

Wolfe, a diminutive southern fop, his brilliant powers of observation and phrase-making honed by malice, claims to adore New York and to relish big-city life – but his earlier writing had already made clear his contempt for liberals, his loathing for modernism, and his dainty aversion to the people he once archly called "the coloured brethren." (To me, what made New York great had everything to do with its liberalism, its eager espousal of modernity in the arts, its intellectual energy and melding of diverse peoples . . . but that view belongs to another chapter.) He early idolized Napoleon and later glorified the Reagan-era astronauts; in *Bonfire of the Vanities*, only the macho Irish cops whose brutishness comes to them naturally emerge unscathed. The blacks are gutter criminals, cold-eyed charlatans, or "pimp-rolling" homeboys, (the "pimp roll," Wolfe explains, is the exaggeratedly springy, swaggering walk of ghetto males); the Jews are pathetically transparent publicity hounds, corruptly self-seeking under a thin veneer of populism; the old-money Yankee WASPs are weak, waning, and cowardly, forced to swallow the dominance of the overweening *nouveau riche*.

Bonfire's protagonist Sherman McCoy is a bond salesman so successful that he surveys Manhattan from his Wall Street tower and intoxicatedly imagines himself a "Master of the Universe." He has everything that New Yorkers allegedly dream of: a sumptuous Park Avenue co-op, "imperious posture," elegant WASP schooling and connections, a $1 million income, a $48,000 black Mercedes roadster, a thin, socially correct wife, a pretty little daughter with the upper-crust unisex name of Campbell, and a sexy Southern mistress whom he meets for assignations in a rent-controlled brownstone flat just a few blocks from home.

Sherman's fall from this state of grace is stunningly swift and hideously inexorable. Picking up his mistress at Kennedy

Airport, he drives back to New York, makes a wrong turn off the Triborough Bridge into the Bronx and, lost and panicky, finally has an accident in which a black youth is injured.

In the court case that follows, McCoy becomes a helpless pawn in the corrupt political and careerist games of prosecutors, lawyers, black "poverty kings" and agitators, TV newscasters, and the tabloid press. We follow the various white players into their clubby restaurants, their Versailles-style dinner parties, their *faux* antique offices and summery Long Island beach clubs. And we follow McCoy in his increasingly dishevelled and sweating downward spiral, into the seedy downtown offices of criminal lawyers, into a Bronx jail, and into ultimate ruin.

In the course of one magazine interview, Tom Wolfe compared himself favourably to Addison, Steele, Thackeray, Balzac, and Dickens, but these large ambitions are undermined by the smallness of his vision: "perfect journalism," he told an interviewer in 1962, "would deal with only one subject: status." That credo still seems relevant to his journalistic novel of 1987. But if you define New York in those terms, as wholly about raw power and greed, a struggle for dominance through money and political leverage, then you are left with a very narrow and grimy lens through which to view urban life. There can be only two states of being: gloating conquest or abject debasement. There can be only two kinds of human being (but only one sex that counts): successful conquistadors and failed ones. Tom Wolfe brings a vindictive energy to this view of New York, and within its distorted frame, he's racily convincing.

I lived at the very centre (geographically) of Tom Wolfe's New York, and though the real world I inhabited there was as different from his as day from night, I know he had the details right.

Our apartment was at the epicentre, one of those stodgy old Park Avenue buildings fashioned for spacious and discreet comfort. A rotating guard of affable doormen manned the lobby with its forest-green leather couches where no one ever sat. They sprang to greet tenants with unfailing smiles, a ready hand to snatch shopping bags or suitcases, a uniformed arm already upraised as they rushed to flag a cab or meet the arriving limo with an umbrella. (A superfluous touch, since a green canopy reached from door to curb over the carpeted path across the sidewalk. No resident ever need be touched by the elements.)

The rich understand how to arrange their comforts. The Park Avenue doorman is neighbour, confidant, self-effacing servant; he manages to convey sincere regard and eagerness to please while muting any unpleasant undertones of either obsequiousness or democratic assertiveness. Until you have experienced the doorman's daily ministrations, smoothing your way in or out with nearly invisible human solicitude, you cannot imagine the aura of snug well-being he imparts.

(For one thing, the doormen are the eyes and ears of the building; they keep running lists of who's in and who's out; they forewarn you on your arrival that your husband is upstairs meeting with four diplomats, that your daughter has just arrived with her school friends, or that your son said he'd be back late. They keep extra keys in case you lose yours, relay messages to your nearest and dearest, and are always there to receive packages, deliver mail and newspapers to your door, or chase after your escaping cat.)

Everything hums in the well-run Park Avenue co-op. The elevator is indeed, as Wolfe described it, panelled in glowing mahogany, plushly carpeted, a little leather seat in the corner for the languid, and equipped with a button marked "C" to alert the doorman that you are on your way down and want a cab to be waiting. (We, Canadian neophytes, had lived there a year before we divined the purpose of the C button.)

The butcher and the baker arrive quietly at the kitchen door, supervised by an ever-alert "back elevator man," to hand over grocery orders to the cook. The building handyman comes at a summons (relayed through a private phone to the doorman and thence to the back) to change light bulbs or help move furniture.

■

Only gradually did I begin to comprehend the rules of decorum that control the tenants' behaviour and maintain their silky assurance of status.

It was September; New York was still sweltering, and I had but recently arrived. I found myself sharing the elevator with another tenant, a woman swathed in approximately two thousand dollars' worth of beige, and an unguessable sum of daytime gold jewellery. She flicked a cool glance at my bare legs and sandalled feet and evinced a tiny grimace of a smile, wavering between disgust and amused condescension. "No stockings, I see."

"Never before the snow flies," I chirped with an ill-calculated grin.

A month later, Manhattan still sweltered. Madame Beige in the elevator, me still in sandals. "You must be chilly without stockings," she minced.

These two remarks were the sum total of all conversation ever addressed to me in three years of riding that elevator. Diplomats, as I could not have guessed then when I was so new to the company of the super rich, were considered undesirable. Most co-ops, whose boards of directors grill every prospective buyer, no longer admit diplomats, who may bring "too many parties" or even security guards in their wake. Furthermore, a woman who violated the meticulous dress code of the upper crust was a threat to the entire tone of the building.

We were astonished to receive a letter from the building management company reminding us that "household staff" must never, under any circumstances, use the front elevators. We were incensed by the insult to our cook and our housekeeper, and we replied acerbically. The management company was baffled. "But how would *you* feel if you were going out for the evening and had to ride in the elevator with some woman dressed in rags?"

This was my first real glimpse into the bizarrely paranoid inner life of the more-than-rich; they are shaken by the mere sight of anyone within their bubble who isn't equally wealthy. Furthermore, their hold on reality is extremely tenuous. Only a lunatic could have imagined our cook and our housekeeper, intelligent, briskly competent, and impeccably groomed, as "women dressed in rags."

Wolfe had this part right: the utter emptiness of the new rich. No one in his book ever reads books, sees a play, argues about ideas, acts out of compassion or tenderness or altruism. No one volunteers to help the homeless: there are no homeless in the book (and no real-estate developers, either). Status is everything, and expensive real estate is the outward sign of status achieved. The co-op dwellers of Park and Fifth avenues maintain the brittle façade of high status by screening new applicants for ownership with exacting standards. I learned about this world in the pages of *Avenue* magazine, a five-dollar publication so glossy that you could use just one of its thick pages to prop a wobbly table leg. *Avenue* was delivered free to our door because its publisher lived in our building; reading its articles, I learned that if you wished to buy one of these $6 million co-ops, you must not be a gaudy entertainer, an unindicted ex-president, an heiress like Gloria Vanderbilt who co-habits with a black entertainer, or "one too many" of an undesirable ethnic group, since some co-op boards try to prevent their building from "tipping" by limiting the number of Jews. Your children must be enrolled in the right private schools, you must dress with conservative and expensive taste, and you absolutely must be able to show the co-op board your stock portfolio, representing a minimum of $30 million in liquid assets.

If you pass all these acid tests, you may be admitted to the hallowed precincts where fourteen-foot ceilings and heavy draperies hush the sounds of the streets below, and where the mere mention of your zip code (10021) will guarantee reverent attentions from the merchant class.

It's a mellow October afternoon, a day when Wall Street has taken a nosedive, and Luca Donovic is enjoying the sunshine on his wraparound penthouse terrace on Park

Avenue. He is beaming at his floppy roses with the old-fashioned scent, at his ripe strawberries, at his view. Ah, the view. The russet and gold of autumn in Central Park, the far banks of the Hudson River.

"Fifth Avenue is nice," he says reflectively, "but the people who live there are stars and entertainers, you know, new millionaires. Park Avenue is, well . . . the ultimate."

Luca Donovic can smile, because a stock market crash means nothing to him or his pretty, dark-eyed wife, Anna. Their three little girls, from their sunny terrace playhouse, can look down placidly on those nervous Fifth Avenue millionaires. The Donovics live here rent free. In perpetuity.

Luca Donovic is the superintendent of his building. There are thirty-four owners of the gigantic old apartments here, and they will do just about anything to please a superintendent who is honest and friendly and faithfully calls the plumber when the ancient pipes leak on the Aubusson rugs. Among the things the co-op board did to please Luca, who came to New York fifteen years ago as a penniless Yugoslavian youth, was to knock together twelve servants' rooms to make him a glamorous apartment. They knew Luca was worth it, because he had been the building's handyman for five years, cheerfully changing light bulbs in ceilings too high for dowagers to reach.

Reliable Park Avenue supers are so cherished, according to *New York* magazine, that several of them are similarly housed in penthouse apartments with greenhouses and even gold-plated taps.

If I tell my New York friends about Luca, I will see their eyes glaze with real-estate lust. They can't help it. (My own eyes are somewhat glassy.) Real estate is an obsession in New York; the first question anyone asks on being introduced is not "What do you do?" but "Where do you live?" Gentle souls admit to scanning the obituaries to be the first to spot the demise of a neighbour with a coveted apartment.

The housing crisis (I know someone who paid $500 a month to sleep on a friend's living-room couch; forget about even a modest two-bedroom apartment if you don't have $2,500 a month) has added a new layer to the cumulative mythos of Manhattan. Tama Janowitz made a reputation and a fortune with her first book, *Slaves of New York*, about women who couldn't leave their boyfriends because they'd lose their accommodation.

Now, apartments have become a prime factor in the pattern of marriage. Divorcing couples insist on staying in the same apartment but splitting the turf: one gets the bedroom, the other gets the living room. "I've seen fights over shelves in refrigerators," one lawyer told the *New York Times*. Couples are working out a whole new sociology of separate-but-together hostilities.

There's a metaphysical aspect to apartment divorce. Neither spouse wants to move out because not only is an apartment rarer than rubies, it's also a potential ruby mine. Most buildings are converted to co-ops sooner or later, and, in order to mute tenants' protests, the developer usually gives them a low "insider" price. Profits are legendary; some people sell their newly bought co-ops for twice the insider price. Who would give up a potential windfall like that? So now lawyers are debating whether future profits, if and when an apartment goes co-op, are part of the marital assets and subject to equal division, even if they come long after the divorce.

Economists in New York talk about "wealth maximization," while the city toys with the idea of putting the homeless in floating hostels built on barges. (Barges are the latest solution to everyone the city doesn't want. Floating prisons already exist. One day, all those barges will be gentrified and sold as co-ops.)

All the world's cities have gone speculator mad. In Tokyo, young couples are delighted to buy a two-bedroom apartment for $280,000, just a two-hour commute from their jobs. In Toronto, my son, a student, calls in triumph to report that he's found a ramshackle, third-floor walk-up over a restaurant, to be shared with two others, for only $1,500 a month. Students now spend more time working to pay for housing than they do studying.

Watching the homeless shuffle along the Manhattan sidewalks (nearly four hundred city children are in foster care for the sole reason that their parents have nowhere to live), I conclude that the most pressing task facing government – any government – is to start thinking hard about where people will live.

Not everyone, after all, can aspire to be a superintendent.

A dazzling address is just the beginning for the New Society. A man who's just made a quick fortune (like junk-bond trader Michael Milken, with his $500 million "earned" in one year) must also have a stick-thin young wife who will be the visible token of his ascendancy. Her surface must be plastic-perfect, because her role in life is to flaunt her husband's unlimited wealth (hence, power) on her back. To achieve physical perfection is exhausting and expensive work: it requires an army of personal aerobics trainers; plastic surgeons and up-to-the-minute spa directors; couturiers; "image" consultants; highly exclusive florists to surround the queenly one with distinctive arrangements; jewels and furniture with historic overtones, acquired flamboyantly at auction; interior decorators with established upper-class taste, preferably the European-educated daughters of old money.

Naturally, an entire world of merchandising has sprung up to cater to the new wealth. Its name is Madison Avenue.

Dashing up Madison Avenue to my dentist, I could swear that the merchants spray the air with perfume. Or maybe it's just the scented presence of the Beautiful People, who, after lunch amidst orchids at Maxim's or Le Relais, waft up the avenue in a blur of mink, suede, and Opium.

Upper Madison Avenue – more exclusive, more intimate, more cosmopolitan and seductive than Fifth – has become their playground. And its allure is potent. Even if you have never before lusted after a crimson art-deco evening bag or a cunning silver pocket flask, you may find yourself drooling just a little. Madison Avenue is so outrageously, arrogantly, unself-consciously luxe that it has the power to mesmerize you with its own values, even if only for a few blinding blocks.

It's a street of contradictions. A pleasant small-scale jumble of nineteenth-century brownstones, Madison still wears an air of sunny gentility from its earlier days, when butchers, bakers, and linen drapers catered to Old Money. A few old-time shops linger on, a study in complacent understatement or expensive, comfy bad taste – like the florists Christatos and Koster, who think nothing of displaying a ghastly Thanksgiving turkey centrepiece made up of painted mums and heather.

But almost daily a new European boutique opens for business behind a renovated curve of glass and sleeking of brass. Ungaro, Valentino, Sonya Rykiel, Kenzo, Isobel Canovas, Yves St. Laurent, Pratesi, Cartier. The prevailing tone is one of ostentation with a hard, serpentine edge. Alligator purses abound. Fred Leighton's window has a diamond *pavé* dragon-fly the size of a lobster, a ruby-studded praying mantis, gemmed lizards, and emerald-eyed snakes to twine around your neck. Shamelessness is *de rigueur*. In a town house where Imelda Marcos once lived, a young entrepreneur opens a shop selling gem-studded shoes for $15,000 a pair.

Gold is the unabashed favourite colour of the new Age of Greed. Chunks, strands, and swaths of gold; gold lamé jackets, gold-scalloped evening gloves, gold-trimmed velvet boots at Charles Jourdan; dark gold with a sullen gleam in the trendier shops; even gold sneakers at

■

Tennis Lady. "We must not be afraid of snobbism and luxury!" was the gleeful cry of Diana Vreeland, former editor of *Vogue* and fashion guru to the Nancy Reagan social set. What but snobbism, indeed, can explain the mink pompons, looking like mutant bacteria, that are dotted all over the puffed scarlet sleeves of a Givenchy evening gown?

On Madison Avenue, it's clear that nothing can stand firm against the vortex of neo-consumerism. Counter-culture styles are swiftly co-opted here. Poverty is the inspiration for modishly tattered rags on one set of mannequins. Others sport chin stubble and spiky hair. Mannequins wear a universal sneer; traditional ones, at Jaeger, have hard chins and mean hair-dos, à la Thatcher; trendy ones, at Skin, are gold, hairless, and splattered with multi-coloured paint that makes them look as though they're decomposing. And at Moga, a nice touch of seasonal satire: the mannequins hold naked rubber turkeys, with boxes of Stove Top stuffing propped around their ankles.

At the Gertrude Stein Gallery (no actual relation to the writer), a poster showing a naked woman surrounded by paintings quotes the author: "If you are not rich, either you buy clothes or you buy art," but one doubts whether such a difficult choice confronts Madison Avenue art collectors.

At one o'clock, a long line-up is waiting at the Whitney Museum to see the John Singer Sargent show. "Oh, the fabric!" the spectators murmur in front of Sargent's elegant, satiny portraits of etiolated society women and art patrons.

The crowning emblem of the avenue is the frothy Rhinelander mansion, now richly renovated to house Polo/Ralph Lauren. Everything – the dark panelling, the baronial clutter, the air spiced with potpourri and warmed by open fires – is carefully calculated to showcase Lauren's idea of landed gentry clothes and *ancien régime* furnishings.

No blatant, gluttonous gold here. Lauren aims for a higher tone: Greed with Breeding. A camel-hair throw, for example, reverses to mink for $15,000; a soft crush of maroon velvet covers a duvet; a chalk-striped, dark-grey bed cover (the boardroom look for bedtime) is $1,450. The portraits of ancestors (whose?) and hunting dogs; the colours of claret, pewter, terracotta, and forest green, all whisper "New Old Money."

When you stagger out to the street at last ("He was carrying a Macy's bag, but he *looked* well-dressed," a doorman is remarking to a colleague), you feel sickeningly sated, as though you've gorged on pheasant.

Of course, even the Croesus-rich Park Avenue woman who shops Madison Avenue has not fulfilled her duty to her husband until she is established in the ranks of the most exclusive level of society, the *grandes dames* of the charity establishment.

Like a fading Greek chorus, the really old money watches the antics of the new and laments, laments the passing of the old. (Well, sort of old. Aristocracy in America mostly goes back only as far as the looters and plunderers of the nineteenth century.)

My one personal brush with the original aristocracy opened my eyes to deeper and deeper layers of snobbishness. It is the custom, apparently, for the women of the Colonial Dames of America (all of whom are descendants of the Pilgrims) to invite the new Canadian UN ambassador's wife to tea at the Colony Club, directly across the street from the official residence. The Colony Club was founded in 1903 by Daisy Harriman and a group of other socialites because, as Harriman explains in her 1923 memoir, her husband absolutely forbade her to stay at a hotel when she came up to town one summer when her New York home was being wallpapered. The women needed a place "to stop in town," to telephone, and "to have parcels sent."

Inside, I was at once alerted, by the paper-thin shabby rugs and aura of skimpy gentility, that I was in the sanctum of the true upper-crust, who would rather die than flaunt. In a dim little sitting-room, my five hostesses made gentle and vaguely bemused conversation while we took tea. A maid in an apron offered triangles of cinnamon toast snuggled in a napkin on a tray. I racked my brains to remember my mother's teachings in ladylike behaviour, and, on being insistently offered my fourth triangle, politely refused.

"Oh, do eat up your toast," snapped one of the dowagers, "so we can have dessert."

The women reminisced about life in an earlier New York: skating in Central Park under the watchful eyes of governesses, carriage rides to church, supervised walks in the neighbourhood. And one of them cried at last, "Oh, Madison Avenue! All ruined now. Simply overrun with foreign shops."

So much for Ungaro, et al. If the new society wants to reach the heights, mere shopping will not do. Reactionary sports are important, too: polo, riding to hounds, and, above all, riding side-saddle. Barbara Tobler, editor of *Brides' Magazine*, confided the thrill of it to *Avenue*: "When I want to go back to a time that is simpler and prettier, I ride sidesaddle. It's fun and very romantic. You feel pretty and old-world." Tobler, whose husband is a corporate president, prances in Central Park in "an authentic eighteenth century apricot wool habit with plumed hat." Tracy Topping, a side-saddle competitor in horse shows, shares her secret of success: "Get out there and be as snobby as you can. Wear the air of a lady, very proper, very English, one of the royalty." And Patsy Topping, no relation, sums up the *nouveau riche* woman's attitude for *Avenue* with a gush of self-revelation: "The most perfect thing is to look absolutely marvellous on the horse, look everyone's dream of what a woman should be."

Looking everyone's dream of a woman requires the aid of couturiers, a fashion that reached its height in the mounting hysteria about the extravagant French couturier Christian LaCroix in the fall of 1987, within days of the Wall Street crash. Julie Baumgold, the journalistic acolyte of Tom Wolfe, covers the antics of the new rich for *New York* magazine with the same Wolfian tone of awed excitement laced with contempt. "Clothes of such brilliant luxury and defiance probably haven't been seen since the eighteenth-century French aristocrats rattled in carts over the cobblestones on their way to the guillotine," she wrote, urgently cataloguing the collection's cabbage roses, petticoats, bustiers, four-foot skirts, feathers, swags and garlands, farthingales, and hoops.

But women who buy $30,000 dresses (and the fuchsia shoes and the diamonds to go with them), women who submit themselves to the grotesqueries of the "erotic, the nipped waist, high heels, ruffles, exposed leg and bosom – the self-conscious eroticized woman," in Baumgold's words, are not doing it for their soul's delight. They must be seen. It is up to them to be pictured in *Women's Wear Daily*, to be chronicled by Baumgold and lionized by Suzy, the *Post*'s gossip columnist; it is up to them to signal their husbands' wealth to the world and to climb in society, so that the wealth can achieve the patina of social prominence and acceptability.

Hence the mania for charity events. According to *Avenue* magazine, my social gospel, the competition for the chair of annual charity balls is so costly and so vicious that it makes a presidential campaign look like tea at the Colony Club. Large donations and tireless socializing are the prerequisites. From early fall until early spring, *Avenue* listed at least one major social event (on behalf of an art or a disease) every night of the year. Women like Blaine Trump and Carolyne Roehm, Gayfryd Steinberg and Kimberly Farkas, women with Filofaxes who simply *long* to dine at home at least one night a month, slave over the details of lavish parties at the Metropolitan Museum of Art, the New York Public Library, the World Financial Center's Winter Garden. Their favourite florists give interviews to the press, confessing their pettish and very exclusive peccadillos: "No *American* flowers . . . only exotica from Europe."

Floral extravagances can cost $350,000 for a really topnotch private party. When the children of the new rich marry, they tend to do so in well-documented frenzies of expense; one $3 million society wedding featured custom-made shoes for each member of the bridegroom's retinue.

Talking to *Avenue* magazine, two of society's *emaciati*, Mai Hallingby and Kimberly Farkas, who between them in 1987 chaired galas, boating parties, masquerades, luncheons, auctions, and fashion shows for the Lenox Hill Hospital, the Boys' Club, the Angel Fountain in Central Park, the Metropolitan Opera, the Citymeals-on-Wheels, the New York Ballet, the New York Philharmonic, and the Seeing Eye, summed up the tenor of the times.

"I must say that whatever your political affiliation, I don't think anyone entertains as well as the Reagans . . . it's an art they've fine-tuned," Kimberly said. They predicted, despite the crash, only the faintest paling of the new extravagance for the coming year: "Short hem lines, smaller poufs . . . romanticism . . . the women's movement is sort of out . . . convertible cars . . . drapes on the floor, very opulent and lavish decor . . . More is more! Basically, you're talking about great wealth, and that is still here."

Socialites may quiver secretly, but they admit no public qualms when even the mightiest among them is taken away in handcuffs. After Boesky, after Milken, *Avenue* magazine blithely did a resort-like guide to the nicest white-collar prisons, meticulously rating recreational facilities and cuisine.

And still, the public couldn't get enough of the antics of the rich. Of course, it helps when the rich own the public-relations vehicles with which to glorify themselves. Peter Price, whose wife publishes *Avenue* magazine, was one of the triumvirate that bought the *New York Post* from Rupert Murdoch. Malcolm Forbes, no slouch at self-promotion himself, not only publishes *Forbes* magazine but gives his honoured visitors money-green neckties inscribed with the slogan "Capitalist Tool." Now and then, Forbes judiciously lends his yacht *Highlander* to semi-public events, like a luncheon for ambassadors' wives, to which I was invited.

Each guest on the spectacularly sleek yacht – a 151-foot, seventeen-room, fourteen-bathroom ship – is given a glossy colour brochure detailing the Forbes shipboard inventory:

■

the landing pad on the deck for the matching green helicopter; the antique furniture and Impressionist paintings; the specially designed, spankingly nautical uniforms of the galley crew, complete with little crossed gold knives and forks on their shoulder flashes.

Donald Trump, a billionaire who built his fortune on the strength of unsavoury real-estate deals and tax breaks (financed, of course, by the lowly taxpayer), is daily glorified. His smug and petulant mug sulks from the covers of glossy magazines; newspapers rush to print details of his hour-by-hour boasting and self-congratulation; his autobiographical *Trump: The Art of the Deal* was an instant best-seller. Trump's yacht, Trump's helicopters, Trump's airlines and casinos . . . breathlessly, the magazines record every gleaming toy. America, led by its fatuous former first couple, is in love with money.

Unfortunately, the trickle-down theory of Reaganomics works only for social values, not for actual wealth. As the gulf between rich and poor steadily yawned wider throughout the 1980s, the masses (those who weren't homeless) were glued to television programs like *Lifestyles of the Rich and Famous* or *Dynasty*, eagerly soaking up the attitudes of the same élite that was wringing them for cash.

Towards my first Christmas in Manhattan, as loudspeakers everywhere pumped out hymns and carols over the heads of frenzied shoppers, I walked over to F.A.O. Schwartz, New York's best-known toy store, to see operant conditioning for the junior crowd.

> Past the teddy bears he races; past the construction sets, the giant walk-on piano keyboard, the hand puppets, and the life-sized baby elephant, and screeches to a halt at last in front of a floor-to-ceiling display.
>
> "There it is, Daddy!" he shouts, his five-year-old face glowing with cherubic joy. "I seen it on TV!" Ah, the innocent dreams of the young. Here, in New York's premier toy store, he has found his heart's delight.

It is Voltron, Defender of the Universe, a giant robot "armed with powerful weapons to defeat the incredible army of evil." Voltron's "friends" are the monosyllabically macho Lance, Keith, and Hunk, plus the lovely blonde Princess Allura. Voltron's head is helmeted; his feet are armoured cars; his hands are tanks; his Zarkon Zapper laser cannon "wreaks chaos and fear throughout the universe," and on his mighty chest he wears a golden cross.

If there is a strange echo of neo-conservatism's worldview here, with its intertwined themes of religiosity, militarism, and strict gender roles, that should not surprise us. Toy manufacturers, bless 'em, are ever alert to the *Zeitgeist*; this year's playthings look as though they were designed by a special Hanna-Barbera team of Jerry Falwell, Phyllis Schlafly, and Caspar Weinberger.

Still and small is the Voice of Women, oldest of Canada's peace groups, which is protesting against the purchase of war toys this festive season. The group's modest leaflet, arriving in the mail, sent me out to reconnoitre the toy departments of Manhattan. I went with a small doubt in my heart. War toys, I thought, say more about the adults who design and buy them than they do about children, who are notorious for ignoring adult purposes in their play. Well I remember the GI Joe who sneaked into our house in the Trojan horse of a birthday present, and who subsequently led a damp and peaceful life as a deep-sea diver in the bathtub.

Besides, I thought, I, too, had played cowboy bang-bang games as a child, and I did not grow into a warmonger.

What I saw in the toy stores, however, changed my mind. Fast away the old year passes, and hail the new, ye lads and lasses. What's new is that the lads and lasses are now in a space-war frenzy, whipped up by television cartoons whose entire content is written and designed to promote merchandise spin-offs. The way children play with these toys, according to some parents and teachers, is virtually scripted by the cartoons. We fondly think of children's play as free-wheeling, creative, using toys in ways undreamed of by their makers. But now, when children cavort with Voltron or He-Man, Master of the Universe, they tend to use these power-crazed heroes exactly as prescribed, mimicking the precise story line and language of the commercial cartoons.

And the story line is just so rigid, repetitiously, revoltingly bad. Outer space is not a mystery, but a battleground; heaven is the good guys' fortress with "gun turrets, holographic stun cannons, detention cell and swivelling anti-gravity howitzers," and that bright star shining in the east is probably the Evil Network's space station, complete with removal rocket platform.

True, such toys will not automatically turn a child into a slavering killer. But, unlike in Yuletides of yore, this year's Toyland is monolithically military, and the glorification of male violence is overwhelming. You'll be hard pressed to find mass-market toys that don't fit the formula. The good guys all have "space bunkers" with awesome weapons; their goal is universal dominance; their hair is blonde; their muscles bulge; their vehicles have fangs, claws, lasers, and "14 removable bombs and missiles." They wrap themselves in American patriotism; Big John Studd, the wrestler doll, is spangled in red, white, and blue; GI Joe is billed as a "Fighter for Freedom."

Just a step behind the star warriors are a bevy of sexily corseted Aryan princesses, like She-Ra, girl-friend of He-Man. She-Ra has a plastic dollhouse to match He-Man's fortress, but hers is a dainty domain, atwinkle with "crystal bed and canopy, vanity with a mirror, chandelier, plush rug, and double crystal door for grand entrances."

I was mesmerized by She-Ra's enemy, the black-haired "Catra, Jealous Beauty," minimally decked out in black fur tail, a cat mask, and a "twist and turn waist for scratching action." Poor Catra; perhaps she snarls in feline envy because she has glimpsed, just one floor down, the luscious pink habitat of Barbie.

Gender stereotyping has wiggled and simpered back with a vengeance. Great Shape Barbie is awash in pink, from her dream convertible to her exercycle. Her consort, Lookin' Great Ken, no mean narcissist himself, comes with a business suit and a credit card, no doubt to pay for Barbie's expensive whims. Barbie kindles a frankly materialistic *Dynasty*-style awe in her admirers. Two young women from Brooklyn stopped to gape at her while I stood nearby. "Lookit, her gown is by Oscah de la Renta," breathed one. "Git ouda hya," marvelled the other.

Toys have always reflected adult norms and preoccupations, but never, it seems to me, has the range been so obsessively narrow. Banished to a remote and dusty corner are all the active toys – skates, blocks, Meccano, chemistry sets, puppets – while, flushed with the Christmas spirit, the children rush past to the good stuff advertised on TV, eager to play out the parables of Power versus Ultimate Evil, Ram Man, Heroic Warriors, Attak Trak, Man at Arms, Warrior Beasts, Blazing Swords, Star Cruisers, Mighty Crusaders with Mighty Punch Action Arms. Christian symbolism links hands with Mars. Joyful all ye nations rise, join the triumph of the skies. From outside on the street, the Salvation Army's unarmed Santa Claus sounds a feeble "Ho ho ho."

Ivana Trump, it is faithfully reported, solved the mad, hectic dilemma of buying children's Christmas presents by sending the little ones over to F.A.O. Schwartz with their nanny, who was equipped with a note pad to record the princelings' cries of admiration and greed. Snap! All Ivana had to do then was to call the store, and, guided by the "ooh, aah" list, order everything wrapped and delivered.

It would be untruthful to pretend that I lounged about my Park Avenue eyrie in virtuous detachment, untouched by this atmosphere of glitter and greed around me. In fact, no one is untouched by the sheer overwhelming thing-ness of New York, where immense reservoirs of charm, skill, and merchandising wit are deployed to make you yearn for possessions.

A young British journalist came to see me when she arrived in New York to begin research for a television documentary on the Imperial Capital. I admired her silk scarf. She blushed. "I don't know what's wrong with me," she stammered. "I just arrived yesterday and today, walking up the avenue, I just had to buy something. Anything! It was like a fever; I've never felt this way!"

No one is immune. Around the corner from me, Bloomingdale's gleamed and beckoned like an Aladdin's cave filled with exotic treasures – which, indeed, it is; whole Third World nations depend on selling their goods to Bloomie's, with its $1 billion in annual sales. And in my mail came more blandishments: upscale catalogues from purveyors of down comforters, hand-dipped chocolates, elegant leather goods, and, most insidious of all, designer gadgets.

Saturday morning mail! Can you believe it, fellow Canadians? Yes, New York Saturdays have an extra glow, a little frisson of satiety, when the bundle of mail clonks down in the foyer. And this morning, O happy harbinger, comes my Hammacher Schlemmer catalogue.

Hammacher Schlemmer is the Taj Mahal, the *ne plus ultra* of gadgetry; for years I've been scouring the U.S. magazine ads for their tantalizing drawings of electric bagel slicers, secret-compartment picture frames, and self-stirring saucepans. And now, here I am, mere blocks away from the source and fountainhead, and privy to their quarterly catalogues.

In a controlled consumer frenzy, I read the fine print under every item. Lightly I pass by the $199 Electric Inertial Cracking Nut Press, but not before studying its workings. As Hammacher Schlemmer takes pains to explain, the nut rests between a cracking piston and a cold-rolled-steel anvil; an electric current draws a steel arm through a solenoid to strike the aluminum cracking piston, which in turn hits the nutshell.

Bracing, isn't it? You may never have pierced the mystery of the microchip, but here you have mastered a sturdy little nugget of technojargon. Even better, Hammacher Schlemmer does not leave you thrashing about in sloppy indecision; it has its very own institute, which tests every gadget and pronounces it, with Olympian certainty, the Best or the Only one of its kind in the world.

The mere thought of possessing the world's most versatile programmable home answering machine, the world's most powerful flashlight, or the Only Self-Configuring Wine Rack, makes me feel like the captain of my destiny.

And that really is the romance of gadgets: the heady conviction of the perfectability of human life. It's a nineteenth-century sort of excitement (that's when sailors coined the word "gadget," actually), and I come by it honestly, because my mother loved a good, ingenious gadget, too. A gadget promises to smoothe life's irritating corners, to impose pristine order on a frazzled household, and to make dull work twinkle by with a smug little gloss of glamour.

The point of a good gadget is not necessarily the gleam of advanced machinery, but its wit of invention: a lead pencil was a heck of a gadget when someone first dreamed it up. In a life that often seems out of control, my gadgets are tiny oases of clever coping: my twenty-five-cent Chinese back scratcher; the book rack for the bathtub; the antique apple corer and peeler that winds the peel off in one long spiral and sprongs the naked, sliced, cored apple into the bowl; and even (especially) my computer, which has already erased, rewritten, and respaced the above words three or four times with boggling speed. My ultimate gadget of the moment is the modem, a little black box sitting on my desk. When I finish writing this, I

∎

will type a few code letters into my computer, and the modem will chew up these words into little invisible electronic fragments, hurl them through a thousand miles of air without bumping into anything on the way, and rematerialize them on my editor's screen in Toronto.

Such moments of serene power and control are all too rare in life, which is why I am addicted to the Hammacher Schlemmer catalogue. I admit there are excesses, a soupçon of electronic overkill. I do not really need the "only personal environmental sound machine," which can lull me to sleep with sounds of surf, waterfall, or rainfall ("adjusts from gentle to driving intensity" – a bit sinister, that). I am not charmed by the Sonic 2000 Rodent Eliminator. Alas, I am too far past the stage of early motherhood to have use for a pink-nosed cuddly lamb that soothes baby with transistorized thumps and gurgles. And personally, I doubt that I will ever be in the frame of mind to start the day with the world's only talking bathroom scale, which announces, in a "clear, digitally synthesized voice" how much I weigh and how much I have gained or lost since last time – and then, the smarmy hypocrite, tells me to "have a nice day."

Nevertheless, I covet the three-in-one buffet utensil, combining fork, knife, and spoon, to eliminate one of life's slipperier embarrassments. And imagine the ecological superiority that could be yours if you were wearing a solar-powered pith helmet that blows a cooling breeze on your forehead as you push through steamy jungles. Electrically heated socks, a cunning magnetic window cleaner that shines both sides of the window at once (uses barium ferrite ceramic magnets) – my temples throb with visions of scientific order.

True, I could not really use a Schmeckenbecker Putter, complete with built-in compass, rabbit's foot, a level (to help me "read the greens"), and hundred-centimetre tape mcasure for disputed putts. I have, after all, never been on a golf course in my life. But its mere existence reassures me with a vision of a tight and tidy life on the links.

It is the same impulse that once made me palpitate to own a clockwork chicken rotisserie that was gathering dust in a French antique shop in a remote countryside. It was, I argued with my sceptical family, the selfsame kind of chicken-winder that had so excited the great food writer, Brillat-Savarin. The family argued practicality, the difficulties of transport, and the extreme unlikelihood that I would ever wish to roast a chicken on a clockwork-driven spit in front of the open fire in my Canadian living room.

I have, however, never forgotten the darling and coveted ingenuity of that French chicken-winder. It gives me a perverse pleasure on this Hammacher Schlemmer Saturday to find in my dictionary that the sailors who invented the word "gadget" had a few other words for it, among them being "wim wom," "timmy-noggy," and "chicken-fixing." Perhaps they, too, had come upon a clockwork rotisserie in their wanderings and had been moved, like me, by the inexhaustible inventiveness of the human mind faced with a boring job of work.

Consumerism is never quite as innocent as all that; I was fooling myself. The lust for the unnecessary makes fools of us all, and nowhere more so than in a city like New York, where the extremes of human existence rub up against each other like sandpaper on silk, and each extreme – bloated wealth and suppurating poverty – is a direct expression of consumer capitalism.

And consumer capitalism, we should not forget, is the unexamined backdrop to *The Bonfire of the Vanities*. As an economic and political system, it has an epoch-making marketing tool at its command: television. Thanks to TV, consumerism confounds Marx. Conditions get worse, the masses suffer more – especially the black masses – and nothing happens except more crime.

Julie Baumgold to the contrary, no tumbrels are rattling over the cobblestones. If there's a Manhattanite Madame

Defarge plying her needles at this moment, she's probably knitting a cheap knock-off of a Bill Blass sweater. The poor, the mad, and the homeless are as dazzled and transfixed by the material society as Tom Wolfe's high rollers; glutted on television, they seem incapable of reasoned revolt. Every consumerist obscenity documented by Wolfe in *The Bonfire of the Vanities* (his hero Sherman McCoy's tedious obsession with shoes, for example) is neatly parallelled by a matching, down-market phenomenon in the ghetto.

That fact came home to me with dismal clarity one night in 1986 when I watched a much-ballyhooed TV documentary about black families.

The young black man grinned conceitedly into the CBS camera. "I got strong sex urges, see?" he said, happily explaining his six illegitimate children by three different women. "I got strong sperm."

He could have been cast by the Ku Klux Klan; you couldn't find a black American more perfectly calculated to arouse loathing, contempt, and fear – in short, racial bigotry.

But it was CBS and its celebrated newsman, Bill Moyers (certified as a "liberal" in a *New York Times* rave review of the program), who had picked him. The show, a much-touted two-hour documentary called *The Vanishing Black Family*, focused on young unmarried mothers in a New Jersey ghetto. The mothers, all living on welfare, told Bill Moyers they blamed welfare for their ills; "welfare makes me lazy," one said.

I watched the show with mounting disbelief and rage. But I shouldn't have been surprised. Ever since I moved to New York, I've noticed a crescendo of sanctimonious concern about the number of black children (57 per cent) who are illegitimate. Not a week passes without another editorial or think piece about the ravages of welfarism. It is a theme song in perfect harmony with President Ronald Reagan's stated game plan for next fall's Congressional elections: an all-out attack on welfare that, according to Republican theology, saps young mothers of their initiative and robs them of their "freedom."

The attack on welfare is a thinly veiled assault on the black poor. What is most surprising is the degree to which everyone is going along with this newly popular cant. The CBS documentary, which never once examined the causes of the hopelessness and apathy of these jobless black youths, ended with a round-table discussion in which all the participants were black. And they, too, echoed the weeping-crocodile tones of Moyers's narrative. "We must have a return to mo-ral values," trumpeted the Reverend Jesse Jackson. A police chief and a Harvard professor chimed in with ringing exhortations to "spiritual regeneration," savouring each syllable as though they were sucking candies.

The only one who talked any sense at all was Dr. Eleanor Holmes Norton, professor of law at Georgetown University, who tried to remind the others of some economic realities.

The truth is that since the early 1970s, the black family has been rapidly disintegrating under the crushing pressure of a changing economy. There are no jobs for the men. When those teenage ghetto mothers tell CBS that they can get along without husbands, they are voicing a bitter truth: the men will never be able to support them or their children, anyway.

As Walter Stafford, a black economist with Community Service Society of New York, explained it to me, blacks are overwhelmingly concentrated in the hard-hit public-service and hospital industries in this city. In the wake of savage public-service cutbacks, blacks make up 55 per cent of New York's unemployed. Meanwhile, manufacturing jobs have permanently disappeared, and there are virtually no blacks in the financial and technological industries. Even as the economy "recovered," unemployment rose to 39 per cent among New York's black youths; it was 44 per cent in 1989.

■

"They've got nothing – no jobs, no hope," Stafford said. "All they've got is their vanity."

The constant yap and yatter about "family values" is all the more ironic in a country where every possible avenue of support for black families and black ambition has been under remorseless attack by the federal government.

Reagan and his ideologues cut back Head Start and job training programs, eliminated all poverty housing aid to cities, made a legal assault against civil-rights enforcement and affirmative-action laws, and even undermined a food-supplement program for impoverished mothers, despite firm proof that it improved the health and potential of newborns. All this while the black infant mortality rate is double that for whites, and rising.

Sex-education and family-planning clinics have been forestalled by right-to-life activists, even in counties with soaring teenage illegitimacy rates. Aid to college students has been slashed. Black enrolment in colleges and universities has fallen severely.

Black high-school students already have a 50 per cent drop-out rate. How deeply this is due to sheer despair can be seen clearly in one anecdote: five years ago, a white millionaire giving a commencement address to a grade-six class in Harlem impulsively promised to pay all their tuition fees if they went on to college. All fifty-two of those astounded students are still in school and doing well enough to qualify for college admission.

The average black child in America will spend at least five years of his or her life in direst poverty, in neighbourhoods where drugs and crime may seem to offer the only surcease from pain and defeat. Ghetto life, wrote Dr. Eleanor Holmes Norton last spring, is "predatory," a "circumscribed culture" that ruthlessly demands conformity. A permanently jobless underclass lives there, hungry, stinted, steadily growing but apparently invisible to the white population.

It is as though a greedy white America, rushing towards material success while yipping over its shoulder about family values, were surrounded by a vast, silent Soweto. I asked Walter Stafford what he thought. "These kids," he said, "you see them up in Harlem wearing their Gucci T-shirts. They're not rioting. That's the thing: they want in, they want to be part of the economy."

Somebody better start working on that soon. All the preaching in the world about family values – and all the welfare cutbacks that can be contrived – won't change a thing. A population without work or hope for the future is a danger to itself and to its society. "Yes," said Walter Stafford, "Americans should be afraid."

And that, pre-eminently, is what Tom Wolfe captures so brilliantly: rich white America's lurking terror of its black people. Reading the chapters of phantasmagorical horror – the dark and the panic on a highway ramp in the Bronx when McCoy has taken a wrong turn and is stopped by two black youths; the gruesome helplessness of his fear and humiliation when he is thrown into a holding cell with black criminals – for the first time, sitting in my safe and serene bedroom, I felt cold trickles of horror down my back. Horror of black vengeance and random violence. New York, outside my window, seemed huge and menacing.

This is not the same matter-of-fact daily alertness I had learned to practise in my three years of exploring Manhattan on foot; this is emphatically not the pragmatic, reluctant wariness of suspicious-looking minority men that even non-racists must adopt in New York City. No, Wolfe's singular literary achievement is to create in the reader, with his exaggeratedly urgent prose, a formless horror of *all those blacks up there in the ghetto*. The novel replaces reasoned subtlety of perception with nightmarish dread.

To free oneself from the story's irrational grip, you have only to sit back and reflect that it whips you into a state of fear

by documenting the plight of a rich white man who is persecuted by the entire machinery of white media, justice, and
law enforcement – all at the behest of black mobs manipula-
ted into a frenzy by unprincipled black leaders. This is the
reverse of truth: it is blacks who have been persecuted and
senselessly killed by trigger-happy New York police in
recent years. And while it is true that black con men exist,
they are funded, controlled, and publicized by the all-white
media and the corrupt political machine – not by weak-
kneed liberal Episcopalians, as Wolfe would have it. And
though the city occasionally yields to outcries of injustice
from minority groups, it is much more common that white
injustices are covered up and exonerated.

But *Bonfire*'s inversion of reality is consistent with Wolfe's
incomprehensible belief that, as he told journalists, "It is
blacks and Hispanics who have the real power in New York."

The ruthless pursuit of quick, stupendous profit that has
enriched Wolfe's New York beyond mortal comprehension
has created its own shadow, its own paranoid nightmare, yet
no one seems to make that analysis, or act on it. No one
mentions black history and the whole sorry mess of American
guilt: slavery's vast devastation of black family, black roots,
black stability; a heritage of ruthless oppression and bigotry. In
the scale of history, it's only a blink of an eye since blacks were
chattels, and only a nanosecond since I was a teenager and read
about white southerners lynching Emmet Till.

It's no longer fashionable, however, to mention historical
causes. Bill Moyers, liberal, can fit right into Reagan–Bush
America by denouncing black promiscuity, black irresponsi-
bility, and everyone nods sagely. It is not legitimate, apparently, to talk about a nation besotted by wealth and material
goods, media that grovel worshipfully before billionaire
crooks, a presidency that financed major cocaine dealers in
return for help for its favourite insurgents, or an eight-year
reign of voodoo economics that gouged the poor to pay the
rich, while deliberately and self-righteously dismantling the
civil-rights and affirmative-action mechanisms that had
helped black Americans climb out of the ghetto – or at least

■

guaranteed that they didn't starve on the very borders of Babylon.

Wolfian fear of blacks is self-perpetuating. The same white Americans who cluck their tongues over the "disintegration of the black family" were stampeded into voting for George Bush in the course of his openly racist election campaign. They have bought for themselves a continuation of the Reagan era that so grievously exacerbated the black-white gulf.

As I left New York for Canada, I was sure the violence that, throughout the 1980s, the blacks had inflicted on each other in their ghettoes would begin to leak into Manhattan. And within the year, "wilding" found its way into the New York vocabulary, as black teenagers rampaged through Central Park to rape and brutalize – with what perfect fulfillment of Wolfe's pattern – an investment banker.

The Bonfire of the Vanities exposes the eggshell fragility of white privilege in New York. Its immense, best-selling popularity is due partly to its appeal to *schadenfreude*, the pleasure people take in another's distress. Just the way many Canadians obsessively hate Toronto's arrogant economic power and gloat over Toronto's troubles, so many Americans loathe and resent New York as the cause, rather than merely the emblem, of American dilemmas like affluent "liberal" decadence and racial violence.

Wolfe's hypnotic hold over his readers owes some of its force to that resentment, but even more, I think, to its portrait of minorities. As savage as the book is about Park Avenue potentates, at least it does them the honour of probing into their cowering psyches. Not so for blacks: they are seen from without. Demonized.

The Bonfire of the Vanities, by describing the most blatant effects of eight years of Reagan while declining to think about causes, is part of the problem. Seizing on the visible detail – those flapping running shoes on the scary pimp-rolling teenagers on the subway, the calculating ambition of the prosecutor – it clinches the cliché, deepens despair, feeds the rancorous little flame of angry fear.

■

115

I had a different perspective. I saw the black criminals as the absolutely inevitable product of American capitalist culture, brought to its overwrought epitome in the New York of the 1980s. Those Central Park "wilders" are all-American kids, raised on the American credo of macho violence and sexism. The mayhem they wrought that night was like the F.A.O. Schwartz Christmas display come to life: he-men proving their virility by forceful domination over a woman who was seen by them as a mere object. Attak Trak, Master of the Universe, Big John Studd. Showing Princess Allura what's what.

When I first came to New York, Bronx and Harlem schoolteachers were struggling to feed and clothe their hungry students. By the time I left, three years later, a significant shift had taken place. Bronx and Harlem schoolteachers were banning chunky gold jewellery in class (too many hallway muggings and stabbings) and talking about setting up metal detectors at the school doors to keep out the huge influx of weapons.

The black kids had discovered their way up and out of poverty; they had latched on to the entrepreneurial American dream. In their own resourceful, street-corner way, they were doing just what the Boeskys and Milkens had done. They had discovered crack, and were making it big until they got caught.

CHAPTER 4

.

Black New York

Part of my personal mythology of New York was that it floated free of the entrenched racism of so much of the rest of America. I rejoiced to see black faces in the crowded streets; sought out the paintings, novels, and poetry of the Harlem Renaissance, that artistic flowering in the proud black "city" of Harlem in the 1920s; visited the Studio Museum in Harlem and the Schomburg Center for Research in Black Culture; listened to black jazz musicians in bars – and found myself, for the first time in my life, having to try hard not to be nervous of some people just because of their skin colour.

I was appalled by the irony. I'd arrived in the heart of cosmopolitanism only to be forced into a racial awareness that shamed and outraged my deepest convictions. Crossing Washington Square Park at dusk, I was accosted by a ragged black man who asked me for a light. Politely, I held a match for him while he dragged on his cigarette. Just as politely, with a little half bow, he thanked me: "And I'm sorry if I frightened you, speaking to you in the dark like that." We could have stood all night apologizing to each other for the crimes of our respective races and not been able to undo the awfulness: this man had felt called on to excuse himself for frightening me with his blackness.

The tension and distress about racial divisiveness shows up in daily encounters. One bitter winter night, a crowd of us attended a literary reading at LaMama, the experimental theatre on the Lower East Side. Afterwards, walking up the Bowery near East 3rd Street, the site of one of the more wretched shelters for homeless men, we were stopped by a black panhandler. "Excuse me, ladies . . ." and he segued into a preposterous, aggressive exaggeration of a black accent, "could you spare a dollar to he'p send a po' black man back to Africa?"

■

The satire aimed at our likely bigotry – and the manipulation of our guilt – was so wicked that we all burst into excessive laughter. He collected enough dollar bills from us to set him up for a splendid evening with the illicit indulgence of his choice.

As a newcomer to the city, I saw it as integrated: black faces are part of the visible mosaic. Only slowly did I learn to make more educated assessments, and to realize that there is a huge gulf dividing the classes in New York, just as Tom Wolfe describes it. The upwardly mobile black population – and thanks to the civil-rights agitation of the 1960s, there *is* a substantial black middle class – blends seamlessly into white New York. My children's black friends lived, in every way, just as white New Yorkers do. But between all of us and the black poor was an unbridgeable chasm. No one I knew had friends in the ghetto. The only links were those fleeting encounters with panhandlers and the homeless.

New York streets present a constant reminder of that impenetrable ghetto world and its horrific effects. You don't notice the ordinary black people quietly going about their business – and I hardly need to make clear that even the ghettoes are filled with hard-working black people struggling to lead a decent life – but you quickly learn to be alert to and wary of the street-corner loungers with their shiny jackets and high-topped sneakers, or the solitary men hanging around in doorways. In a way, they are black because they are poor; their race is noticeable only because their poverty has made them into a menacing underclass.

The drug dealers working the crowds are everywhere and blatant.

"Smoke. Coke. Smoke," the loose-limbed youngster mutters as he walks swiftly along the curb, jostling through the crowd of shoppers.

"Crack. Crack. Crack," whispers another young salesman.

On certain well-known streets throughout New York City, the "steerers" are hard at work rounding up cocaine customers for the local dealer. For every customer he brings in, the steerer – often a teenager, sometimes as young as ten or eleven – gets a discount or a fistful of dollars towards his own crack purchase.

The other night in New York, the four top stories on the eleven o'clock news featured cocaine: a bar-room shooting, the killing by a crack dealer of a twenty-two-year-old police officer in an alley, the sudden death of an athlete on the eve of his wedding, and the arrest of yet another cocaine-dealing football player. And all this within days of the cocaine death of University of Maryland basketball star Leonard Bias.

Crack, much featured in the media these days, seems particularly sinister. Though cocaine soared in popularity in the past decade, its price and the peculiar means of ingesting it (snorting through the nose or cooking it down in a complicated chemical ritual to obtain a smokable residue) kept it in the realm of rock musicians, athletes, and other highly paid members of society – like middle-class professionals.

But crack is creepily democratic: in the year since it has appeared on the streets of New York, it has swept the market. Soon it will be rampant in Canadian cities. Crack is simply cocaine in a form highly accessible to youngsters: you can buy two button-size chunks of it in a tiny plastic vial for ten dollars, put it in a two-dollar glass water pipe (available in the local candy store), and smoke it. Within seconds, the drug hits the brain.

"It's as though you've just had the best food, drink, and sex you've ever had," according to Daniel Langdon, public education director of Phoenix House, New York's largest drug-treatment program.

Within ten minutes, however, the user is experiencing an equally intense low as the high wears off. "As soon as they're coming down, they're thinking of how to get the money to get their next dose," said Bob Ellis, who works with troubled youths at Project Dome. Crack, it appears, is not only the most potent, but also the most psychologically addictive of drugs on the street. Mr. Ellis says that 95 per cent of the teenagers he now accompanies to court are using crack. He has dealt with addicts as young as thirteen.

At the Twenty-fourth Precinct, in the same area, however, Sergeant Kevin Kilcullen of the Street Narcotics Squad said that most of their hundreds of "low-level street arrests" are of users and dealers aged eighteen to thirty. The police, like others in the field, are anxious lest the press sensationalize crack.

But it's hard not to sensationalize, because the facts are blood-chilling. Everyone agrees that crack is epidemic – that it is rapidly becoming the drug of choice, that its use spreads across all class and racial groups, and that its effects are devastating.

"Crack users only think about their next smoke. There's immediate drastic weight loss," Sergeant Kilcullen says. "They neglect to eat, to wash – you bring them in and they're so filthy you can't sit in the same room with them."

As Mr. Langdon points out, "vacuum cleaners" (cocaine snorters) last, on the average, a year to eighteen months before the most addicted are driven to seek treatment. Crack users are crumbling in six to eight months.

Mr. Langdon warns against parental panic, citing the known progression from tobacco to alcohol to marijuana to harder drugs: "Very few kids will fall from total sobriety into crack use."

Frighteningly, though, models of adult sobriety are scarce. There are twenty-five to thirty million drug abusers in the United States. "Getting high," however you do it, is an accepted recreation.

New York has an additional problem. Court space and judges are in such short supply that a low-level user or dealer can be arrested forty times before he or she actually does time in prison. Cracking down on crack has meant that more police are deployed on the street to make more and more utterly meaningless arrests.

Solutions vary. The police want stricter sentencing and more jails; Mr. Langdon stresses more preventive education and compulsory treatment rather than jail.

Mr. Ellis, who admits to moods of despair about crack, thinks kids are immune to such education. "They have nothing else to do – even subway fare and a movie on a hot night costs more than brief oblivion through drugs – and anyway, kids think they're invincible." He thinks the government ought to sever economic aid to the countries that produce and export cocaine. "But they put politics above the lives of our kids."

It is hard to keep a balanced perspective when you're living in the midst of a drug-soaked society, but an article in the *Wall Street Journal* by Dr. David F. Musto, Yale professor of psychiatry, suggests the long view. In the 1880s, he says, cocaine was cheap, pure, legal and a social craze. You could buy cocaine cigarettes at every corner store. Not until people were damaged by addiction did cocaine's public image become loathsome; it was banned by law; within a decade, its use had died almost completely.

Where does that leave us? Cocaine is already illegal in the 1980s. And maybe we are already beginning to change our minds about it; maybe crack will tip the government towards tougher international measures. First celebrities died. Now kids are dying, and soon we must move from tolerated illegality to concerted and furious rejection.

The crack crisis escalated like a brush fire in a wind storm. Within a year of that 1986 column, crack psychosis accounted for 50 per cent of emergency mental-hospital admissions; crack dealers were, according to *New York Newsday*, operating openly from more than a thousand city-

■

owned apartments, and it had become clear that it was minority and poor youths (not the "all classes and races" cliché the experts had earlier relayed to me) who were leaping into the flames.

While magazines wrote breathlessly about Princess Gloria von Thurn und Taxis gyrating in her mink bolero at the most wild and wonderful night-clubs and soirées, eleven-year-olds in Brooklyn and the Bronx learned to stuff their pockets with money, money, money by selling crack. Subways got cleaner (black kids now had better things to do than salve their egos by spraying graffiti everywhere), and crime got worse.

The kinds of violence spawned by crack were so crazy, so far beyond the known patterns of criminal behaviour that they seemed like bulletins from another planet: twice within months – in two separate incidents involving two different women and their children – a young mother was arrested for holding down her six-year-old daughter to be gang raped, in return for a few vials of crack. A young man was arrested as he lay nonchalantly in bed, arms behind his head, snuggled up to the torn and shattered corpse of his girl-friend's three-year-old son. In a crack trance, the man had awakened, seized his gun, and fired thirty bullets into the sleeping child's body.

Every single day in New York's boroughs, some school kid or toddler or barber-shop owner or welfare mother is caught in and killed or maimed by the madly spraying cross-fire between rival crack dealers. It's easy to forget, in the state of anxiety induced by these news stories, that it is ordinary black citizens in black neighbourhoods who are most trapped, most beleaguered, most threatened by the surrounding lawlessness.

Like most New Yorkers I knew, I raged inwardly at the geometric progression of the disasters afflicting the black community, read the papers braced for the latest horror, supported progressive organizations and politicians ever more ardently – and, like everyone else, traversed the scorched earth and hideous streets of the Bronx in a locked car, and only on my way to the airport.

■

Like Tom Wolfe's anti-hero, I, too, had taken a wrong turn off the Triborough Bridge on my way into Manhattan one night, driven down a badly lit ramp, and found myself in a shadowy, tangled landscape of menace, an unknown Third World where the dark figures looming under shattered street lights amidst the detritus of wrecked cars and garbage looked like potential assassins. Nothing in Canada looks like this: bonfires in old oil drums casting lurid light onto impassive faces, sagging tenements crumbling into rubble and ruins, barbed wire sprawling in pointless tangles across empty lots where even the garbage is ancient and decaying.

The South Bronx, to most Manhattanites, is more menacing than a war zone. The people are complete strangers: we can't read their signals, their body language, their intentions. A friendly wave can look like intent to murder. The terror one feels must be exactly analogous to the terror of a black person in a white Mississippi town of the forties and fifties: you feel anonymous and targeted precisely because of the colour of your skin. Dehumanized: it doesn't matter what your feelings, ideas, principles might be. Isolated: because of your colour and class, you can have no expectation of the routine support or safety that comes from being a fellow citizen.

Middle-class black people often feel this way, too. By and large, they are invisible in New York – nurses, day-care workers, lawyers, musicians, actors, secretaries, teachers, and civil servants; among colleagues of any colour, they are professionally at home. Their blackness is less important than their middle-class qualifications. But in the street, anonymous, they become invisible in a different and more sinister way: raising an arm to hail a cab, they are infuriatingly ignored. Cab drivers are afraid of them and pass them by, wilfully not seeing them. Yet when they venture into the Bronx or other ghettoes, where they know their class will mark them out, they are as wary as any white.

In the past few years, race has become the sharp splinter of bone caught in New York's throat. It's not that most New Yorkers hate black skin; that atavistic kind of revulsion belongs to the deep south. Indeed, white Americans have made the *Bill Cosby Show* the most popular program on television, eagerly seeking the reassurance that blacks can be just as unthreateningly, lovably, smugly middle class as everyone else. No, it is the black poverty and crime the political system has created that New Yorkers hate. Blacks, whites, and Hispanics are united in their pessimism. White fear and resentment, long simmering, erupted into public view when Bernhard Goetz became a celebrity, and in the three years since then, race lines have hardened and despair deepened with every headlined crime.

Bernhard Goetz, the weedy vigilante who shot four black youths on a subway train when one of them asked for five dollars, has been acquitted of all but one relatively minor gun-possession charge.

The jury rushed to give TV interviews, revelling in their allotted fifteen minutes of fame. (Indeed, three of them lined up for Goetz's autograph after the verdict was announced.) Astoundingly, they revealed that during all the months of complicated and controversial evidence, they had never "seriously" considered that Goetz might be guilty of anything but illegal gun possession. Even more astoundingly, they dismissed Goetz's videotaped confession, because, said one juror, "the guy had been driving around for nine days." In that confession, Goetz seemed to be in a passion of crazed self-righteousness, babbling that he "wanted to murder them . . . make them suffer as much as possible." He considered gouging out their eyes with his key ring, he told police. He described how he stepped up to one seated youth and said, "You seem to be all right. Here's another," and shot him, too. The jury said they "basically discounted that."

Goetz's defence was that New York is different from anywhere else; that it is reasonable to use "lethal force" in self-defence on a subway train when someone asks you for money. Goetz, who entered the car and sat in the midst of four boisterous black youths, said he could tell by the gleam in Troy Canty's eye that they were going to "play" with him. So he promptly shot them.

The jury (ten white and two black) found his response to be reasonable. Of course, six of the jury had been crime victims themselves, and the odds are fairly good that their assailants were black. (Blacks make up nearly one quarter of New York City's population, but 50 per cent of murderers and 47 per cent of their victims are black.) I'm pretty sure, given the sorry history of American crime and jurisprudence, that the jurors would not have found it "reasonable" had a black man briskly shot four white youths with an illegally owned weapon.

"Race didn't enter it at all," one juror told the television cameras. "We never even considered race."

Denial on this scale takes the breath away.

The whole episode was a racial one. Beginning to end, none of it would have happened if all the parties had been white. The Goetz incident highlighted the fear that whites have of blacks. When it turned out that all four of the black youths were thugs with criminal records, Goetz seemed wholly justified in the public mind. But Goetz didn't know who they were when he shot them. They didn't threaten him, show a weapon, or even rob him. Just because they were young black men in the costume and postures of the ghetto, Goetz felt justified in assuming the worst, and shooting.

History is filled with this kind of reversal. You trample your enemy, then blame him for being squashed and bloody. South Africa brutalized its black majority for a century; now that some of them are fighting back, the white rulers say: "You see? They're violent. We have to suppress them."

Americans enslaved blacks, wrenched their families and history apart, spent generations oppressing, lynching, and debasing them, and now are finally vindicated. See? Black youths are all criminals.

Fear of blacks is real in New York. In the Soweto to the north of glittering Manhattan, millions of the dispossessed are lurking in the dark. They grow up so bereft of hope or opportunity that drug peddling, prostitution, and mugging seem like regular workaday jobs.

No one can honestly deny that the fear exists. When I'm alone on a New York elevator or subway platform and a black man in a windbreaker enters, I hold my purse tighter. He knows it. I know he knows. The fear and the anger are poisons to both of us and to all of society.

My desperation when I wrote that column about white fear of blacks was borne out during the 1988 presidential election, when George Bush's campaign knowingly cultivated that fear in order to win power. Though the prison-furlough program is widespread in the United States – originally begun, in fact, by Republicans, and flourishing under Ronald Reagan when he was governor of California – the Republicans gleefully used the case of Willie Horton (a black man who committed a savage rape while on furlough in Massachussetts) to destroy the electoral hopes of Massachussetts Governor Michael Dukakis.

The fear is twisted tighter and tighter by the media, by authors like Tom Wolfe, by politicians like George Bush who use it like a thermal to ride easily to power. When celebrated authors and even presidents legitimate racist attitudes, it is not surprising to learn that in 1988, a New York state rifle club awarded a plaque of honour to Bernhard Goetz. Goetz seized the occasion to crow that he was grateful to "the four horrible animals" he had shot for being so vile that they proved his righteousness.

Every television station, every newspaper, became obsessed by the need for more "shock camps" where black youths convicted of drug offences could be put through an exaggerated version of military boot camp. Ritual humiliation, physical and emotional violence, military discipline: yes, that's just what these "animals" needed.

What could three months of shock camp change? Could such a camp give black youths the skills to get a job on Wall

Street or even to graduate from high school? Could it change the filth and ruin of the ghettoes, the pervasive corruption that bleeds the city of billions of tax dollars every year?

It seemed to me not accidental that unashamed animosity to blacks should increase just as New York wallowed in the excesses of the Trumps. Ivana, the *Times* reports breathlessly, has begun to order custom-made suede shoes emblazoned with the Plaza Hotel's logo to give away to friends and favoured clients; mayoral candidates vie with each other in calling for more cops, more jails, tougher sentences. As the extremes grow more breathtaking, the media strain to find new expressions of outrage and disgust for the black people they show to the white public.

A black man from a welfare hotel pushed a dead baby – dead from blows and burns and abuse – in a stroller as an aid to his begging. A black woman from the same welfare hotel savagely beat a three-year-old boy into a coma; it was three in the morning, and the weary child had apparently refused to continue panhandling. Ed Koch made a *cause célèbre* of Joyce Brown, a schizophrenic black homeless woman. He wanted her hospitalized against her will. On television, he ranted about how she lived on the street "in her own urine and feces." For several weeks, as the Joyce Brown case dragged on, the media harped on feces. Intentionally or not, they reinforced the subliminal link between New York blacks and filth.

Then there were the Central Park rapists, the nightmare come true. Donald Trump took out a full-page ad in all the city's daily newspapers, with a huge headline demanding the return of the death penalty. The text of the ad wallowed in nostalgia for those halcyon days before civil rights, before police had been undermined by charges of anti-black brutality, when families could "stroll the streets" or "sit on their stoops." (According to Trump, it seems, it's the weakness of giving in to black demands, the effeteness of overdoing civil rights, which caused black crime.) "I no longer want to understand the anger of these young men," Trump wrote – as though he ever had. Instead, he "wanted to hate them." The ad was one long tantrum by the city's richest man, a public incitement to open racial hatred worthy of Mississippi in the 1960s.

And, as though to fan the racist flames, there arose the Reverend Al Sharpton, whose porcine image was unavoidable all the way through the winter of '87 to '88. That November, Tawana Brawley, a black teenager from a small town in upstate New York, was found half-naked, smeared with dog feces (that image again), crouching in a green garbage bag behind a public housing development. She claimed that she had been abducted by six white men in a van, some of them police officers, who raped and abused her for four days before dumping her.

It was evident from the first day – evident at least to this mother of teenagers – that Tawana Brawley was lying. You had only to see her once on the television news, patently pretending to be asleep on the family couch while her mother unconvincingly ranted against white racists who "did this to my baby," to know that the whole story was fishy. The hospital announced that it had done exhaustive tests and found that though Tawana seemed to be suffering from some sort of emotional trauma, there was absolutely no evidence of rape or intercourse. From the beginning, there were broad hints from neighbours and acquaintances of the family that Tawana had simply run away to see her imprisoned boyfriend, and had concocted the abduction story to avoid a beating from her reportedly brutal stepfather, a convicted murderer.

The Reverend Al ("Lamb of God") Sharpton of Brooklyn leaped onto the case within days, appointing himself Tawana's spokesman, guardian, and official representative. From that moment, no one had access to Tawana or her family except through Sharpton. He was already known to the media as one of the more repugnant con men in the boroughs. He had, apparently, a long record of sleazy manipulations. The *Village Voice* documented his history of creating lucrative "phantom" protest movements that capitalized on black pride and outrage. It revealed his shake-downs and ticket-scalping scams that preyed on successful black boxers and entertainers like Michael Jackson (apparently, he would threaten prominent black performers with black protests and pickets outside their shows unless they gave him large numbers of tickets to "distribute"); his role as an informer for the FBI; his youthful tendency to fleece his black peers (in high school, he arranged a raffle "to honour Martin Luther King" and then rigged it so he won the cash); his lifelong involvement with the corrupt side of black local politics. Ideologically, Sharpton is a chameleon – or, as the *Voice* called him, "a flimflam man . . . a quick-change artist . . . a clubhouse hustler."

Sharpton clearly has a genius for opportunistic self-invention; he's a Twainian villain of fakery and bombast, in his unscrupulous quick-wittedness, battening off racial conflict, playing white guilt and white racism against black loyalty to one of their own. The *Voice* describes a typical Sharpton scam: when Jesse Jackson enraged Jewish voters in New York by embracing PLO leader Yassir Arafat, Sharpton quickly teamed up with a Jewish Brooklyn city council member to form the "Congress of Humanities" to "improve black-Jewish relations." Evidently, Sharpton hoped to create a new source of public donations. When the black community instead supported Jackson, the Congress evaporated into thin air. "When the press was gone, he [Sharpton] was gone," said one close observer. The clash with Jackson didn't prevent Sharpton from later trying to involve Jackson in the Tawana Brawley affair (Jackson steered clear), but then, shamelessness is the essential talent of con men.

Sharpton staged noisy protests, for example, outside Bernhard Goetz's apartment house; later, apparently without a qualm, he was a "key organizer" in the black community for the two public figures who were Goetz's most ardent admirers: Republican Senator Al D'Amato and black Reaganite Roy Innis. (Incidentally, through Sharpton's meddling in Brooklyn politics, one can glimpse some of the corruption of Brooklyn's political machine, which has kept black voters divided and powerless in that borough where they are now a majority. Every black politician who struggles

■

to represent his or her community with integrity is sure to be opposed, harassed, and sometimes defeated by more opportunistic black politicians whose pliability wins them the powerful support of the white political machine. Sharpton's dalliances with an assortment of suspect black politicians is emblematic of the way whites can still divide and rule in the midst of a black majority.)

All this posturing self-advancement could not be possible without the media. Every controversy, every protest involving black New Yorkers, found Sharpton horning in, grabbing the spotlight from legitimate leaders. He never hesitated to insult or libel them. During the Howard Beach controversy, when New York was in an uproar after a gang of white youths in Queens chased three black men out of their neighbourhood, causing one to be killed on a highway, Sharpton called respected Manhattan Borough President David Dinkins "a coon" for meeting with Ed Koch to discuss how to calm racial tensions. His insults got more play than the substance of the meeting.

When Sharpton appointed himself and two prominent black lawyers, Alton H. Maddox, Junior and C. Vernon Mason, as Tawana Brawley's "advisers," local media, therefore, already had his measure. And from the first moment, Sharpton's tactics were outrageous. Without a scrap of evidence, he named a local law-enforcement official as being one of the alleged rapists. His colleague Alton Maddox said that the state attorney general, Robert Abrams, "masturbated over Tawana's picture." Sharpton insisted that the Brawley family not co-operate with the investigation of the alleged crime or speak to the press. Tawana was hidden away, incommunicado, with relatives upstate, and her mother took refuge in a church.

It was a media carnival: the reporters and the cameras egged Sharpton on, leading their broadcasts with his latest (and constantly escalating) scurrility. Now and then, we would see Tawana's face, sullen, confused, and evasive, as she rushed past with her praetorian guard. But mostly it was the ludicrous Sharpton, with his paunch, his preposterous blow-dried mane of hair, his gold chains and insolent sneers, who loomed large on the screen and whose words were blazoned in headlines. No one was surprised when a traitorous associate of Sharpton's told the papers that Sharpton had boasted, "We beat this, we gonna be the biggest niggers in New York." At black rallies in support of Tawana, Sharpton raked in cash donations. Whenever the story flagged – as it had to, since Tawana never spoke and no evidence of the attack was ever found – Sharpton stepped up his accusations. At one point, he claimed that officials were "covering up" the true facts of the rape with the help of the IRA, the Ku Klux Klan, and the Mafia.

Slowly, as Sharpton successfully whipped up the black community's feelings of anger, more responsible black leaders in Brooklyn lined up beside him, linked arms with him when he organized a "Day of Outrage" demonstration to block subway trains with a sit-in, and even, briefly, went to jail with him when the protest leaders were arrested.

Those community spokesmen may have been reluctant to join with Sharpton, but perhaps they had little choice. The media barrage reaches hurricane force in New York, where they daily generate stories that become national news. Their impact at the storm centre is overwhelming. You cannot reach out to your own constituents, sway public opinion, or raise "serious" money, without the co-operation of the media. And the media were giving all their attention to Sharpton. Although 52 per cent of the black community told pollsters they disapproved of Sharpton, none raised their voices publicly against him. For them, after all, Tawana Brawley represented all the black women whose lives were shattered by rape and whose fates were ignored by the white press. Sharpton, the black voters knew, was right in claiming that the entire judicial system is weighted against blacks, though wrong in his wild charges against individuals. As trapped by Sharpton's charade as Tawana herself, the black community, most of them mortified, held their tongues.

My first reaction, watching the egregious Sharpton nightly on the news, was to despair of the black community's judgement. Where were the responsible leaders? Had they all been assassinated, silenced, or bought off? Gradually, as I began to understand the media connivance with Sharpton ("He's a master at the sound bite," they would explain sheepishly after each of Sharpton's gross diatribes), a more sinister and depressing analysis occurred to me.

Without the Sharptons, the black community would have no access to the larger public; in their angry frustration, their political impotence, they have to go along with the clownish impostor who can at least command public attention for their claims. And in focusing on Sharpton, in helping to create him, the white media, intentionally or not, allow the white community to dismiss the disquieting spectre of its own racism. Who can take seriously the charges of systemic discrimination, police brutality, judicial unfairness, when Sharpton is the one to voice them?

(Now, two years later, with Sharpton muted by criminal charges, the black community has managed to reach the media more constructively. After a full month of ghoulish stories about the Central Park rape of the white jogger, and after anguished black outcries that the rape of black women is never even reported, the *New York Times* belatedly carried a feature documenting the twenty-eight other first-degree rapes or attempted rapes that had occurred in New York during that same week. All twenty-eight rapes were committed against black or Hispanic women. None had been reported by the press.)

Sharpton is worse than the "Al Charlatan" derided by Mayor Koch; he is a living weapon against his own people. At this writing, in the summer of 1989, Sharpton, Mason, and Maddox are under official investigation, and Sharpton has been charged with fraud. A New York grand jury long since found that Tawana Brawley's story was false; a judicial panel is now determining whether her advisers knowingly made false accusations.

But during the whole long fiasco, the conservative newspapers treated Sharpton as an authentic voice of the black community, without once writing about his parasitical

■

schemes to defeat, embarrass, or defraud less publicized but more respected black leaders. New Yorkers were encouraged to see Sharpton as representative of all blacks.

There is only one liberal daily paper in New York City: *New York Newsday*. It was *Newsday* that broke the story that Al Sharpton had been wired by the FBI so he could act as an informer on black leaders and activists in Brooklyn. *Newsday*, unlike other media, followed up this revelation with a strongly written and well-researched series of articles on New York's black communities.

If anything remained of my tattered vision of New York's ebullient, tolerant diversity, the feature story by reporter Nina Bernstein about eleven-year-old Daryll Davis finished it off. Daryll is only one of 650,000 black children in New York City, but his life is agonizingly illustrative of the more than half of those children who live in drastic poverty. A nice-looking, skinny kid with big, worried eyes, Daryll is one of five siblings, all with fanciful names like Ebony, Tawana, and Tyran. (Names, at least, are free.) They have different fathers; Daryll has never met his. The best "stepfather" he remembers was a junkie and a convicted murderer who stood up for him against school-yard gangs. Daryll's mother struggles against hopeless odds: trying to stay off welfare, she went to night school and finally landed a construction job as a labourer. When the job ended, she had to re-apply for welfare, but her application was lost in a computer blip. The family simply went hungry.

Daryll's family moved five times in three years; each move meant chaos, the squalor of shelters and welfare hotels, a new school and new harassment from classmates who have learned to despise "hotel kids." Once, Daryll's mother took an overdose of sleeping pills. "Daryll shook her awake," writes Bernstein. "'We're hungry,' she heard him say. 'Are you going to cook?'"

Daryll's life is a continual hunger – for love, stability, warmth, food, self-respect. He dreams that the father he never met will be found, will be rich, will give Daryll a limo. When Daryll cried instead of defending himself against

Bronx street bullies, his mother first defended him, then beat him herself. At age eight, Daryll learned to fight back, with fists and even with bottles.

One day, Daryll looked out the school window and saw his apartment in flames. He was frightened about his cat, but the teacher told him that firemen would rescue it. No one was hurt – except the family cat. "The cat, the only cat we had, my favourite, but it died," Daryll told the *Newsday* reporter. He was almost as upset by the disillusionment. "The teacher told a fib to me, and I was dumb enough to believe it."

The family poked about in the ashes to rescue blackened belongings; neighbourhood kids, used to such tragedies themselves, gathered around to watch as Daryll found some shrivelled pieces of a plastic toy. An older kid looked at Daryll's face and warned him roughly, "Don't cry."

The family was put up in a temporary Bronx shelter, and Daryll went to the public school across the street where, for once, the teacher loved him. "He was fantastic. His verbal abilities were fantastic. I was so excited to have this kid," the teacher told Bernstein. That lasted three weeks. When the family was moved into a more permanent shelter in Harlem, the city refused to pay bus fare for Daryll to commute to the Bronx.

And so another new school. On the first day, Daryll came home silent and withdrawn. "What happened?" his mother asked. "Gossip," Daryll mumbled. "Talking about my sneakers and my jacket. Telling me I look like a bum. They called my sneakers 'skippies'."

Bernstein interviewed community workers who have dealt with thousands of these bruised, nomadic, depressed children. They told her that poverty in America was more cruel now than ever before.

"I don't think kids knew they were poor when I was growing up. Now kids know they're poor. The media tells it to you. Your sneakers tell it to you. You can taste it. Television has defined what adequacy is all about – a Cadillac, the right sneakers. And the more you lose emotional things – an intact

■

family, for example – the more material things you need to fill up that void."

Daryll has watched his mother insulted and abused by the system; he has been preyed on by bigger, more hardened black kids; school has betrayed and humiliated him; like a refugee in wartime, he has been cold and hungry and frightened; he has lost his belongings, his roof, his stability, time after time; he has been herded like a lost animal into the vast warehouse shelters where, every night, beside his mother and sisters and brothers, he was surrounded by copulating couples.

To survive, he will have to turn his sadness into rage. In a year or two, perhaps, he will be dealing crack or mugging strangers or "wilding" in Central Park – what is sacred to such a child? – and then the Donald Trumps and Al D'Amatos can call him an animal; the papers can call for more shock camps.

At the moment, Daryll is still a hurt child, mourning for his cat and all his lost fathers, worried about why people killed Martin Luther King, learning from Sunday school that maybe "poverty is a punishment from God. Maybe all the poor people did something wrong."

What Bernstein does in her story, and it's all too rare in New York media, is to stay with her subjects long enough to let the reader understand a little of their inward lives, their struggle to make sense of so much deprivation and disorder, their doomed efforts to overcome. It would be easy to make a villain of Daryll's mother, Elaine, who has often hit him "too hard," but such easy judgements lose their power to satisfy when you overhear Elaine's ruminations, her defeat and guiltiness, her longing to do better, and to move her children to a racially mixed neighbourhood where "people respect each other a little more."

Daryll, too, speaks more resonantly than he realizes when he sums up for the reporter what he knows about Jesse Jackson: "He's a black leader, and he's still alive."

Jackson has an extraordinarily high recognition level among poor black children like Daryll Davis who may know almost nothing of other politicians or current events. In the three years leading up to the 1988 presidential election, Jackson was the one ray of light and hope for people like Daryll and his family. Jackson was the one identifiable hero who was constantly on their television screens, speaking into their ghetto living rooms with passionate concern for *them*. From the vantage point of Canada, Jesse Jackson may have seemed like a demagogue, another southern preacher of dubious integrity. But living in New York, where the raw misery of so many black people is daily paraded on the streets and in the news, I found myself understanding the Jackson phenomenon in a new way. His was the one clear voice heard above the media babble, his the one strong black presence that embodied hope for those living in desolation.

All my friends in New York are talking about Jesse Jackson; he's the one startling phenomenon in this dispiriting contest of wary bureaucrats.

"The Democrats can't put him on the ballot or they'll lose. They'll lose the white working class, the Catholics, the Jews, and the racists."

"If we don't put him on, we'll lose the blacks."

And: "If he had become the Democratic candidate, they'd have killed him."

They mean "kill" literally, as in Kennedy and King. And every New Yorker I know, regardless of other views, agrees with this instantly. "They," the potential assassins, are variously the oil billionaires, the weapons merchants, the cocaine runners, the contra lovers, the white supremacists – all the rich, rabid, and trigger-happy cabals with lines running into Washington. An amazing country.

"But if he could have been president . . ."

Drop this into a conversation, and all talk stops. It's as though all the campaigning, controversies, and torn loyalties until now have distracted everyone from imagining this biggest "if."

Once the thought occurs, though, it's dazzling. A black president. A sudden radiant vision of the one thing that might heal this country's sickness of open racism, white fear, and black despair in hopeless ghettoes.

Overwhelmingly, ordinary people in inner cities (where the murder rate is surging) say that the number-one election issue is drugs. Picture a black president who takes it seriously, a populist who crackles with platform energy when he talks about jobs, housing, schools, rebuilding the crumbling cities. Picture a black president in office, and you can almost imagine racism slinking back into the shadows, and black kids blooming into optimism before your eyes.

On a rainy Monday morning before the Tuesday primary, under the swaying red paper lanterns in a Chinese senior citizens' hall on Mulberry Street in Little Italy, ripples of electric joy went through the audience when young Asians – as many women as men – rose to speak about their involvement in Jackson's Rainbow Coalition. The speakers were beaming, bursting with a new sense of racial pride and political entitlement. And when someone mentioned Mayor Ed Koch, a hiss rose from every corner of the hall.

Koch, the Ego That Ate Manhattan, has acted like a wild man with his anti-Jackson vitriol, his once-popular brazen schtick slipping over into divisive and widely criticized hysteria. People here think he's snapped his elastics. The city is physically disintegrating from corruption and neglect, and the mayor is racing from subway stop to subway stop, literally shrieking his attacks on Jackson, while his foolish annointed one, Al Gore, tries to slip away, stiff-faced with embarrassment.

Koch's diatribes were interpreted as racist by almost everyone. Jews, traditionally progressive voters here, ignored him and voted for Michael Dukakis. But many voted for Jackson, too. It was not an easy decision, even for the most liberal minded. In the 1984 presidential race, Jesse Jackson pitched himself almost exclusively to an unconvinced black electorate, embraced the anti-Semitism and authoritarianism of Louis Farrakhan's Nation of Islam, called New York "Hymietown" and "a city where people steal things," and ran around the world promiscuously hugging assorted terrorists and dictators.

Since then, he's worked earnestly to distance himself from those excesses. On foreign affairs, he sounds measured and sensible. Besides, the press, partly due to the usual lazy habits of pack journalism, have harped so shrilly on past misdeeds that one almost began to feel sorry for Jackson – who, after all, grilled Richard Nixon about his bigotries, or Ronald Reagan, for that matter? – and to admire his endless restraint in answering those questions.

It's not clear how much of Jackson's moderated viewpoint on the Middle East is mere election strategy. Just last December, for example, in a lengthy interview with the serious, progressive Jewish bimonthly, *Tikkun* magazine, Jackson expressed such a mishmash of historical ignorance, such a welter of biases and double standards, that he seemed to undo years of effort.

Still, had I been a U.S. citizen, I probably would have joined my friends in voting for him. For whom else could one vote? Al Gore, Son of Barbie and Ken, the man who voted against crucial measures to support the Equal Rights Amendment and against funding for abortions for poor women? Manager Mike from Michigan, whose most forceful feature is his eyebrows and whose utterances are as pallid as Pablum?

As a preacher, Jackson is a man of reactionary social instincts. Asked about teenage pregnancy, he once said that teenage girls "walk around as hunks of sex, and then boys fall for the bait."

My teenage daughter and I are still howling with laughter over that one. Still, he's a man who can learn: he's been arguing, with evident conviction, for all the key women's issues on jobs, pay, child care, and, though he's personally against abortion, reproductive choice. He's the

■

only candidate to have laboured at the grass roots and to have won support from the homosexuals, the dispossessed, the poor, the workers, the alienated, the racial minorities, and the progressives; he represents a sizeable constituency, and he's done it all from the outside, without big money or the media, dignified even under vicious attack.

I can't help noticing these days how the black people of New York are reacting to Jackson. On Park Avenue, striding past in Dress for Success suits, they're proudly sporting his button on lapels. Outside the hall on Mulberry Street, in the rain, amidst the police cruisers with their flashing lights and the phalanx of guards and the press of curious Chinese shoppers, there were little black kids jumping straight up in the air to get a glimpse of the candidate over the heads of the crowd: "Jesse! My man Jesse!" they yelled, their faces alight.

To many Americans, Jesse Jackson is almost tragic. He's come farther than any other black man before him, and roused a kind of dizziness of rising hope in the black community. Nobody can tell if it's his own flawed character, his populism, or the deep-dyed racism of the United States that has stopped him short. He will sorely try the souls of Democrats in Atlanta. A black man has led his ragtag band through the desert and is standing on the heights at last, looking at the Promised Land, forbidden to enter.

The truth is, there can be no happy ending to this chapter. Race relations in New York are at their lowest, bitterest ebb since the civil rights agitation of the 1960s, and there is no possible amelioration in sight. The solutions are political and economic, and Americans – Tom Wolfe's greed-besotted New Yorkers among them – are unwilling to make those changes, as the most recent election showed.

The people I knew in Manhattan, white and black – the writers, teachers, lawyers, international civil servants at the

■

UN, the librarians, nurses, and AIDS volunteers – were both doggedly idealistic and despairing. They were excited by Jackson, aware as they were of his shortcomings, because they still want to believe that economic justice, healing, and racial harmony are possible. Nothing I saw in New York gave me any reason to hope such dreams were achievable – nothing except for the perseverance and resolute open-mindedness, despite everything, of those New Yorkers.

To live in New York, of course, is to live in a state of permanent, ongoing cognitive dissonance. A *New York Times* poll in the summer of 1989 showed that both black and white New Yorkers are depressed and pessimistic about racism in their city. At the same time, progressive New Yorkers are still more progressive, more open, more tolerant than any other people I know. My friends fit this category; thanks to them, it was possible to live in the midst of so much drastic social wrongness, and still feel stirred by New York's possibilities.

CHAPTER 5

•

Moments of Grace

GREETINGS FROM THE HOUSE OF WEYHE 1929

Scene: a Fifth Avenue mansion. A cocktail-party buzz fills the lofty room. Squashed into a corner near the immense Gothic windows overlooking Central Park, I admire the richly panelled walls, the grand piano, the ceiling exuberantly carved in grapes and cherubs.

I'm a little confused. This is the living room of a writer – a *feminist* writer. Merely by sending money to a few municipal causes, subscribing to some faintly progressive magazines, and signing petitions at public political rallies, I've ended up on a thousand mailing lists, which is how I've been invited to this fund raiser for Bella Abzug, crusading *grande dame* of the New York Democratic party, whose recent congressional bid left her a loser and in debt.

"Gosh," I exclaim naïvely to a woman standing beside me near the window. "I never knew that Shere Hite [our host and owner of the panelled living-room] was a *rich* person."

The woman laughs in surprise. "Well, of course she's not a rich person. She earned this with her first book, *The Hite Report*," she responds.

We all know that the stakes are higher in New York, but this is when revelation blazes across my mind: ordinary writers, people like me, might, by luck and connections and being in the right place, shoot for glory. New York is a nerve centre: magazines, newspapers, and television networks, agents, publishers, writers and reviewers, criss-cross and overlap like live currents. At any moment, connections can spark, and a writer can rocket instantly into the blinding glare of international celebrity. Bingo: celebrity equals dollars, more dollars than most Canadian writers, though perhaps of equal ability, will ever see in their lifetimes.

The breathtaking volatility of fame and wealth is what explains the frenetic outgoingness of New York literary society. A friendly contact with someone who knows a book editor at the *New York Times* can mean, one golden day after a favourable review appears, a potential fortune. Hite's original success had nothing to do with such contacts, so far as I'm aware, but the splendour of her material success helped me to understand the pace, the publicity seeking, the strategic back patting, occasional viciousness, and ceaseless jockeying that are notoriously part of New York literary life.

Writers are drawn here by New York's centripetal force – or by the presence of other writers, the proliferation of jobs in the language trades, and the sense of being at the centre.

Few of the other writers I met or knew in New York enjoyed anything like Shere Hite's lucky strike; nevertheless, they stayed and persevered (despite the harshness of the economic struggle) because this is where everyone else is.

The scene: a vast and amiably shabby Chelsea loft. The place is crammed with women. Again, I'm a stranger, invited by someone who knows someone to come to a reading at the home of novelist Esther Broner. The point of the gathering is to raise money to help along a struggling writer, Marsha Freedman, who was once a feminist member of Israel's parliament. Freedman, in fact, was one of the *roman-à-clef* characters in Broner's exhilarating semi-surreal feminist novel, *A Weave of Women*.

We listen to the reading, we put money in the plate, the babble of talk rises to the high ceilings. I find myself standing near the long dining-room table, facing a vivid woman with a witchy bush of black hair: Esther Broner. "Oh, I loved your book," I exclaim unoriginally, and introduce myself.

"Darling person! Here." She grabs an apple from a basket on the table and presses it into my hands. "Have an apple! Come to dinner!"

Just this simply and luckily, I'm swept up into the welcoming arms of what my son affectionately calls my "coven," the group of sister feminists who will become my bosom friends and who will enthusiastically draw me into what I think of as my real (as opposed to tourist) life in New York.

■

Circles overlap in New York. Again and again, at public meetings, readings, rallies, plays, living-room discussion groups, and political fund raisers, I will meet the people I met in Shere Hite's living room or in Esther Broner's loft: Ruth Messenger, the one shiningly intelligent and honest member of New York City Council; Liz Holtzman, progressive district attorney from Brooklyn; Bella Abzug and her activist daughters; Susan Weidman Schneider, editor of *Lilith* magazine.

I go to the 92nd Street Y to hear one of my favourite writers, Lore Segal, reading aloud from her novel *Her First American*; a year later, I begin to meet her in friends' living-rooms as we gather to debate the course of events in Israel. Again at the Jewish Y, a centre of astounding cultural programs, I could sign up for Dick Hyman's piano-and-lecture series about the origins of jazz, then listen to him play at one of New York's piano bars, then enjoy his music on the soundtrack of *Moonstruck*.

At meetings of PEN Women, I hear an inspired panel discussion on "women and war"; among the panellists are former Canadian Bharati Mukherjee and Caroline Heilbrun, an academic who also writes mysteries under the name of Amanda Cross. For anyone who reads and whose life is touched by books, New York is a web of connections; people whose written words have enraged or inspired you, informed or entertained you, criss-cross your life – Norman Mailer, looking too small for his suit, awkward at a cocktail party; Nat Hentoff, the *Village Voice* columnist, wildly bearded and in a long black coat that would look bizarre even on a home-less beggar, muttering past on the street; Erica Jong in leopard-patterned stockings; Cynthia Ozick, making angry conservative arguments at a discussion about the Middle East. . . .

The atmosphere is thickened and intensified not just by the presence of celebrities, but by the omnipresence of what, in other times and places, might be called an intelligentsia. At Esther's loft, at meetings in Cooper Union Great Hall, at Middle East peace rallies on the Upper West Side, at counter-culture theatre events on the Lower East Side, I keep meeting the women (and men) who never appear in the New York novels of Thomas Wolfe, Dominick Dunne, Jay McInerney or Tama Janowitz. Viennese therapists, city hall activists, dealers in antique guitars and violins, aspiring actors, theatrical costumers, collage artists, pro-choice lawyers, book binders, writers who meet their friends in the Peacock Café on West 10th Street.

The people with whom I spent my days and nights in New York are neither starving artists nor "social whirlers," in *New York* magazine's phrase. They are in New York because it is the great liberal, creative centre of the continent; they care about politics, theatre, film, books, and music; they pour energy into fighting racism and AIDS; they go out constantly, working at their friendships, turning up at each other's one-woman shows or readings or publishing parties, introducing newcomers to old-timers, writing for magazines and newspapers and arguing with each other.

There are a hundred universities and colleges in New York, ninety museums, thousands of non-profit organizations and agencies, dozens upon dozens of publications, all of them providing a living for a tribe of scribes and politically engaged intellectuals that has not been entirely sucked up into the enclosed world of academe.

The circle of which I became a part is one of thousands; a punk rocker from Mongolia could probably find a sympathetic bunch of fellow Mongolians somewhere in New York. My group of friends was perhaps a little more mainstream than these hypothetical Mongolians; wherever they came from originally, they embody the tolerance, energy, political dissent, willingness to entertain new ideas, rigorous intellectual striving, and cultural ambition that, for most book-reading North Americans, epitomized New York in the first half of this century.

We all turn up at City University of New York on West 42nd Street to hear Tony Morrison read from her work. I see many of the same faces in the banquet hall at the Village Gate when we gather to pay tribute, over a home-cooked vegetarian banquet, to the magnificent short-story writer Grace Paley, being honoured by the War Resisters League for her years of front-line peace activism.

The highlight of the evening, aside from the dancing and the music, came when two friends read aloud from FBI file reports (obtained under the Freedom of Information Act) on Grace's tireless protest activities during the Vietnam War. Unwittingly, those FBI agents had transcribed and preserved for us Grace's brave and vivid sidewalk speeches. Grace's voice, in her stories and poems and, evidently, in those speeches I would never have heard but for the uncomprehending diligence of the Commie-fearing FBI, is utterly distinctive.

Grace's voice is New York to me. It has the unpretentious immediacy, the bite of sardonic humour, the stubborn realism of ideals lived and practised in the most contentious city on the continent. Her prose sounds just like her voice in person, with that deflating Bronx accent, tough but generous wit, the blunt lustiness without any hint of salaciousness; it's smart – too smart to be fooled by phoney sentiment – and off-beat, the sophisticated insight disguised by saltiness. It sounds like ordinary, earthy, common-sense speech, but it keeps stepping off without warning into the shocking space created by poetry.

A whole history of street activism and neighbourhood citizenship is summed up in Grace's fictional voice. People sometimes lament that Grace has written "only" three books of short stories and one of poetry. "Art is too long and life is too short," she had explained. "There is a lot more to do in life than just writing. . . . I think I could have done more for peace if I'd written about the war, but I happen to love being in the streets."

When I discovered a magnificent historical exhibit in Cooper Union Great Hall, I realized that Grace Paley was a legitimate descendant of all that made New York great, and which still echoes in the streets between the glossy condo towers and the Euro boutiques. It is not Tom Wolfe's fault that his glittering, hollow novel is being taken as an exemplar of the "real" New York; he set out to describe the New York that impresses him, which is not the same New York that moves me.

Late at night, in lulls between the shrieking sirens and the subterranean thunder of trains, a small, rhythmic sound comes up to my window. It is the clip-clop, clip-clop of the tourist horse carriages echoing home to their stables along my street. That resonant tick-tock is like a time lever: it pries away a raucous layer of the late twentieth century and lets the ghosts of an earlier era float to the surface.

New York now is mostly about money (that anachronistic carriage ride will set you back twenty dollars a half hour), but there was a time when New York was equally about ideas: passionate, contentious, turbulent ideas.

For the next year (1987 to 1988), those earlier times of turmoil and warring ideas are brought back to resonant life in an exhibit at the Cooper Union for the Advancement of Science and Art. The show celebrates the 128-year history of Cooper Union's Great Hall, a public space that played a pivotal role in New York history.

Cooper Union is a big, solid, Italianate brownstone college that faces down the Bowery in a part of lower Manhattan that is still curiously low-rise, tattered, and sunlit. It's an extraordinary place, the last and only free private college in the United States. All one thousand of its art, architecture, and engineering students are on full scholarship.

The school, and its Great Hall, are the legacy of Peter Cooper, born in 1791, a working-class boy of equable spirit, optimism, and mechanical ingenuity. A self-taught mechanic, he invented America's first railroad steam engine (the Tom Thumb) and made a fortune from new methods of glue-making.

Very much like Charles Dickens, Cooper yearned for the education he never had, and, like Dickens, deprivation awakened in him generous sympathies. When he built his school in 1859, he designed it for the betterment of the working classes, and insisted that it provide equal education to women.

The Great Hall, a noble, many-arched space, was dedicated to public debate. Workers, immigrants, and trade unionists had free access to the hall; eventually, it became a platform for every politician, intellectual, entertainer, and poet who mattered, from Ulysses S. Grant to W.H. Auden, from Woodrow Wilson to Margaret Mead, from P.T. Barnum to Orson Welles.

One of the first public speakers in the Great Hall, in 1860, was a lanky, raw, and nervous Republican who began hesitantly in a twanging Kentucky drawl. The crowd guffawed, but quickly fell into spellbound silence. And when he reached his now famous peroration against slavery – "Let us have faith that right makes might, and, in that faith, let us, in the end, dare to do our duty as we understand it" – they erupted in a roar of approval that swept Abraham Lincoln forth on a wave of popularity right into the White House and the Civil War.

Mark Twain lounged across this stage, cracking jokes about the mysterious content of the American sausage; fugitive slave Frederick Douglass, Sioux leader Chief Red Cloud, and feminist Susan B. Anthony, all eloquently pleaded for justice from this wooden platform.

At the turn of the century, workers flocked to the "People's Institute," an admirable experiment in democratic education: free nightly lectures on history, politics, geography, and literature.

The Hall witnessed tragedy, too. In 1909, the Triangle Shirtwaist Company locked out its workers – mostly young immigrant women and girls who toiled under ghastly sweat-shop conditions to make filmy Gibson Girl dresses. At a meeting in the Great Hall, the Triangle women appealed to the city's other unionized garment workers to support their demands. After hours of dreary debate, nineteen-year-old Clara Lemlich, a Triangle worker, rose to make a now-celebrated speech that

■

began, "I am just a poor working girl. . ." and ended in a clarion call for a strike. Twenty thousand workers followed her. They won a fifty-two-hour work week; only the workers at Triangle were defeated. Two years later, a huge crowd of labourers returned to the Great Hall to mourn the 150 young women burned to death (behind doors locked and bolted to prevent workers from going outside) at the Triangle Shirtwaist Company.

Read poor Clara's words, here where they were spoken, and both the hope and the horror of those times come back in a rush.

There were lighter moments. In 1873, free-love advocate Virginia Woodhull (a former stockbroker and patent-medicine hawker) defied a court ban and eluded a police cordon to speak about women's sexual and marital oppression. Tottering onto the stage in the disguise of an old Quaker lady, she threw off her bonnet and thrilled the packed hall with "an overwhelming inspirational fire scintillating from her eyes." The police were too enthralled to arrest her.

Peter Cooper's idea of an educated citizenry bore fruit. It was here that intense debate finally forced the creation of a public subway system, and here that mass protest meetings began the move to oust the corrupt Tammany chief, Boss Tweed.

Progressive democracy was the great American idea, and it still pulses with vitality in this exhibit. The hunger of workers for enlightenment, and the courage of popular leaders, both recorded here in their own words, still ring with moving conviction.

Until the 1950s – until television – Cooper Union's Great Hall was central to the city's public life. Debate meant something then; it was spontaneous and fiery, and it swayed the electorate. Words had power, and ideas crackled with potential action.

Peter Cooper founded his institution at a time, according to the exhibit, when class divisions split the city, when luxury lorded it over abject poverty, when new technologies and the mass market had thrown thousands out of work, and when the City Council was known as the Gang of Forty Thieves. Sound familiar?

Cooper! Thou shouldst be living at this hour! Heaven knows, New York hath need of thee.

Cataclysmic money – immense, meaningless, stock-market loot – has cast a spell of ostentation over the city. The museums mount ever more stupendous and vacuous special displays (costumes, horses), funded by and playing to *nouveau riche* largesse. Broadway plays become ever more elaborately mechanical and gutted of meaning; advertising, with the enthusiastic editorial back-up provided by the commerce-minded daily press, ensures that regressive spectacles like *Phantom of the Opera* will draw huge audiences. The art market reached frenetic peaks of cynical manipulation and blind excess while I lived in New York: Andy Warhol's cookie jars were auctioned off for thousands of dollars; neophyte painters zoomed into the stratosphere and self-destructed within months; the East Village art scene burgeoned as an underground phenomenon, swelled with instant wealth and fame, and evaporated.

Meanwhile, largely unnoticed by the media, a sturdy small-scale cultural life chugs determinedly on. Much of it happens in weirdly unsuspected places that, like ceremonies in Rome's Catacombs, lend an aura of defiant risk or adventure: the chill and vaulted chambers inside the footings of the Brooklyn Bridge, for example, or rat-trap abandoned schools or crumbling lofts. The Guerilla Girls, anonymous artists in gorilla suits, mount sporadic and hilarious protests against discrimination in the arts; I visited the Clock Tower Gallery in Lower Manhattan to see a show of their work and found myself in a marvellously remote and lambent space at the end of a long corridor in a magnificent old life-insurance building. In the middle of the high-ceilinged gallery room, a rickety winding stair led upward to the clock tower itself. A friend and I climbed up, isolated as spelunkers in the midst of Manhattan, and discovered another humble work of art. We stood in a quiet tower lit by shafts of sunlight, between the four twelve-foot-round faces of the clock. Silently and delicately the pendulum swung in its shaft in the middle of the room. A brass motor, vintage 1895, ticked over smoothly to power the eight-hundred-pound weights. The clock had been restored to magnificent working order by two dedicated citizens, who devoted hundreds of hours of volunteer labour in this private place.

Volunteer labour is vital: the arts and all that pertain to them are, unlike developers and corporations that thrive on public money, drastically underfunded in this city, which depends on them for its vitality and magnetism. Less than one per cent of the city budget goes to the $5 billion arts industry; all but a tiny minority of artists starve and struggle and are pushed to the city's fringes and its abandoned places.

New York is so crammed with creators and performers that even the "amateurs" are professional: an evening's concert of satirical music at Emanu-El Midtown Y on East 14th Street, where the audience perched casually on wooden benches, was a vivacious parade of accomplished stilt dancers, pianists, and the Downtown Chamber and Opera Players. With terrific zest and skill, they romped through excerpts from William Walton's and Dame Edith Sitwell's "Facade"; Paul Bowles's "Music for a Farce"; an entr'acte by Eric Satie for a film by René Clair; and a savagely ironic modernist short opera written by John Becker in 1939, starring characters named Privilege and Privation, with a chorus of "Bums" singing "Ach du lieber bank account." Anywhere else but in culturally top-heavy New York, such an inventive program would have received star billing.

You don't have to live in New York or have a close circle of friends in the arts to discover the off-beat rewards of the city. Many of the more arcane delights our family learned about through reviews of small productions in the *New Yorker* and the *Village Voice*. A tourist who has more than an week-end to spend could stroll into the 92nd Street Y and pick up a catalogue of their spectacular events, public readings, superb chamber music, experimental theatre, and film evenings with famous directors and actors. A close perusal of the smaller ads in the *Times* will lead you to rare jazz concerts at the New School (a progressive university) or unusual readings at bookshops or even hardware stores. (Really. Two branches of the Intuflo Hardware stores regularly hold avant-garde readings amidst the step-ladders and the cockroach motels.)

It was a small *Village Voice* notice that led us to the Lower East Side, where we sat on lumpy cushions on the floor in the ratty converted P.S. 122, to see "A Neoprimitive Opera" about anarchist Rosa Luxemburg; the shoe-string production was bursting at the seams with innovative music, lighting, and stage effects.

Everywhere I turned in New York, artists, performers, and writers were doggedly using unlikely nooks and crannies to go on with their work. A friend took me to join an organization called Poets and Performers, which stages intimate evenings at the Murphy Center for Sport and Art, a converted municipal asphalt plant near the East River. With a name like that, it was irresistible.

Life imitates art imitates life . . . until the mind reels. And a mind that reels is, in a way, the whole point of art.

These reflections came to me as I sat transfixed in the audience at a reading of two plays based on the writings of neurologist Dr. Oliver Sacks. He works with brain-damaged patients in New York, and his book of case studies, *The Man Who Mistook His Wife for a Hat*, has been hailed as one of the year's best.

The audience that night was chock-a-block with artists, actors, and writers – and one young man who barked. Or anyway, it sounded like a bark: a hoarse, explosive shout, at embarrassing and regular intervals.

You could almost hear the audience mentally tsk-tsking. Who would bring such a disruptive unfortunate to a play reading?

But afterwards, the audience, shamefaced, looked with new respect at the man who barked. Clearly, he suffered from Tourette's Syndrome, like one of the patients in the play. Tourettism, with its involuntary tics, spasms, and, as Sacks describes it, "wild excitements and weird, antic humour," made the character's daily life a torture. It also made him a brilliant weekend jazz drummer, gifted with Dionysian flights of improvisation.

Dr. Sacks rose to speak after the reading, and it was clear that he, as much as the audience, was preoccupied with these strange conjunctures of art and life's dis-eases.

A genial bear of a man with an engagingly undisciplined beard, Dr. Sacks noted slyly that "after all, the Oedipus complex was first described in a play."

Behind his public warmth, he is a man of nervous personal reticence and scrupulous intellect. And he worries about the fervour with which his work is being snatched up and adapted by others. "It's a delicate matter whether these case studies are a fit subject for art. It would be deeply offensive if they were used in a melodramatic manner," he told me later in an interview. Already, there have been plays, fiction, an opera, and films based on his almost unimaginably bizarre case studies.

Dr. Sacks calls his work "clinical tales," and it's an apt phrase. His tone is scientifically precise but startlingly unmedical – instead of pompous jargon, a dazzling tenderness and poetic, Kafka-like intensity. He not only studies his patients, he learns from them, and records his sense of awe at their miraculous adaptations.

Dr. Sacks wants to "restore medicine to the realm of human sensibility and moral importance which it should never have lost in the first place. Medicine must talk about the whole person, his world, his human predicament, his fight against illness . . . It becomes inherently dramatic, as, indeed, life is," he told me.

■

Dr. Sacks is that rarest of beings, a non-academic intellectual, who wears his erudition with endearing modesty. An Oxford graduate, he reads the *Oxford English Dictionary* in bed, plays piano, grows tropical ferns, obliviously drops cracker crumbs into his exuberant beard, scribbles endless private notes to himself, and quotes with equal ease from Sir Thomas Browne, Tolstoy, and Schopenhauer.

To read *The Man Who Mistook His Wife for a Hat* is to feel that little closed doors in your mind are being clanged open on scenes of unbearably poignant uncertainty. What do we really mean by identity? By health? By disability? What primitive powers of the brain have we sacrificed in becoming civilized? How free are we?

Dr. Sacks makes you feel these questions right to your nerve endings. And answers emerge from the stories that challenge both our slack lip-service to art and our ideas about curing disease.

A man who suffered a total loss of recent memory has to re-invent himself, moment by moment. "An abyss of amnesia continually opened beneath him," and he was driven to increasingly frenzied fictions. His only peace lay not in treatment or talk but in quiet moments in "an undemanding garden" where, in communion with nature, he could sense himself as real and existing in the real world.

Rebeccah, with an IQ of sixty, was "driven full-tilt upon her limitations" in special-education classes, which nearly destroyed her. But she had strong poetic powers, and flowered as an actress in a special theatre group.

Martin, a childish, disorganized, and tempestuous "simpleton," became calm and fulfilled when allowed to sing Bach in the church choir: "Bach lived for him and he lived in Bach."

And then there was unforgettable Dr. P, the distinguished musician, who had lost all sense of concrete reality. He was unable even to recognize faces of relatives. He went to put on his hat, and tried to lift off his wife's head.

■

He could interpret the world only in terms of extreme abstraction. Confronted with a glove, he was baffled, describing it as a "continuous surface, infolded on itself ... with five outpouchings." Nevertheless, he could function if he hummed constantly. Dr. Sacks describes him at tea ("an edible song of food") cheerfully "humming the last torte." Dr. Sacks's prescription: "Make music the whole of your life."

In our deepest being, Dr. Sacks says, we are creatures who make and sustain inward narratives of our lives. He shows us people in strange and terrible extremities, people whose very minds have been ravaged, and yet who heroically create identities for themselves through stories, music, and art.

No wonder that artists, relegated for so long to the consumer sidelines, have seized upon this work, which, on the basis of scientific observation, sees art as central to life.

So much has been said about the bloated mercantilism of the New York art world that I'm almost embarrassed to say that, for me, art and life seemed intertwined in New York in a way I'd never experienced before. Part of this impression sprang from the cultural ambition of the most ordinary and unlikely people. In the local cigar store, I bumped into the butcher, a man with an untidy grey moustache and a plump aproned belly, reading art magazines on his coffee break. Eagerly, he told me of his plans to create a book of food photography as art: his eyes glistened with visions of perfect pork roulades. A bleached-blond real-estate agent confided that she was researching a book on the history of European witches; a taxi driver played me a tape of his own jazz saxophone compositions.

My friends, too, did not separate their art from their lives. I became one of the Seder Sisters, a group of Jewish feminists who for thirteen years had been creating an all-female Passover celebration. Esther Broner, together with Israeli Naomi Nimrod, had written the original and now-renowned feminist Haggadah. (The Haggadah is the story of the Exodus from Egypt, which is read aloud at a family feast, or seder, on the first and second nights of the eight-day festival; the Seder Sisters celebrate with their own families on the first night of Passover, and gather for the feminist seder on the third night.)

I had read that Haggadah years ago in the pages of *MS* magazine and tried to adapt its spirit and some of its insights into my own family seder. Now, to my delight, I became part of the original group that had touched my life from afar: Esther Broner; Letty Cottin Pogrebin, a founding editor of *MS*, prolific author, awesomely competent organizer, and incisive public speaker; Phyllis Chesler, the feminist psychologist whose book *Women and Madness* transformed our understanding of traditional categories of sanity and madness; artists and teachers Bea Kreloff and Edith Isaac-Rose, whose steadfast humanity and shrewd humour leavened the most earnest debates; film-maker and still-radiant child of the sixties Lilly Rivlin, a member of one of Jerusalem's oldest and most distinguished families. Annual guests at the seder are Gloria Steinem, Bella Abzug (whose lustily melodious singing of Yiddish drinking songs and old religious tunes gives a lilt to the evening), Grace Paley, and a changing group of fifteen to twenty other feminists, ranging from the part-Jewish novelists Mary Gordon and Anne Roiphe to the committed Conservative Jew, Frances Klagsbrun.

(Letty Cottin Pogrebin, writing about the seder for the *New York Daily News*, impishly quoted from her notebooks: the 1979 food assignments for the pot-luck dinner, she said, included Susan Brownmiller, sponge cake; Eve Merriam, gefilte fish; Gloria Steinem, Manischevitz wine; and Bella Abzug, chicken.)

It would be difficult for a professional adult to live and work in New York without at least crossing paths with celebrities. It's not because some of these women are famous that I mention them, but because they became personally important to me, including me with instant warmth in their circle of friendship and in the spontaneous community they had created. As a lifelong feminist, struggling to make sense and coherence out of my non-religious Jewishness, my left-wing politics, my intense commitment to my family and to my work, I had always seen myself as a loner and an anomaly in Toronto. People lead more introverted lives in Toronto, and there is less public activism of any kind, cultural or political. And so, despite all my diverse Toronto friends, I never had a sense of belonging to any group. At feminist meetings, I privately felt more married, more maternal, more Jewish, or more left than others; at Jewish events or left-wing meetings, some part of me always had to be put aside.

In New York, I found a whole community for the first time in my life. Not that everyone shared my precise vantage point, but we had so many convictions or instincts in common. New York was a centre of the feminist movement; over the years, this group fought innumerable battles side by side, battles the rest of us read about from a distance, while engaged in our own local, less celebrated skirmishes. What impressed me about the Seder Sisters was the resilient, emotionally nourishing friendship they formed from their common political causes. Neither wholly private nor solely public, the group knits a close-woven fabric out of the separate strands most of us spend a lifetime painfully keeping untangled.

What's remarkable about the Seder – aside from the fact that these argumentative, over-extended women, all with frighteningly onerous family and work responsibilities, have succeeded in carrying it on so long without rupture or exhaustion – is that it is created anew every year. Tremendous artistic energy is poured into its preparation; the women meet in advance to choose a yearly theme, and each, on the seder night, will make a freshly created contribution. Esther will read, in her intense, poetic whisper, gorgeous new tropes that give surprising shape and depth to our lives as Jewish women; Phyllis, gentle and commanding by turns, will speak in the incantatory tones of a prophet, making anger at injustice into a flashing sword of defiance or a daringly ribald joke; Letty, a tenacious natural archivist, will remember the group's history and tenderly bring it to us in freshly illuminating words that make us see ourselves; Lilly, shining with sweet honesty and magnetic presence, will introduce new, troubling, and touching tangents; Bea and Edith will invent visual symbols and iconoclastic wisdom to bring us back to earth. Depending on the varying guests, the seder talk may be political, lovingly personal, or questioning. But the seder is always a drama, and all our daughters take part.

The Seder Sisters meld their lives, their feminism, and their art all year round. There are other feminist Jewish ceremonies: a rowdy and tearful political "hug-in" arranged by Lilly at Bea's West Village loft, to help Bella Abzug mourn the sudden death of her husband during her ill-fated political campaign; a Channukah party to re-dedicate ourselves to shared values; a mass visit to the Orthodox synagogue where Esther Broner is praying every morning, behind a segregating curtain, to mourn the death of her father. We crowd into the narrow end of the bench allotted to women, and bulge back the curtain (a plastic shower curtain, actually) with our assertive solidarity.

More than anywhere else I've lived or visited, New York seems to invite people to see themselves and their concerns as an authentic part of the cultural brew. Where else would people (well, some of the people) welcome inarticulate, disfiguring graffiti as an authentic expression of the thwarted egos of ghetto youth? And where else would you meet people as charmingly mad as the Janeites?

The music tinkled, the mirrored walls glittered under their swags of peach silk, and the hush-hush of the dancers' slippers, skipping and dipping their way through the Bath Cotillion, blended with the murmur of polite voices and the chime of tea cups. Evening in the Pump Room: slender young women in their Empire dresses; gents in knee breeches and cutaway coats; gentle-faced widows with black lace frills on their white hair.

"No, no, I don't think I'll join the promenade," said Mary Margaret Benson of McMinnville, Oregon, blush-

161

ing modestly and toying with her little mesh purse. ("It's a reticule, really.")

Can this be Manhattan, this delectable facsimile of nineteenth-century Bath? Certainly it can. This is the annual meeting of the Jane Austen Society of North America, and several hundred of the nearly two thousand members, devoted Janeites all, have gathered to enjoy their collective mania. For this evening, the members have turned the ballroom of the Waldorf Astoria into one of Jane Austen's favourite settings: the Pump Room at Bath. Most of them have come in costume and are now relishing a performance of cotillions and quadrilles by the Court Dance Company.

At tables around the dance floor, a heightened buzz of attention heralds a solo hornpipe by a dashing young man with adorable calves; spectators' eyes flash above their owners' fans. This is as sexy as it gets; in Jane Austen's day, dancing was not about sex but about social order, with maybe a little peekaboo flirtation for spice.

"Certainly there are passions," Mary Margaret, a librarian, tells me with a twinkle. "We have violent arguments about Fanny Price, for example."

Fanny is not, as you might assume, a fellow member of the society. No, she was one of Jane Austen's characters – the tediously priggish heroine of the novel *Mansfield Park*. But Austen characters are palpably alive to society members, who have read and reread all six novels and who always call the author "Jane" with sisterly familiarity.

At the mere mention of Fanny Price, a chorus of decided opinion goes up: "A literary wallflower!" "A wimp!"

"This is nothing," confides Judith Terry, a member from Victoria, British Columbia. "Once we were discussing an Austen character named Mary Crawford, who is faintly wicked, and a man jumped up and yelled, 'Don't say a word against her! I've been in love with Mary Crawford all my life!'"

■

Mrs. Terry, who is so elegantly fine-boned that she could be an Austen heroine herself, is a Fanny-loather. She got her revenge on goody-goody Fanny by writing a novel, *Miss Abigail's Part*, a sparky and subversive version of *Mansfield Park* seen from the viewpoint of the servants. It was published early this year [1987] to acclaim in England, the United States, and Canada.

The Jane Austen Society provides its members with the pure pleasure of getting together to talk about their favourite books. "It's like a family shorthand," said Diane Levine. "Before I joined the society, people used to laugh at me for loving Austen. In fact, my husband – my *former* husband – used to say, 'Oh, you and your Jane Eyre.'"

Across the room, I spotted an animated trio of costumed women, one of them wearing what looked like a doily on her head. I approached her to ask about the authenticity of her headgear. "Well, actually, I'd call it a doily," giggled Muriel from New Orleans.

Muriel and her friends, Libby from Boston and Florence from Long Island, met through a Janeite pilgrimage to England. "What a high: we met a real vicar."

None of them, it seems, liked Jane Austen when they were teenagers. "It was too good for us then," said Libby. I agreed. When I was thirteen and first read her, Jane Austen was an infuriating propagandist for my mother's ideas about the importance of being "a little lady." Little ladies didn't shout, whistle, chew gum, swear or argue. By the time I reread her in my twenties, Austen had improved dramatically. Now she was sparklingly funny and wholeheartedly in favour of witty, intelligent, self-determining women.

"She's still right, you know," said Libby. "It's marriage and money that matter."

"Rich or poor, it's nice to have money," agreed Muriel.

"Well, she really wrote about society more than about marriage," said Amina Steinfels. Amina, a gazelle-like beauty of fifteen, won a prize for the best gown, whose delicate flowers she had embroidered herself. She's not only a precocious Austen fan, she's a testament to the literary reach and power of the British Empire. Amina fell in love with Austen when she was nine, in her native Pakistan. She immigrated to New York only two years ago.

"You never meet Austen's heroines after they've been married and had ten kids," said Amina, wrinkling her nose. She wants to study math and literature, and doesn't think she'll get married.

Actually, though all of Austen's books are built on the courtship plot, she herself never married. And in a letter to her favourite niece, she said, "Oh! What a loss it will be when you are married. . . . I shall hate you when your delicious play of Mind is all settled down into conjugal and maternal affections."

The delicious play of Mind is what hooks the Janeites, who have a lot more fun at their conventions than do business or academic types. They're not strait-laced, either. At a panel session the next day, they were audibly delighted by an author of Regency bodice rippers who rewrote an Austen novel, and by a bubbly Virginian who made a musical out of the novel *Persuasion*.

Judith Terry spoke, too, and mused aloud about one of Jane Austen's villains. "Henry Crawford had his faults," she said, "but you can't help thinking how good he'd be in bed."

All the Janeites applauded heartily.

Art is more visibly a part of daily life in New York than in most North American cities I've visited: there are more serious readers on the subways, more street performers, more sculpture and graphic art in the public buildings, and, thanks to conscientious non-profit groups, more and more art being created.

Looking slightly battered on its narrow slice of a traffic island, the giant snail resolutely faces north from the

Flatiron Building, soaring symbol of Old New York, and heads towards mid-Manhattan. At the end of a sturdy rope hitched around its shell, it hauls an enormous two-yard ear of corn.

A plaque identifies this surrealist little parade as a work of art ironically called "Social Progress" by Christy Rupp. People crossing the intersection do a double take, smile, pat the snail, or rush past, bent on their own version of progress.

Public art, despite Christy Rupp's despairing view of human advancement, has taken a long leap from the days of bronze equestrian heroes who stare sternly into the distance, ignoring and ignored by the city dwellers around them.

Art blossoms everywhere in New York these days: murals appear on walls of derelict buildings, cryptic light shows flash between bits of news on the Times Square electronic bulletin board, sculptures puckish or provocative take shape in parks and on beaches.

Nowadays, the movement for public art is often sponsored by non-profit community groups such as the Public Art Fund, which believes in asking the community to help choose the artists, and then sponsors the artists to work right on the site.

Over in Brooklyn, a sunny afternoon spent at Cadman Plaza, outside the State Supreme Court building, showed me how well this works. Lying in a strip of grass in the public square were five telephone poles half-covered with sparkling designs.

"Oh, yeah!" exclaims a passer-by with a surprised grin of recognition. "Bottle caps!"

Thirty thousand of them, to be exact, collected by artist David Hammons from Manhattan bars ("I like the mood in bars"), sorted according to colour, and nailed to the telephone poles in spirals, diamonds, and snazzy zig-zags. When the poles are completely patterned, they'll be set upright, topped with basketball backboards and strung with wind chimes. The work is called "Higher Goals."

■

The day I was there, Hammons was away collecting more bottle caps, and I was free to lean on the park railings and eavesdrop on the passers-by. "I can't wait to see this thing go up," one woman told another as they rushed past to the Italian sausage vendor. "Now this," another woman told me confidentially, "is clearly an afghan or crochet pattern. I like it. It's going to be glamorous."

I was struck by their companionable tone of involvement; these court-house workers have watched "Higher Goals" take shape day by day. It's theirs in a way that master-works in a museum might not be. A cold, religious hush prevails in museums; nobody hums, sprawls, chortles, or exclaims aloud. And the posher private galleries can be so intimidating that once, confronted by a supercilious employee, I passed myself off as an eccentrically rumpled but wealthy collector.

The new wave of public art is bent on bridging this gap: artists, in fact, are now called in to design even the furnishings of parks, plazas, and lobbies. The Whitney Museum has east-side and west-side branch galleries in mid-town, both of them pleasantly accessible from building lobbies. The Whitney, of course, has a lot of outreach to do: it looms over Madison Avenue like a brutal fortress ("Reminds me of the Siegfried Line," a museum director told me) and has enraged its neighbours with its expansion plans.

Its branches, by contrast, are user friendly: my favourite, in the Philip Morris building, draws office workers with the garden chairs and marble espresso bar in the lobby; gulping lunch, they rub elbows with works by Frank Stella, Claes Oldenberg, and Alexander Calder. Young women deep in conversation over their croissants unconsciously mimic the buoyant gestures of George Segal's dancing girls, frozen in motion beside the living ones.

In the intimate little gallery itself, as I enjoyed an exhibition of the Ashcan School – early streetscapes of

New York – the security guard wandered in to peer over my shoulder and enthuse about a moody painting of the El (elevated streetcar). "I used to live right there!" he exclaimed with nostalgic pride.

New York, of course, is one place where art-in-the-open is bound to interact with its public and its environment, sometimes in the most unexpected ways.

On a triangle of park in the middle of Broadway outside Lincoln Center stands "Rostropovich's Tower." As I stood admiring the dozens of lyrical bronze cello shapes towering against the blue sky, a voice asked me, in a rich Parisian accent, "You like ze sculpture?"

It was a silver-blonde woman in her sixties, elegantly dressed, who was feeding the pigeons.

"Yes," I said.

"Rostropovich didn't," she said with regretful finality. "I come here every day to feed the pigeons. One day I see Rostropovich himself – I am a retired opera singer – shaking his head. He says they are too big for violins, too small for cellos." She shrugs tolerantly. "They are violas, maybe, I tell him."

One of the intense pleasures of a metropolis is the possibility of endless discovery. In a city that, however constantly it rips down and rebuilds, goes back to the seventeenth century, there are layers and layers of history and civilization to uncover. Every month, the papers proclaim a new discovery: a Dutch ship unearthed from the mud of what was once the harbour; a household midden of New Amsterdam filled with clay pipes and blue and white crockery. Art, too, is rediscovered: a missing nineteenth-century statue is tracked down to the Peacock Café in Greenwich Village, where it has stood in plain view of the patrons for years; long-lost murals of the WPA (Works Progress Administration, the Roosevelt job-creation program that included artists and writers) emerge into the light when a curious janitor in a public housing apartment chips at the rough paint in the lobby, or an art conservator digs through forgotten files.

Though daily I could enjoy the great and the famous in the grand museums, it was a particular pleasure of mine to follow loose threads that led me to the more obscure. To live in a city so prodigal that the formerly renowned are forgotten on dusty shelves; to live somewhere so rich in galleries, bookstores, and museums that I could make my own unimportant private discoveries through sheer serendipity . . . it was like my childhood dream of finding Indian arrowheads or pirate treasure, only better.

The E. Weyhe bookstore, around the corner from me, lives in its own time warp; once you have noticed it, sandwiched between the liquor store and the Golden Brioche Bakery, you feel there's some disconcerting magic at work. Surely it wasn't there yesterday when you hurried past?

But it was; it's been here since 1923, and soon it will be gone – one more scrap of old New York blinking out.

Unlike the other stores on this stretch of Lexington Avenue, E. Weyhe hasn't disguised its original brownstone character behind plate glass and garish Day-Glo signs. The modest doorway and shop window are outlined by a checkerboard of little yellow and blue tiles; artist Rockwell Kent designed the wrought-iron leafy vine over the door. The first two stories are a soft and fading ochre colour; the top three are painted cream.

It was the shop window that first caught my eye. The books, old and new, are laid flat in rows in a dustily downright style unthinkable to modern merchants. Brown monographs on Gothic architecture. Glossy books about French embroidery. Obscure works on famous modern artists; tantalizing works on obscure artists.

I wandered in one winter day a couple of years ago and found myself in an affable Dickensian clutter. No cash register: some books on a table had been shoved aside to make room for an adding machine, the store's only concession to modernity.

And yet, E. Weyhe was an important way station in American modernism. After Erhard Weyhe (pronounced Vaya) moved his rare-book business here from Charing Cross Road in London, artists began to drop in, and soon Mr. Weyhe had turned the second floor of the shop into a gallery for the kind of serious young modernist who was then scorned by the more affluent and established galleries.

"It was a gathering place," said Gertrude Dennis. She is Mr. Weyhe's daughter and grew up in those cream-coloured upper stories. She's been running the gallery for, she said – politely but determinedly vague – "a long time," and it is indicative of New York's real-estate frenzy that it now makes compelling economic sense for her to close up shop and lease the building to some other, more aggressive, kind of business. [At this writing, however, in the summer of 1989, E. Weyhe is still hanging on.]

It took me a year of browsing in the bookstore before I discovered that you could climb the narrow, creaking stairs to the gallery. But "browsing" isn't the right word. I would sit quietly on the wooden floor behind the sagging wooden shelves, take off my coat, and read my way through a yard or so of books about early-twentieth-century New York artists. The radiators would tick, the pages would rustle, and occasionally there would be muffled cries of delight from some artist or professor burrowing through another shelf and finding his heart's desire.

Weyhe's is the kind of place that makes you feel as though the next book you take down, having sat there unnoticed for half a century, might hold priceless secrets and rare knowledge. Mrs. Libow, who has run the adding machine at the front for twenty-four years, doesn't bother anyone.

When I finally ventured upstairs, a little less ignorant about American art than I had been before, I found Mrs. Dennis presiding over a narrow room, unchanged since

1923. "Lexington Avenue was different then," Mrs. Dennis told me. "Across the street [where there is now an orange second-storey sign for Lexington Luggage] there was Ann's Candy Shop, with little bow windows. It was beautifully kept."

Every year, the Weyhe artists produced a greeting card for the gallery. One of my favourites, from the thirties, is by the wonderful Mabel Dwight, showing the gallery from the inside – Weyhe's curator Carl Zigrosser, leaning against the stack of print drawers, artist Wanda Gag in lively conversation, a cat on the wide window-seat, art critic Henry McBride chatting up Mr. Weyhe. Through the paned windows you can see thick falling snow, and little Christmas wreaths in the windows of Ann's Candy Shop across the way.

Carl Zigrosser later became a curator at the Philadelphia Museum of Art, and an important authority on prints. But back then he was part of the modernist coterie in New York, exhibiting Matisse and Kaethe Kollwitz and Mexicans Diego Rivera and Orozco, and bravely championing Americans like early modernist sculptor John Flanagan, as well as Paula Cadmus, Emil Ganso, John Sloan, Reginald Marsh, Mabel Dwight, Adolph Dehn, and Howard Cook. If you'd wandered in during the early thirties, you could have picked up a signed Kollwitz print for five dollars, a Picasso for twenty-five. Those were exciting years of struggle that seem enviable now that young avant-garde artists are being snapped up and commercialized by sleek galleries and hugely wealthy collectors, and the camaraderie of a more intimate era is almost unknown.

In 1928, for example, when Weyhe mounted a mixed media show, Alexander Calder found that he had left one of his small mobiles back at his studio in Greenwich Village. Artist Barbara Latham, Howard Cook's wife, volunteered to fetch the missing work. She brought it uptown, waving and tangling in the breeze, on the open top of a two-decker Fifth Avenue bus.

■

When the E. Weyhe shop and gallery closes, the thousands and thousands of rare art books will go to a barn in Vermont, where Mrs. Dennis's daughter will sell them by mail order. The prints, paintings, and sculptures will go with Mrs. Dennis to be sold from a more prosaic location. The endearing façade of the shop will, inevitably, disappear into some shiny renovation.

For me, though, Weyhe's will hover ghost-like somewhere near the corner of Lexington and 62nd Street, folded into time, invisible but rustling at me when I pass.

New York is haunted for me anyway; walking around Brooklyn Heights with a friend, on narrow streets unchanged for one hundred and fifty years, Whitman's voice rolled along beside me when we walked down Cranberry Street, where he lived as a child, and passed the corner of Fulton Street, where *Leaves of Grass* was printed. These are quiet streets with simple, tangy names (Joralemon, Pineapple, Cranberry, Orange), and more than six hundred houses built before 1860 remain more or less intact. The watery winter sunlight, the dead leaves whisking and whispering along the wrought-iron fences, the clapboard, fanlights, mews, dormers, and stoops, all breathed reminders of those who lived or visited here: Mark Twain, Charles Dickens, Edgar Allan Poe.

Crossing the Brooklyn Bridge on foot, just as sunset flared, I swear I heard Elizabeth Bishop's "Invitation to Miss Marianne Moore": "From Brooklyn, over the Brooklyn Bridge, on this fine morning, please come flying/ In a cloud of fiery pale chemicals, please come flying. . . ."

We came dazzled off the bridge into twilight, into a strange, vaulted porch whose rhythms seemed hauntingly familiar: suddenly, I recognized it as the Municipal Building from a Don Freeman print showing the same open space forty years ago.

Pausing at a Sixth Avenue news-stand, I'm instantly revisited by the voice of poet Frank O'Hara, buying a paper to discover that Billie Holliday had died.

■

No street in New York is unmarked by poets, novelists, writers of songs or movies. New York is drenched in words.

The lulling drone of sentences rises in the calm, white space of the gallery. Long, curving, melodic sentences, they seem to float; they drift over the woman who lies flat on her back on the grey carpet; they glide past the old man with a flowing, silvery beard who very, very carefully uncaps a plastic cup of coffee, as though not to disturb the sentences in their lazy loop.

"Is it a seance?" asks a puzzled New Year's reveller outside, peering through the window of the Paula Cooper Art Gallery in SoHo.

No, although she isn't far wrong. This is the twelfth annual marathon reading of Gertrude Stein's thousand-page novel, *The Making of Americans*. Beginning on New Year's Eve, it takes fifty non-stop hours and more than a hundred volunteer readers to perform this uniquely New York act of literary homage.

"Children are always thinking are very often thinking that their mothers are very lovely looking and that is very often because mostly the child is always close up to the mother close to her when the child is looking. . . ." The reader's voice is clear, pleasant, conversational, hypnotic.

Gwen Deely, an organizer of the event for the past ten years, told me later that "dancers make the best readers. They have a physical approach, and this is definitely an aural experience." Ms Deely, a musician herself until she had to take a job in a bank, finds the reading "mesmerizing".

"Of course, it's also a literary work of substance; it's filled with poignant and true observations of human nature," she adds hastily.

Stein's huge novel, written in 1908, is so demanding that perhaps this is the only way a normally attentive reader can appreciate it. Last year, I was dragged to the reading by a friend, and we ended up visiting twice. Admission is free, and part of the enveloping pleasure of

■

the marathon is the way people can slip in or out, according to their stamina, while the paragraphs flow on and on, the ideas circling and slowly mutating, the way themes in music are reiterated, the readers deftly following each other as in a relay race. This year, if I weren't at home writing this column, I would still be sitting on the grey carpet myself, entranced by the language that Mabel Dodge said "induced new states of consciousness; it is so exquisitely rhythmical and cadenced," and which the composer Virgil Thomson compared to a finale of Beethoven's.

One of the ironies of Gertrude Stein's career is that she won enormous popular success with her charming *Autobiography of Alice B. Toklas*, a memoir of her life with her "wife," while *The Making of Americans* – which she claimed was the first twentieth-century novel – was virtually ignored.

She wanted to free language from the staleness of custom the way Picasso and Matisse freed paintings from old-fashioned ways of seeing. Indeed, Stein still strikes the ear as astonishingly modernist, and it's no accident that she should be celebrated in New York, where performance art and experimental music have eager followings, and where there is always a tolerant reception for the avant-garde.

Though Stein was celebrated in her own day as one of the first and most influential patrons of Picasso and Juan Gris, as a guru to young writers in her Paris salon (Sherwood Anderson and Ernest Hemingway sat at her feet), and as a powerful shaper of modern prose, she is still known to most people as the maddening and mockable author of "a rose is a rose is a rose."

Not least of the reasons I love New York is that this is the city that introduced me to the real Gertrude Stein. After last year's reading, I went home to Toronto and read her, really, for the first time. I found her memoir, *Wars I Have Seen*, vivid and penetrating. Incidentally, in 1944, eons before Marshall McLuhan, Stein, listening to her

■

radio, concluded that electricity had "made the globe into a village." Her reflections on writing are still shockingly original; her use of naturalist, slangy American dialogue is inspired. ("Howdy," she used to say, scorning pomposity, and "Great Jehoshaphat!")

I also read her explanation of that too-often-quoted sentence about the rose. "Now listen! I'm no fool. I know that in daily life we don't go around saying ' . . . is a . . . is a . . . is a . . .' but I think that in that line the rose is red for the first time in English poetry for a hundred years."

Stein, as she taught Hemingway to do, stripped language of its "excrescences" and tried to make it work in new ways, to short-circuit our dulled habitual responses to the written word. Listening to her prose read aloud, you can hear how it eddies and echoes the way our unspoken thoughts do; she is so sparing in her use of nouns and adjectives that when they occur, they crash on the ear like an unexpected chord.

Poor, stubborn, infuriating genius Gertrude. She is, it seems, fated to be "rediscovered" (in New York, if nowhere else) again and again by a surprised public. For all her reputation for outrageous obscurity, most of her novels are made of sentences so simple that a child could understand them. All it takes is the patience and the openness to read as receptively as we look at modern paintings.

Which reminds me of her typically funny retort to a New York journalist in 1934. She began a press conference with the gnomic utterance: "Suppose there were no questions, what would the answers be." Then she went on to charm her questioners with her clarity and wit. "Why don't you write the way you talk?" challenged a journalist. And Stein asked, as she would undoubtedly have to ask today: "Why don't you read the way I write?"

The next year, I raced to Alice Tully Hall at Lincoln Center when I read that a once-only performance was to be given, in honour of composer Virgil Thomson's ninetieth birthday, of

■

an opera he wrote with Stein, *The Mother Of Us All*. I'd been longing to hear this opera, about the suffragette Susan B. Anthony, and I was in luck: I snapped up the very last single ticket at the box office.

The performance was magic. Virgil Thomson, dapper in a white tuxedo, mounted the stage to reminisce with graceful wit about his immensely happy collaboration with Stein. His only regret, he said, was that he didn't write more operas with her. "But then, neither of us thought, back then, that we wouldn't always be alive."

On that poignant note, the music began, and the audience was rapt: tart, funny, tender, and sometimes heart-wrenching, perfectly matched by Thomson's melodies, the libretto tangled together the battle for the women's vote with by-play about love and marriage and with Stein's playfully elliptical version of political debate. Susan B. Anthony, despite the surrealist goings-on, had a staggering, simple dignity. Caught up on the wave of the audience's intense involvement, my eyes burned suddenly with tears of pleasure and excitement.

I had come alone, and walked (or flew) home alone, on a damp, misty night, south around the dark cave of Central Park and up again to my street, propelled by that intoxicating experience, rare for me, of deep conviction and joy shared with a knowledgeable, receptive audience.

I was often alone as I roamed Manhattan, but never for one moment lonely. Aside from the comfortable unself-consciousness I felt as part of the crowd, there was the quick, spontaneous openness of New Yorkers I met in the course of my work as a columnist.

Liz diLauro, a day-care worker from Queens who volunteered as a human-rights activist, was my contact for a story I did on the native American prisoner Leonard Peltier. Delighted, like most New Yorkers, to meet a newcomer who was infatuated with the city, she instantly invited me to visit her office at a local cathedral. She knew perfectly well that I would be enchanted. Indeed, St. John the Divine, with its extravagant public gestures and its peacocks, its Jewish public-relations director and its vigorous involvement in the life and arts of the city, stood as a symbol for me of the New York I cared about. At St. John the Divine, the pragmatic links arms with the spiritual, eccentricity is embraced along with custom and ceremony, all tumultuous human dilemmas and arguments find a compassionate hearing, and no one questions that a life dedicated to the arts, even the humblest of them, is at home with the sacred.

Thock, thock, thock. It's a soft, resonant sound, apple-wood mallet tapping on chisel tapping on stone. Shafts of sunlight angle across the cathedral close and into the open side of the stone-cutting shed. Just across the yard, the carvers are at work on the finished blocks of limestone. Their drawings of gargoyles, leaves, and demons are tacked up beside them as they chip their private visions into public effigies.

You get dizzy here; time spins around. The cathedral spires, the dreaming sunlight, the quiet punctured by a rooster crowing from the Deanery garden. . . . this could be the Middle Ages.

But it isn't. This is St. John the Divine, called the largest cathedral in the world, on the highest point of land in Manhattan, close by the Latin fringes of Harlem. The stone cutters and carvers are apprentices, many of them drawn from the ghettoes of New York (like Carol, of the Bronx, mother of four, formerly on welfare, now, proudly, a stonemason), and every now and then, one of those Deanery chickens disappears for a neighbour's *arroz con pollo*.

But that wouldn't ruffle anyone's feathers (besides the chicken's, of course) because the Episcopal St. John the Divine, begun in the 1890s, is uniquely medieval in tone, tolerantly contemporary in values, and more alive than any European cathedral I've visited. The neighbours wander in casually to pray, to celebrate high-school grad-uations in the nave, to light a taper at the shrine for AIDS victims, or to work in the organic garden, which grows food for the cathedral shelter for homeless men.

Naturally, a medieval American architectural style has to be invented, and the "American Gothic" ornaments being made under the direction of the English master carver Nick Fairplay are captivatingly original. High on the face of the cathedral, stone blue jays will perch in thickets of cranberry, the faces of blacks and women will stare from the capitals, and West Coast Indian totems will frown among the more usual devils and demons.

The thirteen acres of the cathedral close encompass a whole village of clergy and artisans. Children attend the Cathedral School and local youths train as weavers, ceramicists, and tapestry restorers. The crypt is home to avant-garde theatre and dance troupes, and on special occasions, resident aerial artist Philippe Petit waltzes across a high wire in the cathedral.

I visited the cathedral as a guest of Liz diLauro, whose human-rights office is a whitewashed niche tucked inside one of the flying buttresses of the church. Touring the cathedral in her wake, I felt as privileged as a child exploring a city of secret treasures. We might have been discovering for the first time the artworks strewn casually about the hushed and deserted chapels.

Immense indoor space is rare in New York. From a narrow walkway outside Liz's office on the Triforium (third level), I gazed down the vaulted dim heights of the nave, unseen by the tiny figures walking about more than a hundred feet below. The shadowed silence is mysteriously intimate, as though, if I dropped a whisper, it would sink slowly down to drift around rood-screens and candelabra, to nestle in some unknown ear at last.

We teetered along catwalks at eye-level with the glowing stained-glass windows and found surprising saints there, including Jack Benny and Florence Nightingale. We slipped through elfin Gothic doors and climbed hidden staircases, that curled up through the walls in spirals as tight and private as a snail's shell. Sometimes, almost lost in the labyrinth, I could only follow Liz's voice in the dark: "Up four steps, turn right," until we emerged on the roof leads, cheek by jowl with gargoyles, dusty, exhilarated, and terrifyingly high over New York.

I would be wrong, though, only to emphasize the exotic. St. John the Divine is loved by New Yorkers because it epitomizes the most eclectic and boldly progressive impulses of this city. Bishop Desmond Tutu spoke to a tumultuous welcome here; so have fiery labour leaders, native chiefs, and social crusaders. Under the leadership of Dean James Park Morton, the cathedral has pioneered housing reclamation projects in the ghettoes of New York, blazed a trail in worship appropriate to the "Planetary Age," and celebrated the spirit of prophecy in deeds of political activism. There are women priests at St. John, and besides the traditional services, you may hear Buddhist sermons, Hebrew prayers, Muslim chants, jazz, ragas, or the Gay Men's Chorus.

Last St. Francis of Assisi Day, an elephant, a camel, a llama, and a hawk on the arm of its falconer advanced up the aisle to be blessed by a rabbi, a Franciscan, and the dean. In another church, it might seem like show biz. In this strange community of believers in the oneness of spirit, the moment rang true.

The dean has written about "the feast of religious experience"; to him, the bustle of artisans and artists in the church seems natural because "art is also a moment of grace at the feast." For him, there is something wrong with a church communion where anyone feels excluded.

And it's true that the cathedral is so big, so extraordinary, so multifarious, that it's hard to imagine anyone who would not find something there, in some corner, that touches and embraces her. For me, it was the stone-cutting yard, where male and female stone cutters, black and white, intent on their work, told me that it doesn't matter to them if no one ever sees their creations, high on the cathedral façade. It is something, they said, to be part of a greater whole, something timeless.

In a city so pressed for time and bent on commerce, their modest devotion to craft struck me as one of those moments of grace at the feast.

CHAPTER 6

.

The Art of the Steal

During my first months in Manhattan, giddy with new discoveries and the pleasures of finding new friends, I was dimly troubled by seeming anomalies. Blatant crimes, casually discussed by newspapers, went inexplicably unpunished. In a city crammed with civic activists, the municipal government seemed extraordinarily feckless. Since New Yorkers are notoriously loud-mouthed and demanding, I was mystified by the way they tolerated – indeed, shrugged off – so much bizarre wrongdoing and malfeasance.

Canadians are inherently naïve about American big-city corruption. Not that we think people are better than they are, but we have a different hierarchy of vices. We suspect politicians not of greed but of unseemly conceit. Secretly, we harbour a niggle of contempt for those who have the egotism to push themselves forward as politicians, and surreptitiously we enjoy the day they get their come-uppance. Of course, we assume that there will always be a few politicians who seize their opportunities for illicit personal gain, but the system itself is one we trust. The over-arching authority of Parliament, for example, is not something we question. We may quarrel fiercely over what we mean by "the public good," but basically we believe that our governments – city, province, and dominion – are ruling in our best interests as defined by their particular ideology.

New York (and it is no different in this from other big American cities) cannot be understood this way. A higher, civic good does not seem to exist as a political ideal; perhaps it has withered in the massive shadow of the Reagan trickle-down theory that what is good for the richest must be good for the country. This theory has, in any case, neatly dovetailed with the permanent underlying pattern of New York city politics, which is one of contending interest groups out for their own private welfare.

Only very slowly did this dawn on me. Day by day, I was astonished – in a city of so much energy, wealth, intelligence, and flair – by the regular, spectacular failings of the most elemental measures of safety and hygiene. Beams from construction sites fell fatally on innocent passers-by; pot-holes yawned like craters; motorists careened at demonic speed, unchecked, down city streets and through red lights. The water often ran dark brown. Public schools attained a level of filth and ramshackle grimness unequalled by even the worst Canadian penitentiary. Garbage towered in reeking pyramids. Some tenants evacuated from a burning apartment building in mid-town Manhattan were shepherded to safety across the street, where they stood on a sidewalk grating that promptly collapsed beneath them; several were badly injured in the plunge. Houses under renovation collapsed on workers and inhabitants alike. Water pipes erupted under posh Madison Avenue, flooding the street and the basements of the rich. Bridges on the verge of collapse were closed down, causing massive traffic disruption and economic chaos. Hospitals were reported to be in such a desperate state, with AIDS patients, drug addicts, and victims of violence straining their resources, that I prayed for continuing good health.

And yet I met public servants by the score (teachers, city-hall lawyers, nurses, civil servants) whose energetic idealism and devotion to the city were admirable. How could it be that in the bosom of imperial splendour, with so much talent on which to draw, the mundane order we take for granted in a functioning city simply did not exist?

No matter how familiar a city seems to an outsider, its inner dynamic is inscrutable. So taken for granted are the basic assumptions of the body politic that no one thinks to explain them. Stumblingly, blundering through a series of *faux pas* and naïve misunderstandings, piecing together the bits of evidence floating to the surface in the daily news, listening to the laments of the native born, and persistently questioning, the newcomer begins to understand.

■

What I began to understand is that the basic, unchanging inner structure of New York is corruption itself – or, at least, what a moderately idealistic Canadian would call corruption. Some call it "brokered politics"; Mayor Ed Koch compared it to conducting an orchestra (or maybe the Sing Sing Chorus?); the essence of it lies in apportioning the city's loot to competing interest groups, most of them based on ethnicity, race, or class. Since New York is a one-party town, with no "loyal opposition" to the entrenched Democrats – and since the long-ruling Democrats have built up a complex voting structure that makes it very difficult to vote for anyone but a Democrat – there is no healthy clash of visions, no ongoing political debate about what the city should be.

So, instead, the city is an Aladdin's cave of treasure, a stockpile of lucrative contracts, jobs, permits, licences, and real estate, all to be plundered by whichever politician is the best fixer and grabber for his or her particular interest group within the Democratic party. (There are, of course, some honest politicians. They struggle to survive in a system that makes their civic altruism a lonely and often irrelevant pitched battle.)

To most New Yorkers, this system does not seem reprehensible. It is normal, even patriotic. Isn't it the American dream to climb from immigrant poverty to affluence?

"The citizen looks upon the fortune of the public as his own, and he labours for the good of the State, not merely from a sense of pride or duty, but from what I venture to term cupidity," wrote Alexis de Tocqueville in 1835.

What is the pre-eminent Canadian public holiday? Christmas? In New York, it is Thanksgiving. The day of abundance has no grinches, no dissidents, no non-observers; Christian and Jew, Moslem and Buddhist, newcomer and old-timer, all rejoice in the quintessential American holiday of material well-being and family reunion, with a grateful nod to pilgrim ancestors who had the sense to land on the shores of plenty. Non-sectarian turkeys grace every table, even those of the homeless in their shelters. This is multiculturalism, New York style: each national group delights in its identity, revels in a sense of entitlement as a group, and is utterly confident at the same time of its American-ness, which, to an outlander, seems at such moments to be equated with the freedom to be left alone to make money.

To my surprise, I found such breezy and unabashed materialism rather congenial. For the first time, I understood American boosterism as the glee of, say, a child about to open its birthday presents. Furthermore, no one is unentitled to go for the prize. This is a relief from the more constrained and involuted atmosphere of societies originally based on class privilege, where you can't always know the rules that will admit you to full membership, and where ethnicity may be a permanent bar to true acceptability.

But patriotism as cupidity, and loot sharing as the civic *modus operandi*, can clearly lead down a very short path to pervasive crookedness. In other times, depending on the ascendant immigrant group of the moment, and on national norms and values as well, New York leaders – like mayor Fiorello LaGuardia – have arisen from the hurly-burly of the "brokerage" who could both placate their constituents and articulate a more humane and embracing view of city life. In the time of greed, the Reagan eighties, that was impossible. Money lust ran like a fever through the populace, and all the time I was in New York, marvelling at the brazen Sun King excesses of the Trumps, the Guttfreunds, the Kravises, the Macklowes, I was equally stunned by the brash excesses of the ordinary people who wanted to be like them.

Gucci and Cartier were caught evading taxes, and Leona Helmsley grinned all the way to court when she and her husband, Harry, were nabbed for charging their $4 million house renovations to their business expenses. The Helmsleys own $5 billion in real estate, including the Empire State Building and twenty-seven hotels, and Harry's bonds alone earn $100,000 an hour in interest.

Meanwhile, grubbing away at the grass roots, four sewer inspectors pleaded guilty to accepting $2.5 million in five- and ten-dollar bribes from local plumbing contractors; that's a staggering number of pipes and drains that were so sub-standard the inspectors had to be bribed to issue certificates.

Half the city's restaurant inspectors were charged with extortion; corruption had so thoroughly penetrated the department, from the top down, that the city had to hire an entirely new corps of inspectors and keep them separate from the regular troops to prevent contamination. Restaurateurs, it was said, were tired of having twenty-five-thousand-dollar-a-year inspectors roll up in their Cadillacs to collect their pay-offs.

Maintenance inspectors for the New York school board were more orderly: a decade ago, they held a luncheon at which they agreed on a rate structure of 10 per cent in kick-backs for all contractors working on city school property.

The construction industry is equally efficient. The Genovese, Gambino, Lucchese, and Columbo crime families organized a Two Per Cent Club; every building contract of more than $2 million in New York City had to pay a percentage to the club, to be shared among the participating members. Vince "Fish" Cafaro, a Genovese captain, explaining the system to a Senate subcommittee, said that organized crime controls 75 per cent of the construction industry in the city: "Legitimate guys ain't got a chance." That certainly explains a certain number of falling beams, collapsing houses, and construction-worker deaths on uninspected sites. Mob membership, said Fish with a shrug, "is not good and not bad. But you get respect all over the city."

Respect is important to the sanctimonious, like Father Zorza, a priest who was arrested for conspiring with two hundred others, members of the Sicilian Mafia, to smuggle heroin into the United States – the Pizza Connection ring, as it was known, since pizza parlours were used as outlets. Asked to explain what he meant by "suits" (a suspected code word for heroin) in wire-tapped conversations, Father Zorza explained that he was talking about clothing for the poor. Father Zorza, also accused of art smuggling (he was arrested at the home of a woman said to be "an art restorer"), denied

■
187

everything, including charges that he tried to sell $46,000 worth of stolen tickets to Broadway's *Les Misérables*. Luckily for Father Zorza's reputation, the latter charges were dropped.

Another New York priest, Father Louis Gigante, posted $25,000 bail for accused Central Park rapist Kevin Richardson. According to the *Village Voice*, Father Gigante may get lots of respect all over the city because his brother Mario, a convicted extortionist, is a member of the Genovese crime family. Father Louis has intervened in the sentencing of several accused Genovese racketeers, but his defence of his brother may have been his finest hour. He told the court that Mario was "very considerate, generous, a good character, kind and not violent." According to other testimony quoted by the *Village Voice*, Mario was a feared loan shark who specialized in kicking people viciously in the groin; he told one victim, "I'll send a hundred fucking niggers up to the store if you don't get that money and get it now." He went to jail for eight years.

Actually, so thorough and widespread is corruption in New York that robbery could be called a cradle-to-grave city service.

A high-ranking New York state police inspector was charged with selling fake Vermont birth certificates to would-be illegal immigrants. Twice, FBI agents ordered, received, and paid for – at five thousand dollars each – these phoney certificates. The transactions took place with the state police inspector, outside a Bronx subway station. (A piquant note: the inspector had been in charge of a special agency to investigate ethical violations in the police force.)

Death, like birth, can be wrung for profits. A Brooklyn funeral home was charged on twenty-five counts of illegal trading in burial plots. And the Public Administrators, who handle the estates of people who die without wills, were secretly videotaped stuffing their pockets with cash and jewels from apartments of people they thought had died. (The videotapes were made during a state "sting.")

■

No agency is too sacrosanct, too lofty in purpose and reputation, to escape sticky fingers, or worse. People who work for societies for the prevention of cruelty to children had been allowed since 1875 to carry weapons without a permit and make arrests to protect children. Some enterprising New York Mafiosi took advantage of this little-known law to incorporate their own children's aid society in 1982. It made a perfect front for cocaine dealing and operated in Sullivan County, New York, for six years, until sued by the attorney general.

The state National Guard was headed for some years by Vito Castellano, until he was sentenced to three years in jail for taking $58,000 in bribes from Wedtech, the corrupt defence contractor. Vito had some other interesting business that took full advantage of his role as head of the guard. The guard's armoury, for example – prime Manhattan real estate – rented space for a decade to a private tennis club at ludicrously low prices: eighty-four cents a square foot, according to the *Village Voice*, which pointed out Castellano's suspiciously close association with the tennis company.

As head of New York State's military, Castellano picked up an extra $35,000 a year and a company car as a "consultant" for *Penthouse* magazine; his duties included advising *Penthouse* how to keep its magazine stocked on military bases. Castellano was also in the business of making loans to other officers and did some "consulting" work with military contractors. Castellano is a confessed bigamist – a crime that has a quaint charm in the light of his other activities. Apparently, he married and divorced Dorothy and Linda so many times that he lost track and ended up married to both at once.

Much of New York's corruption has an appealingly comic edge; we laugh against our better judgement. What to make of the news that in the city-owned metred parking lot across from Manhattan's Criminal Courts, some enterprising street hustlers walked in and took over, charging court clientele and officials $5 to double-park their cars – illegally, of course. Or the allegation that Mayor Ed Koch's chef was running an illegal business out of Grace Mansion, the official residence, using the mayor's kitchen, pots, pans, staff drivers, and involuntary endorsement to sell catered food around town?

But usually, corruption is not amusing, particularly when it's the undetected thread in an otherwise baffling story. New York reacted with outrage when Joel Steinberg and Hedda Nussbaum burst onto the front pages, he arrogantly moustached and defiant, she battered into a pulpy grotesque; their six-year-old illegally adopted child, Lisa, had died in hospital after being found comatose at home.

Ambulance workers had found Lisa on the floor, where Steinberg had left her to go out to dinner the night before after clubbing her with a metal exercise bar. A baby, Mitchell, was found roped to a chair and chewing on a bottle of sour milk; the walls were spattered with blood and excrement.

Ten years before, Nussbaum had been a sparklingly pretty woman with dark hair and intelligent eyes. She had a college degree in English and a job as a senior editor of children's books at Random House. When she was arrested, she had a smashed nose, grotesquely swollen and bruised lips, grey, unkempt hair, a broken jaw, nine broken ribs, and gangrenous wounds on her legs. Her eyes were glazed. Joel Steinberg was described by those who knew him as a swaggering, domineering blow-hard. A criminal lawyer who defended accused drug dealers, he boasted about his huge fees and his knowledge of fine wines. When the police arrested him, they found crack pipes, cocaine, hashish, and $25,000 cash. The filthy apartment had only one single bed; evidently, the children slept on a couch or in a playpen.

Steinberg was eventually convicted of killing Lisa; charges against Nussbaum had been dropped, on the grounds that she was so destroyed by drugs, fear, broken bones, brain damage, and degradation that she could not be considered culpable. Nevertheless, rage and controversy were constant for more than a year, throughout the trial and after: should Hedda not be held accountable for imperilling her children, failing to protect them? How could a white, middle-class couple at such a desirable address – a beautiful old brownstone on West 10th Street in Greenwich Village, a house where Mark Twain once lived – descend to such brutality?

The pattern of blaming is always illuminating; like the magnesium glare of a rocket, the path of blame throws a sudden revealing light on blamer, blamed, and bystanders. Here, in the heart of a privileged neighbourhood in Manhattan, a woman had been savagely beaten for ten years; two small children lived in squalor; one of them had clearly been abused for a long time. Whose fault? The press focused obsessively on the mother; when children are hurt, mothers, not fathers, not even if the fathers are the killers, are secretly felt to be most guilty. Mayor Koch instantly blamed the neighbours, raging about their apathy, their cruel indifference to the child's obvious suffering.

The public took up his cry, simultaneously indulging in an orgy of sickly sentimentality over Lisa. Letters addressed to "Our Little Angel" were left at the door of the town house, along with candies, toys, scented candles, and hate mail accusing the neighbours of not doing enough.

As it happened, the murder had a double frisson for me: not long before the murder, I had visited an old school acquaintance who lives in the same town house, in the ground-floor flat. When the neighbours came under attack, I phoned her. According to her, she and two other neighbours can account for at least twelve phone calls to police and child-welfare authorities in the couple of years before the murder. Three times, city social workers answered the summons; they found "not enough evidence" for prosecution. Police were there frequently; there were never any charges.

My friend painted a grim picture of a woman around whom a noose was tightening. By 1982, Nussbaum was often turning up for work in bandages and dark glasses. There were frequent absences; finally she was fired. For the past four years, Nussbaum refused to see her family. When neighbours called police after a beating, she cowered behind the closed bedroom door.

■

"She was a ghost," my friend said. "She was gone, the flame was out. She only went out late at night for groceries, scuttling along even in cold weather with hardly any clothes. Even the groceries made no sense. I'd see her come back with more Häagen-Dazs ice cream than any freezer could hold. You felt you were hurting her just by saying hello. We're sure she was heavily drugged all the time to stand the pain."

Why did Mayor Koch rush into print blaming the neighbours? Why did police insist they knew nothing about the couple before the final call? Why had city social services never acted? Given the record of corruption and patronage in every city agency and service, it's at least possible to speculate that there could have been pay-offs: Joel Steinberg, cash in hand, answering the door. As for the social workers, however earnest and dedicated they may be, they work for one of the city's most overburdened and underfunded agencies. Like most municipal services, it is likely weighed down with at least some incompetent supervisors who owe their jobs to political patronage. Whether they are bribed or just indifferent, such patronage appointees corrupt everything around them. Files can be misplaced, or simply find their way up to the supervisor's desk, where their journey ends. Political whims and grandstanding ploys – instant new programs initiated after a disaster – can disrupt the entire work-load of an already harassed agency.

Setting aside the larger story of woman-blaming and society's niggardliness about paying for children's services, the most illuminating thing about the death of Lisa was the mayor's haste to put the blame where it would do least harm to his administration.

Publicly, at least, there was never any challenge to the role of the police, the ease with which lawyers arrange illegal adoptions, the inaction of the Human Resources Administration (the agency responsible for child welfare), or the non-existence of any public agency to reach out to women known to be battered.

The mayor's talent for quick-draw quotes and colourful bluster saw him safely through this and a dozen other scan-

■

dals. For me, Ed Koch epitomized the structural corruption of New York politics, even though no one has ever accused him of taking an illegal dime.

> As the rulers of democratic nations are almost always suspected of dishonourable conduct, they in some measure lend the authority of the government to the base practices of which they are accused . . . To pillage the public purse and to sell the favours of the state are arts that the meanest villain can understand and hope to practice in his turn.
> – Alexis de Tocqueville, 1835

I came to New York last fall in the midst of the mayoral election campaign here, gawking like a greenhorn at the American style. Publicly, unabashedly, Mayor Ed Koch boasted of his lavish war chest, and no one wasted so much as a shrug at the fact that most of the $7 million came from developers with projects needing approval from New York City. A big yawn. Business as usual.

Now, less than a year later, New York has staggered through a winter of ghastly revelations, corruption after corruption boiling up through the cracked surface of political life. Though Mayor Koch's popularity is still immense, and though he has escaped personal implication in civic crimes, one senses a chastened air at City Hall.

The first break came with the bizarre and pathetic attempted suicide of Queens Borough President and Democratic party boss Donald Manes; by the time he succeeded in killing himself, on March 13, 1986, the first of dozens of investigations, charges, and arrests against public officials had begun.

It quickly became clear that almost every branch of municipal government is sullied by incidents of fraud, racketeering, bribery, and influence peddling. Officials of the Parking Violations Bureau took bribes from collection agencies in exchange for contracts to collect delin-

■

quent parking fines. The chairman of the Taxi and Limousine Commission was fired when it turned out that he played fast and loose with $100,000 taxi licences, known as "medallions." The business development commissioner was fired for owning stock in a company that received city financial aid. Now a member of the planning commission has been called before a Bronx grand jury to explain why he privately represented an accused murderer and racketeer in a series of real-estate deals.

Breath-taking gall marks some of these crooked transactions: fat contracts handed out to non-existent companies, for example, or, as *New York* magazine reports, awarded to businesses with known organized crime connections. Nothing has escaped the larcenous attention of enterprising crooks, not hospitals, school buses and lunches, public housing, cable television, poverty programs, a proposed Grand Prix race-track, parking garages, tow-truck contracts, credit unions, garbage incinerators.

And all this doesn't even touch on the matter of campaign contributions.

Why is corruption so common in so many American cities? The first clear cause is the lack of strong political opposition.

"The trouble goes back to a deeply-rooted one-party system," a strategically placed City Hall insider told me. "There's a Democratic party clubhouse in every district, and no opposition party. You just can't get elected without the party machine. [The clubhouse, as he didn't bother to explain, is so powerful because it can deliver the vote, and it can deliver the vote because it buys the voters' loyalty with jobs, advancement, favours.] Once you're in power, you owe favours: to the machine that got you in, to the developers that gave you money. And every elected official can fill literally dozens of important official posts – deputics, advisors, heads of agencies, lawyers, commissioners – with political buddies."

In New York, only the doggedly muck-raking *Village Voice* newspaper, the Harlem-based *Amsterdam News*, and the toughly principled Democratic council member, Ruth Messenger, have held out against Mr. Koch's brash charm. Despite howls of self-righteous outrage from the mayor, they have steadfastly questioned, probed, attacked.

But these are lonely voices in the overwhelmingly powerful clubhouse atmosphere. Back-room cronyism seems to make local politicians feel immune to discovery. They've extorted bribes and pillaged the public money with no apparent sense of shame or terror: how else to explain the *bonhomie* with which politicians openly carouse with and do favours for known gangsters?

Ms Messenger thinks that conflict-of-interest laws aren't tough enough: "State and municipal legislators who happen to be lawyers are free to appear before many public agencies in their private capacity as lawyers," she told me. She also regrets the lack of press vigilance, and the almost universal media acceptance of Koch's boosterism: since the fiscal crisis of the mid-seventies, whatever crass megadevelopment Mayor Koch says is good for the city is applauded as though by trained seals.

Another cause is plain greed. Self-interest and the pursuit of the buck are sacred items in the American political credo. Contemporary robber barons are uncritically admired for their glamorous success, and even loved as public benefactors.

But why, I asked my City Hall informant, is the electorate so lethargic about the gargantuan thievery of its tax money? His answer took me right back to de Tocqueville.

"Simple," he said. "The ordinary people hope they're going to benefit. Remember Tammany Hall and the ward-heelers? The party looked after its grass roots." Not every citizen yearns for a bit of pay-off, of course, but the poisonous acceptance of corrupt patronage is so entrenched that the voter's only response may be a defeated shrug.

From a U.S. vantage point, Canadian cities look pretty good. Nearly all our city councils have outspoken opposition members. As pesky or trouble-making as they may appear to the establishment or to complacent voters, they are our saving grace.

Still, we dare not rest on our relatively shiny laurels. It may seem tiresome to insist on public disclosure of campaign donors, accountability of appointed officials, limits on election spending, rigorous scrutiny of public contracts and patronage appointments, and stern conflict-of-interest laws . . . but the alternative is appalling.

Of course, one reason it takes so long for a newcomer to understand the extent of corruption in New York is that so much of it is tolerated as benign. Mob control of certain industries is accepted with a shrug; most New Yorkers know that the Mafia pimps, sells drugs, steals, and murders, but their fund of indignation over this seems long since exhausted. Besides, the criminal presence is part of New York's excitingly dangerous edge: when a Mafioso was assassinated on the sidewalk outside Spark's Restaurant, a sumptuous steak-house on the East Side, crowds thronged to ogle the spot for more than a week. Compared to the unpredictably savage crack gangs, organized crime seems almost benevolent to New Yorkers, who gratefully mythologize it. Repeatedly, I was assured that Staten Island was a marvellously safe place to live, since "the mob patrols the streets there," or that Little Italy was a safe place to stroll because the "Mafia protects its own."

Municipal corruption has its scribes, story-tellers, and myth-makers, too. No tabloid is complete without its Irish male columnist – Jimmy Breslin at the *News*, Pete Hamill at the *Post*, Dennis Hamill and Dennis Duggan at *Newsday* – whose special tone (established long ago by Breslin) is tough-guy, blue-collar, indignantly populist, macho about sports, and knowing about crime. For them, cops and criminals are the local version of cowboys and Indians; even though they earn their living by the sissified white-collar task of putting words on paper, they can prove their ballsiness by rubbing shoulders with the working guys in the local saloon, riding the range (the streets and the subways), and showing their exaggeratedly nonchalant familiarity with the engaging varmints and rascals who hang out at the borough hall. At frequent intervals, these hard-boiled newspaper guys pass on to us (the wide-eyed local yokels) the latest colourful lingo they've picked up on the streets. The tradition began with Damon Runyan, and the tradition says that these "hard guy" criminals are not supposed to do real harm. They're local colour, funny like in the movies, admirably honest in their cynical view of human nature.

Hence Jimmy Breslin's howl of fury when the Queens scandal began to unfold and some of Breslin's favourite local characters were revealed to be seedy crooks. In *City for Sale*, Jack Newfield and Wayne Barrett, two of the city's most dogged chroniclers of wrongdoing, describe how Breslin had been close personal friends for fifteen years with Queens lawyers and political hacks whom he though of as picturesque and quoted frequently. When Breslin learned of the Parking Violations Bureau scandal, very early on, from the desperate characters who were about to be unmasked, he wanted to scream, he told Newfield. He, Breslin, had delivered an emotional eulogy at the funeral of Shelley Chevlowe, "a legendary [Queens] rogue . . . a bar owner, city marshall and bail bondsman," and, as it turned out, a bribe collector for Donald Manes, the Queens Democratic party boss and borough president. At Chevlowe's funeral, after weeping at the graveside along with Breslin and others, Manes approached one of his bribe payers and told him who would take over from Chevlowe as the bribe collector.

From the moment he learned this sharp little fact, Breslin played a key role in unravelling the skein of lies and cover-up, feeding bits of strategic information and clues to the prosecution through his column. "I had to prevent the worst possible crime from occurring – public embarrassment to Breslin," he told Newfield. "Later I felt rage and betrayal . . ."

■

The complicated and sordid story that spun out from the Manes suicide is told in riveting detail in *City for Sale*. The bit players are as hilariously awful as the columnists always portrayed them: Geoffrey Lindenauer, the quack sex therapist who conducted orgies in a borrowed office; a mink-coated Manhattan psychiatrist married to a former Miss Ohio, who took cash and cocaine bribes to write fake disability certificates for city employees; Herb Ryan, foot-soldier for Manes, who boasted expansively to an undercover agent to whom he had proposed a series of lucrative fixes, "This is a way of life"; convicted embezzler Dominick Santiago, who changed his name to Nicky Sands and got appointed by Koch to a senior city position.

It takes Newfield and Barrett more than four hundred pages to describe the dizzyingly complex interlocking schemes of lawyers, businessmen, mobsters, politicians, judges, trade unionists, congressmen, celebrities, and low lifes who conspired to enrich themselves, sometimes by millions of dollars, by robbing the taxpayer. So many were so ruthless and unashamed, so rapacious, so infinitely skilled in finding ways to circumvent the law, that one can only conclude, with Vince ("Fish") Cafaro, that "the legitimate guys ain't got a chance."

Two characters in the book take pride of place: Meade Esposito, the all-powerful boss of Brooklyn, and Ed Koch. Esposito was long suspected by the FBI (and nearly everyone else) of being an actual Mafioso. At the very least, he had extremely close ties to mobsters in every area of corrupt unions and businesses in New York. A rough-talking, funny, shrewd, implacable, and obscene character, Esposito was the champion fixer. As Brooklyn Democratic boss, he had hundreds of patronage jobs at his disposal; his lackies were everywhere; he appointed judges, commissioners, board members of public agencies; he anointed candidates for high office and defeated those, like Brooklyn congresswoman Liz Holtzman, who wouldn't play the game. In his eighties, convicted on several counts of fraud and bribery and sentenced to two years' probation and fined half a million dollars, Esposito has the consolation of the $5 million he gained during the Koch years. He's spending his probation mostly at his summer home in the Hamptons. For years, he exercised almost absolute power; now he relaxes in affluent, though somewhat shadowed, splendour.

A newcomer to New York can't help but be perplexed at first: how can it be that obviously criminal types, whose horrifying felonies are often casually reported in the press, go from triumph to triumph unscathed? How can notoriously sleazy characters like Roy Cohn, the McCarthyite lawyer who openly boasted of influencing the judge who sentenced the Rosenbergs to death, be a "celebrity" in New York, fawned over by the literati and party-goers of every political stripe? Sydney Zion, often described as a "liberal" journalist, wrote a friendly biography of this crooked lawyer whose elegant Upper East Side town house office was, as Newfield and Barrett describe, a "hub of mob activity," and who skimmed millions from city parking-lot leases, bribes, and pay-offs.

One answer, of course, is that between them, the mayor and the Democratic machine have the power to appoint Criminal, Family, and Supreme Court judges. Roy Cohn, "indicted more often than any of his clients," according to Newfield and Barrett, was never convicted; it helps to have appointed the judges who hear your case. (In New York, not only judges but even district attorneys and special investigators may be mob or machine appointments.)

The power of patronage is bottomless. FBI agents told Newfield and Barrett that so many thousands of possible witnesses owed their jobs to Meade Esposito that for decades they could never make a case against him; they were always "an hour too late or a dollar short."

And the ultimate answer is that corruption transcends politics; the Republican Cohn, for example, schemed to gain control of the corrupt Democratic machine, and exercised power in city politics through his henchman and law partner, Stanley Friedman, arch-criminal and boss of the Bronx Democrats. Politics in New York isn't about politics; it's

■

about money. This is so widely accepted that notoriety easily slides into celebrity; Bess Myerson, a former Miss America and the city's Culture Commissioner, thought nothing of consorting with a gangster type eighteen years her junior, who, while he was with her, enjoyed $150 million in city sewer contracts.

The exception to all this, it seems, is Ed Koch, whose ego and lust for power transcended the more common vice of greed. In 1977, Koch campaigned as a reformer; a little-known liberal Congressman, he astonished his mayoral supporters by energetically siding with anti-black bigots in local controversies, injecting the irrelevant issue of capital punishment into the city campaign at a time of anti-crime hysteria, and skilfully using an entirely phoney "romance" with a celebrity, Bess Myerson, to defuse rumours that he might be gay.

But something more fateful happened, by Koch's own account, during that first winning run for the mayoralty. Since he had publicly lambasted corrupt machine politics and the "gangster" (Koch's word) Esposito, he could hardly seek the support of the all-powerful Brooklyn pol. Secretly, therefore, he met with Esposito to ask for his covert support. In return, Esposito asked Koch to "take his phone calls," a code for responsiveness to patronage demands. The deal was struck; the word went out. The "anti-machine" Koch was elected, and promptly put into power the long list of Esposito's men. To read *City for Sale* is to marvel at the ten years of Koch's endless blustering, lying, evading, covering up, attacking, and dodging in order to protect the corrupt commissioners, board members, and powerful public officials he had installed at Esposito's command.

Meanwhile, New Yorkers cherished him for the same qualities they value in themselves: his sandpapery wit, the elbows-out competitiveness it takes to "make it" in Manhattan, his cocksure and ebullient boosterism about the city he claimed to have saved from the dark days of the near bankruptcy in the mid-seventies. When the scandals began to explode around him, he kept the voters distracted with sleight-of-hand diversions. One day he would be insulting visiting Soviet children on a peace mission to New York by telling them their government was "the pits"; then he'd be lecturing Ireland or Nicaragua about their politics; he rushed around the city personally nailing up no-smoking signs while his transportation commissioner, his Parking Violations Bureau chief, his chef, his taxi commissioner, and his chairman of the Health and Hospitals Corporation (Koch's former personal assistant), to name only a few, were busily looting the public treasury. Bridges, ambulances, highways, and hospitals creaked, groaned, and collapsed as their public guardians used them as personal fiefdoms to enrich themselves.

Koch was skilful at exploiting racial and ethnic frustrations. He campaigned among blacks saying he would advance them in city jobs and keep open a threatened Harlem hospital; once elected, he closed the hospital and whipped up animosities between blacks and Jews. He promised advancement to Italians, too; when some of his corrupt appointments were criticized, he ranted about the critics' anti-Italian prejudice.

Koch's much-vaunted "Talent Bank" is a case in point. It was supposed to be a unique mayoral initiative to promote women and minorities in city positions. By 1988, it was clear that the quiet little operation in the basement of City Hall was not a Talent Bank but a patronage machine, where an Esposito and Friedman confederate, Joe DeVincenzo, colour-coded job applications according to which party boss had recommended the person for the city payroll. Just as in Oliver North's White House basement operation, frenzied paper shredding occurred below stairs when the scheme came to light.

No taint of money-grubbing ever touched Ed Koch. The public's faith in him eroded as it became clear that he must have known what was going on, but his only personal brush with greed was his yearning for a really extravagant limousine. Koch loved the brute power of being klaxoned around, through, and above New York's traffic in police helicopters and speedboats, but the official car fell short of his grandiloquent dreams. He once suggested that the police confiscate a drug baron's stretch limo for him; he ended up, to the delight of the press, being chauffeured around in a Cadillac that turned out to be leased at bargain rates from a mob-affiliated Brooklyn car dealer.

The sheer magnitude of the corruption scandal protected Koch, to some degree, from public anger. In the bewildering maze of trials, hearings, investigations, reports, and indictments, few noticed that, as the *New Yorker*'s tireless City Hall reporter Andy Logan pointed out, Koch's administration had been receiving clear and detailed warnings about the Parking Violations Bureau corruption for four years before the scandal became public, and chose to ignore them. The sleaziest crook of all, by all accounts, was Stanley Friedman, Bronx Democratic boss and a flattering, clinging shadow to the mayor, now serving a twelve-year jail sentence for his key role in the PVB crimes. Friedman had a sign in his office: "Crime doesn't pay – as well as politics." Koch seems not to have noticed.

Koch heatedly defends the principle of patronage, as well he might, with twenty thousand city patronage jobs – an immense power base – at his disposal. More surprisingly, journalists have actually defended corruption as a way of life. A profile of Koch by Marie Brenner in *Vanity Fair* carefully positioned him as a "pragmatic" politician, "one of the last of the great breed of city Democrats," against the "fanatical" reformers and "ideological" journalists who attack him. ("Ideological" is the neo-conservative Koch's favourite put-down of his critics, as though having ideals were childish or stupid, or as though neo-conservatives don't have an ideology.) His deal with Esposito, Brenner says, was "shrewd," a giving up of "reformist ephemera" in order to "come of age." Roger Starr, formerly the city's housing commissioner and now the *New York Time's* editorialist on urban affairs, has written that "graft is an important safety valve against the possibility of an ineffective government." Starr warmly recollected as "heroes" the building inspectors who took bribes in Starr's family's business.

■

Even critics on the left have a stubborn allegiance to brokered politics, with its inevitable cronyism and mutual back scratching, which gave immigrant workers their footing in New York. Jim Sleeper, a left-wing urban critic and an editor of *Dissent* magazine, writing in the *New York Observer*, scolded reformers like Liz Holtzman and Carol Bellamy for their "purity". Successful politicians, he said, have to be "seasoned", have to learn to "rub elbows, do favours, wait their turn." It is deeply unfashionable, embarrassingly naïve, in New York, even on the left, to argue for a politics of principle. "The public business," wrote Sleeper, "trades on personal weakness and commercial interest, not principle."

Given such a rooted acceptance of urban pragmatism, it is no wonder that Mayor Koch howled angrily and uncomprehendingly at heckling crowds – "Why are you out to get me?" – long after most of his corrupt colleagues were in jail.

New York's deepest corruption, after all – the real-estate racket – is not seen as wrong. With hardly a peep of protest (by and large, New Yorkers support his approach to development), Koch has presided over the most massive and unscrupulous theft from the public since the days of Boss Tweed. Even the "government consumed at the highest levels with graft," in the words of Newfield and Barrett, pales in comparison with the depredations of the real-estate industry.

Real estate is the biggest game and the worst criminal scene in New York. Real estate is the oil, the gold, the uranium – the infinitely exploitable natural resource – of the city, and the city pols and gangsters who sucked millions out of the public treasury look like sardines compared to the looming bulk of the city's killer whales, the development moguls.

Typically, New York real-estate developers of the killer ilk start with small felonies. Take Samuel Weinberg, whom the *New York Observer*'s Tom Robbins called "a one-man crime wave in two boroughs." When Weinberg pleaded guilty to racketeering (specifically, to mail fraud to further an arson-for-profit scheme) in 1987, the federal prosecutors had a long list of past crimes in his file. As a landlord eager to evict

■

tenants, Weinberg "solicited henchmen to assault and rape tenants" and "engaged in anti-Semitic and racist intimidation" (many of his tenants were elderly Holocaust survivors; he ripped down their Channukah decorations and erected a large metal cross); he allegedly exposed his genitals to an elderly woman, and finally pleaded guilty to burning down one of his own buildings, causing third-degree burns to one man and injuries to several firemen.

All this came to an end in 1984 when the Brooklyn Democratic machine made him . . . a judge. Even after he was indicted in 1986, he continued to serve on the bench, according to Robbins.

Criminality is by no means unusual in this field. During my stay in New York, developers would be lionized in the glossies, written up as patrons of the arts, fawned over and admired, and indicted the next week. Gerald Guterman built fancy co-ops in Manhattan and amassed a huge private art collection, which he housed in a fifty-room $14 million mansion in the suburbs, until he was sued by a business partner over a missing $17 million.

Harry Macklowe has a renowned art collection, too. Art is crucial to developers; an elegant and famously expensive collection can perfume the most fetid ill-gotten gains. Huge wealth is pointless in itself; it has to be flaunted, publicly envied; it has to buy you the grovelling subservience of journalists, television stars, and politicians before its true savour can be appreciated. The quickest way to achieve the desired social lustre is to buy paintings and antiques; once the instant reputation as a cultivated billionaire is in place, it is not difficult to consolidate your social position by huge donations to, and board memberships at, the most august museums. Such Olympian social connections can tap new sources of wealth and a pleasant sense of invulnerability to prosecution or ostracism.

Harry Macklowe survived early accusations of fraud and various other controversies before his master-stroke. In 1985, just two days before a new law went into effect banning the destruction of single-room occupancy hotels, Macklowe rushed to knock down four buildings, two of them SROs, on 44th Street, in mid-town. He neglected to get permits. The wrecker's ball swung with such haste, under cover of dusk, that the gas had not been turned off and the sidewalk was unprotected. The city was outraged.

A tide of homeless humans had washed through the streets of Manhattan. When Mayor Koch took office in 1977, the word "homeless" barely existed; the two thousand unsheltered adults in the city were known as "winos," or, in the case of the women, most of whom were emotionally unstable, "bag ladies." The two thousand have multiplied to about eighty thousand today, many of them working-class and welfare families for whom affordable housing simply does not exist. Many blame the mayor's "zoning-for-cash" policies.

The Macklowe case is a perfect illustration. The SROs were never elegant, but they provided a roof, stability, and often a modicum of decency. Under Koch, the city government tackled its fiscal problems by turning itself into a clearing-house for the developers. Anyone who could put together the money to build a luxury building could also buy special zoning concessions from the city to ensure massive profitability. The SROs, as well as older rental buildings of every kind, were smashed down, and gleaming co-ops and condominiums rose in their places. As the crisis of the new homelessness became unendurable, the city finally moved to prevent any further demolition of the remaining SRO stock. This is the law that Macklowe was attempting to evade. But in Koch's New York, you only have to honour the law if you have no cash flow. Macklowe received no punishment for his depredations; he simply paid the city a $2.5 million buy-out fee and went right on building his glossy Hotel Macklowe. (And Mayor Koch returned Macklowe's $10,000 campaign contribution.)

In another case, fifty tenants of an East End Avenue building sued Macklowe for physical and mental injuries they suffered in a gas explosion; they had to go to court again to force him to restore hot water and utilities weeks after the

■

explosion. "He didn't buy that building because he wanted a six-story tenement," Macklowe's lawyer explained to the *New York Observer*. Eventually, Macklowe got the tenants out, paying some and evicting others.

Every year, twenty-seven thousand tenants are evicted, mostly illegally. The wealthy are not disturbed by the way the unwealthy are inexorably being pushed out of the city: "Nobody has a *right* to live in Manhattan," a distinguished man, a former speechwriter for Jack Kennedy, told me at a dinner party in his elegant Central Park West co-op.

Nor are many of them fretted by the way the Koch administration has decided that the city – its history, culture, architectural legacy, streets, and sunlight – all are for sale to the highest bidder.

At that same Central Park West dinner party, I listened deferentially (though with some sense of irony) as the power-ful investment banker Felix Rohatyn, who controls the city's supra-governmental budget agency, expounded on the dangers to America of foreign investment. He proposed, as I recall, some form of foreign investment review agency to preserve American independence. The talk moved on to city corruption. I remarked how stunned I was to learn that Mayor Koch, in the virtually uncontested 1985 election, had collected $7 million in donations, mostly from developers. Rohatyn turned his thickly spectacled gaze on me in surprise. "But those were campaign contributions," he explained impatiently. "Exactly! That's corruption!" I exclaimed. He looked at me as though an exceptionally stupid beetle had crawled across the tablecloth and blundered into his line of vision. He did not deign to reply.

It seems self-evident to New Yorkers that rights accrue to money. If the developers have money, it would be sacrilege to thwart their plans, especially as the city has virtually no plans of its own. Under Koch's rule (the City Council is little more than a rubber stamp), developers have been not only allowed to buy their way out of the most flagrant zoning violations, they have been encouraged with breath-taking tax abatements. The more greedily the developers snatch these goodies from the public purse, the more they are admired for their skill and daring.

Unfortunately for the city, the time of Koch coincided with the time of Reagan, who brought in a depreciation allowance for developers that made already wealthy men into billionaires. (You don't need much "art" to make a fortune when government designs laws to let you get away with fiscal murder.) In the booming 1980s, no major developer in Manhattan paid a cent in federal tax. Beginner tycoons like Mortimer B. Zuckerman benefited, too: his net worth soared to $250 million during the Koch-Reagan heyday. While Washington stringently cut back infant-nourishment programs for ghetto babies, allowed corrupt officials to loot the Housing and Urban Development department with reckless abandon, and raised the tax share paid by the poorest workers in America, billionaires like Helmsley and Trump multiplied their treasuries while contributing not a cent.

Donald Trump, whose childish egotism is outmatched possibly only by Koch's, boasts of his prowess in his self-hyping *Trump: The Art of the Deal*; more aptly, it should have been titled *The Art of the Steal*.

The son of an affluent developer from Queens, Trump wanted to make his mark (alas) on Manhattan. His first big deal, the one that launched him as a major force in the city, was a run-down hotel on 42nd Street. Trump managed to buy the hotel without investing a cent of his own money; with the help of the thoroughly corrupt Stanley Friedman, he also managed to obtain a forty-two-year $160 million tax abatement, the largest in the city's history, according to journalists Newfield and Barrett. Well-launched at taxpayers' expense, Trump immediately became a client of Friedman and Roy Cohn, and a large-scale contributor to some of their dirtier manipulations of city politics.

Over a ten-year period, the city's developers enriched themselves by $1.3 billion through the city's golden-handed tax breaks. Similar mutual enrichment schemes between politicians and construction and land moguls have recently come to light in some Canadian cities; the difference is that in New York they are not considered a scandal.

Not only is it seen as unremarkable for the city to fund the developers and for Koch to act as their errand boy, but uncontrolled development is considered by the majority of voters to be a sensible way of encouraging New York's economy. Of course, most of their opinions are based on the constantly reiterated development-is-good theme advanced by the media. Publishing, electronic media, and real-estate empires are intertwined.

But the vast majority of New York's population has not benefited from the boom in luxury condominiums and office towers. Small-scale industry (light manufacturing, printing, the garment trade, theatre and the arts, and thousands of small stores) are driven out, to be replaced by giant corporations and their white-collar employees; not only do thousands of valuable blue-collar jobs disappear in this unnoticed erosion, but the hopes of the working class for betterment vanish, too. What happens to the city's fabled vitality, its fertile thronging together of aspiring and diverse peoples, its populist and dissident energy, when only the wealthy can live in its shining towers?

Worst of all, of course, is the deepening of the chasm between the incalculably rich and the destitute homeless. Though Mayor Koch advised people who complained on behalf of the homeless to "see your priest if you feel guilty," most New Yorkers I met and observed cared passionately. Many worked regularly at soup kitchens or shelters, suppressing as unworthy their fears of tuberculosis or worse. Almost everyone in my circle of friends kept tabs on the homeless in their neighbourhood, carrying pockets of change, bringing blankets or food, joining organizations to lobby for low-cost and public housing. Shortly after I came to New York, shocked at the spectre of those who lived on the streets all around me, I set out to learn more about the crisis of homelessness caused, in large part, by Koch's pandering to developers at all costs.

Over the doors of Grand Central Station are carved three Greek gods, representing the Glory of Commerce, Moral Energy, and Mental Energy. Eighty years ago, New York City proudly claimed those virtues as its own. Today, Commerce is still in its glory. Moral and Mental Energy, however, are dying or dead. This city's forty thousand homeless bear witness to that.

Few Canadians would believe the horrific sights that are shrugged off here as routine. One evening last week, I carelessly clattered down the stairs of Grand Central Station to a lower concourse and abruptly stepped into a scene from Dante's *Inferno*. In a vast, dim hall, mine were the only echoing footsteps. All around the floor, mis-shapen figures crouched silently by the walls. Nothing moved but a few heads, lifted to stare at my intrusion.

About three hundred people live in this station all winter. Many of them are too immobilized to make it outside to the food lines and shelters. "Severely swollen legs are the results of being on your feet all the time and sleeping while sitting up," a young worker from the Coalition for the Homeless told me. "Eventually, the condition can be fatal." Every night at ten o'clock, coalition volunteers hand out sandwiches, apples, and cartons of milk to those who cannot walk as far as the doors.

Outside, on a dark side street named after Cornelius Vanderbilt, two hundred of the mobile patiently line up for the coalition's food packets. By their feet shall ye know them: this group wears sneakers and even work boots, not the bundled rags on the feet of the severely deteriorated. These are mostly young men, many of them black and Hispanic, recently jobless and still wearing their decent work clothes.

They step up silently, one by one, to take the food. Many avert their faces. They look ashamed, angry, and frightened. When the food runs out before half the line is fed, only one man shouts despairingly. The rest seem numb. Standing in the dark beside the empty food van, I want to howl.

The homeless are everywhere in this city. About eight thousand will bed down this winter in city shelters in armouries, abandoned prisons and warehouses. A thousand men sleep in one vast drill hall, patrolled all night by security guards. Thousands more sleep in stations and doorways, in cardboard boxes and on newspaper nests over sidewalk steam vents. Women with young children sleep in the hallways of welfare offices or on the Formica counters. Dozens live in the emergency rooms of psychiatric hospitals, sleeping upright in the plastic chairs.

New York City officials, it seems, have neither the moral nor the mental energy to confront the policies that have created this nightmare. In "rescuing" the city from bankruptcy by allowing unrestrained development, Mayor Ed Koch encouraged builders to tear down thousands of low-rent units to raise shining towers of expensive condominiums. The evicted – including many pensioners and families – cannot find other places to live. Another hundred thousand are living doubled up, camping out in the already cramped living rooms of relatives and teetering on the edge of homelessness.

"People who have worked all their lives just can't believe it's happening to them," said Deborah Mashibini of the Coalition for the Homeless. "They tell me on the phone, 'But you don't understand . . . I'm not like that.' And then they're on the street."

The lack of housing is not the only cause; would that it were. Seventy per cent of ghetto youths drop out of school and straight into joblessness. Reaganomics has hit hard; welfare is so tight that most recipients must choose, as I was repeatedly told by street workers, between a roof and food. Cut-backs in psychiatric services have been severe: six thousand discharged mental patients live on New York streets, and it is now virtually impossible to get even a psychotic admitted involuntarily.

The city administration does not want to "encourage" the homeless to seek public housing, for which there is a three- to nine-year waiting period, so it deliberately provides minimal and sometimes catastrophically bad shelter. The city often funnels the money through private, profit-making hands. Homeless single mothers, for example, are put up in Times Square hotels, where the city pays landlords up to $3,000 a month for two rooms with no kitchen – and where mothers must pay forty cents extra for the hot water to warm a baby's bottle.

Ten thousand children are living in welfare hotels where prostitution, drug deals, rats, theft, filth, and violence are normal. Toddlers have been raped and infants have died violently in these pest holes. Last year, the Holland Hotel alone (with a thousand health and building code violations listed against it) made more than $3 million profit.

For those who prefer the streets to dubious shelter, the downward spiral is swift. University graduates are pawing through garbage here. "How can you get a job if you live on the streets? You need clean clothes, car fare, the strength to get to interviews. And what if an employer says, 'We'll phone you'?" Ms Mashibini said.

I went out with Susan and Mike from Midtown Outreach, which sends social workers onto the streets to help the chronically mentally ill. In the Port Authority Bus Terminal, Susan and Mike check on their psychotic regulars, who are slumped on floors and benches, and coax them to seek treatment. Then they spot someone new hiding behind a pillar to rifle a garbage basket. Bobby: stringy blonde hair, bizarre clothes, eyes wild like a scared horse.

"I did twenty years in a hospital outside Philly," he tells them jerkily. He's been a month in the bus terminal. He thinks the police are stealing his veterans' cheques. Mysterious voices torment him. "It's nearly Christmas. But Bobby's all right. Bobby gets Christmas presents," he yells defiantly. Gently, they tell him the address of the nearest shelter. "I'm not walking anywhere more than two blocks," Bobby shouts. "I got holes in my shoes."

"Ninety per cent of the people on the streets are mentally ill," Susan told me. (Others put the figure at forty per cent.) "The more capable get into shelters. But these folks can't help themselves."

And the city, state, and federal governments *won't* help them. Thank heaven for the sturdier social conscience of Canada. It's unthinkable – isn't it? – that our citizens, newspapers, and elected members would ever let homelessness escalate to this sickening extreme.

Mayor Koch grew more and more irascible as public pressure about homelessness increased. The federal government, he correctly pointed out, had slashed public housing funds, and restricted its cash payments to cities for housing the homeless to short-term accommodation only, hence the insane expenditure on welfare hotels. The country's senile president, apparently unaware of his own policies, mused aloud when told of the welfare hotels, "I wonder why these cities don't build permanent housing?"

When the federal government cut even those payments in 1988, Koch finally initiated a plan for renovating some of the hundred thousand city-owned abandoned apartments. By the late spring of 1989, only 4,152 families (with nearly 8,000 children) were still left in the hotels and shelters, and some of the more rancid had been closed down. But the city-owned apartments, many of them in undesirable areas of the outer boroughs, bore the stamp of municipal inefficiencies caused by corruption: sloppy workmanship, no hot water, lack of heat, doors without locks. An estimated seventy to ninety thousand New Yorkers remained homeless.

All over the city, church and volunteer groups, and even private developers with social consciences, were homesteading, rebuilding, or constructing affordable housing, projects that the city could easily copy on a larger, more meaningful scale if it had the will.

Instead, Koch continued to rail against his detractors. When the Coalition for the Homeless successfully sued the city to provide shelter, a new theme developed: "It's a plot," the mayor began to say. "They want to bring the whole system down." In a way, he was right. The "whole system," as elaborated in the Koch regime, is a cabal between developers, financiers, and politicians to plunder the city like a strip mine, extracting maximum profits for the haves and pushing out the have-nots. So complete is their control of government and media that practically no one talks about planning; almost no one dares to suggest that the city's people have a right to enjoy the environment in which they live and work and to have some say in the design of public places.

Catching Trump's priapic impulses like a disease, the city ignored the public good and pushed developers towards gigantism. When the prime site of Columbus Circle was to be redeveloped, for example, practically the only requirement the city demanded of private bidders was that they erect the tallest building possible in order to pay top price to the city. Only because the proposed tower would have cast a monstrous shadow across Central Park, in the midst of Manhattan's most élite residences, was the first plan rejected. Celebrities like Bill Moyers and Jackie Onassis joined with the respected Municipal Art Society to force the city to back down.

For the most part, the depredations go on unchecked. Despite the more lurid aspects of the mid-eighties civic scandal, this is the real corruption built right into the structure of New York City: there is no government in any real sense of the word, merely a sprawling and politically bankrupt machine for enhancing the wealth of the real-estate industry and consolidating the petty power of egomaniacs like Koch.

The visible marks of this degeneration of a once-great city are everywhere. Brute hulks thrust their way up to the sky, blocking light, wrecking the coherence of the street below, and dwarfing the human-scale buildings crouching at their feet. The poverty amidst great wealth increases exponentially. Bloomingdale's shoppers wade through a Third World miasma of uncollected garbage, pot-holed streets, and whining beggars.

■

Hard-liners and power brokers express contempt for such concerns: ceaseless change, they say, has always been the spirit of the city. By change, they mean the tearing down of buildings. Whether political change can come in time to save what's left is less clear.

CHAPTER 7

.

Children of New York

One of the most moving and powerful elements of Jane Jacobs's analysis of city life (in *The Death and Life of Great Cities*) was her fluent, natural, unself-conscious observation of the way children live and play in the city. Her lucid description of their lives, and the lives of those adults who care for them and relate to them, in street, park, and neighbourhood, lent an extraordinary and practical rigour to her analysis of how cities work. It was revolutionary, and it partly explains why that book, first published in 1961, reads with such freshness and timeliness today.

Urban essayists and travel writers rarely pay attention to the lives of children, perhaps for sheer lack of access. For me, however, involved from the first day with schools – all three of our children went to school in Manhattan – it was a completely natural focus of attention, and, as it turned out, revelatory.

New York children live in worlds unimagined by the outsider. New York children do not go trick or treating on Hallowe'en (except in occasional apartment buildings where adults have organized it as a special event); they do not racket around town on their bikes, play street hockey, or offer any freckle-faced clichés of innocence to lazy adults who haven't bothered to rethink their image of childhood in thirty years.

New York kids, from penthouse to welfare hotel, from shtetl to ghetto, are little shock troops of contemporary urban life, taking for granted the extremes of the city into which they are born and dramatizing those extremes with their unquestioning adaptation.

On a Sunday afternoon in Williamsburg, Brooklyn, in the community of Hassidic Jews just one subway stop from Manhattan across the Williamsburg Bridge, I might have been in a pre-war European shtetl – except for the obvious solid comfort of this ultra-orthodox enclave. Young women in elaborate wigs, or with their hair wrapped in kerchiefs, strolled up and down the wide, sunny, low-rise shopping streets, each one wheeling a pram and trailing a clutch of little girls. An early 1950s shopping street, geared to family life: homey little shops, lots of children's shoes, baby equipment, cooking pots, fancy household ornaments, mechanical rides – rocking horses, Bambi – outside the stores to amuse the children. The little girls swarming in their mothers' wake had shining long hair in tight pigtails, long navy coats of good wool cloth, dark stockings, and sensible shoes. School-girls strolled together, arm in arm, giggling and whispering in Yiddish. The shop signs are in Yiddish; books and news-papers are in Yiddish. Despite the spectacular fecundity of the women, no little boys were in evidence anywhere; the streets simply seethed with old-fashioned femininity. When I asked shopkeepers about this, they shrugged evasively. To ask the little girls would be unthinkable – the presence of my two friends and me strolling the streets was obviously causing a storm of curiosity and nervousness. Even the boldest of the girls were evidently afraid to look at us.

Finally, a real renegade, age about eleven. She bolts past, protected by a clutch of girl-friends, snorting with sup-pressed hilarity as she shouts mockingly in heavily accented English: "Oooh, handsome man!" at the one male in our trio.

We catch up to her. Blushing and excited, she asks: "What are you, tourists?" This is such a safe, closed, isolated world that she can't imagine why else we might be there. When we ask about the boys, we learn that all – even the four-year-olds – are in school. Girls, lesser creatures, need not attend school on Sundays.

Just across the river, New York's upper-class children are no doubt arriving back from a country house or departing for their week at prep school; their lives, glimpsed mostly in the pages of magazines, are a highly conscious, conformist grooming for future privilege.

The middle class, however – the ones I knew best – are, in a way, the luckiest. There are incredible pressures, to be sure. In a city where fame and fortune are glitteringly immediate possibilities and remarkable tenacity is needed just to hold one's own, high-achieving parents are beset by anxiety for their children to do well. Top schools are seen as the key to ultimate triumph, so there is ferocious competition for spaces. Naturally, since privileged placement and success at each level supposedly lead to admission to top schools at the next level, parents with their eye on Harvard begin to worry about the school ladder when their offspring are still in diapers. The pressure on admissions to favoured pre-schools is now so intense that magazines feature interviews with pre-primary "play coaches" who advise on the best toys, games, and exercises to prepare a three-year-old for admission interviews. "Ask your housekeeper to play some good video-tapes," advised one such guru in *New York* magazine, suggesting that parents buy all the Winnie the Pooh video-tapes because they teach "vocabulary and manners."

Virtually all middle-class children in New York, black and white (and even many of the lower middle class), attend private school; one might expect them, under such competitive stress, to be in a state of neurotic collapse by high school. Undoubtedly there are casualties, but the teenagers I knew had an easy poise and self-esteem that defies such predictions. Their small schools afford an intimacy, a degree of personal attention and a sense of identity that, combined with native street smarts, make New York children breath-takingly confident and outgoing. High-school youngsters inhabit what is virtually a mobile small town; in a city of eight million, it's extraordinary how many other private-school faces a Manhattan teenager will know and meet at local teen hang-outs. Since they don't have cars or shopping malls, uptown teenagers congregate at the Sheep Meadow in Central Park, where each school group lounges together, or at Tekk's pool hall, or in a favourite vegetarian restaurant in Greenwich Village, or over spectacular ice-cream desserts in an Upper East Side café called Serendipity.

By the time they're in their mid-teens, they're living New York's night life, sashaying out at eleven o'clock, queuing up outside the clubs, dancing with friends (each private school dominates a favoured night-club), drinking, and coming home in cabs.

This sounds more dissolute than it usually is; the clubs are merely the big-city equivalent of the shopping mall, a place where (if you dress right or have one of the many passes distributed around the city) you can get in free and spend as many hours as you like in the company of your peers. New York teenagers relish the new. At the centre of consumerism, they are preternaturally alert to the newest slang, fashion, music, dances, and innumerable quirks of personal style that continually define and redefine status and identity. They know perfectly well that their freshest fads will be picked up and imitated six months or a year later in suburbs and towns across the continent.

Despite the high cost of teenage amusements, the danger of muggings, and the exhausting demands of ambitious schooling, most of the New York teenagers I met would scorn to live anywhere else. They treat Manhattan like an endlessly fascinating small town where the comfort of familiarity is exempt from its usual corollaries of boredom and restriction.

Our youngest daughter, Jenny, spent her high-school years at the United Nations International School on the East River, whose student body is made up mainly of the children of international civil servants, plus (about 40 per cent) local middle-class youngsters. Upper-crust youth from élite schools like Dalton and Brearley tend to associate with each other exclusively; United Nations students, on the other hand, had loose bonds with similarly middle-class teenagers at less exclusive private schools and at Stuyvesant and Bronx High School of Science, two public schools for the gifted. Most of them went to night-clubs to hang out with their school friends; they also worked on weekends at the Metropolitan Museum of Art; one starred in a soap opera; another cut records with his band. We bumped into one of Jenny's class-mates lugging her cello along West 57th Street. "Going to play Carnegie Hall?" we joked. "How did you know?" she asked, wide-eyed. Another schoolmate conducted his own

■

symphonic composition at Carnegie Hall after winning a national competition.

New York offers unparallelled opportunities for a culturally alert or energetic youngster. Jenny arrived in New York at age fourteen with a passion for theatre. That summer, she was already working as a backstage gofer at an off-Broadway hit. One job led to another: she supervised the wardrobe for a low-budget comedy (the job included bringing the costumes home every night, washing, mending, and ironing them); made the props and operated the antique lighting board for an off-off-Broadway show-case; worked as a stage-hand on the Lower East Side (that meant building the stage); put on a black dress and frilly white apron to work as an extra in the New York production of *Tamara* and serve food in faked Italian (*"Biscotti, signora?"*) at intermission.

Life for most middle-class teens in New York is expensive, but interesting, exciting, and fun. "You feel like part of a moving, competent mob," reflects Jenny, asked to remember her time of bopping around Manhattan with her pals. The mob, of course, starts out with advantages: these are the children of people lucky, clever, or successful enough to cling to apartments in Manhattan or the better parts of Brooklyn.

Just forty blocks north, life begins at the polar opposite of all this energy and ambition. In Harlem and the Bronx, teenagers do not get weekend jobs at the Met, or a chance to write symphonies. But that, too, is a complex truth. To see the poor children of New York only as future muggers is to yield to another kind of racism. Poor neighbourhoods are also filled with families struggling to win for their children even a hundredth of the opportunity that showers upon the lucky children of the middle class.

When angry citizens demand that the authorities "do something" about poor public-school achievement, or youth gangs, or crack, they forget the ecology of ghetto life. The disadvantages – which will later show up in school failure, truancy, and crime – begin before birth, with infants who are malnourished in the womb, and therefore born small, and therefore more vulnerable and less developed, and therefore

■

not as potentially bright. In ghetto apartments, teenage mothers who do not know how to feed themselves properly, let alone their infants, may also not know how to feed their minds. In a world of day-to-day survival, in which just picking up the welfare cheque to buy the groceries may mean an exhausting journey across town, a six-hour wait in a welfare office, and endless hassles, creative play and stimulating conversation are not high on the priority list. By the time such a child reaches kindergarten age, the disadvantages have thickened and intertwined like a thorny hedge. And yet almost nothing is done to halt the cycle by offering supports to young mothers of infants; instead, the accepted American wisdom is to make welfare conditions harsh and punitive to "discourage welfare dependency."

It's true that New York spends more money and effort on social services than any other city in North America. But too much of it is misdirected, misspent, wasted. And the problems are multiplying like bacteria: AIDS has become a heterosexual disease primarily in the black and Hispanic communities; by the winter of 1989, it was estimated that, in New York, a hundred thousand intravenous drug users, their sex partners, and their babies were infected with AIDS. In some of the poorest minority districts, nearly half the babies born are HIV positive; at the same time, the number of damaged and low birth-weight babies being born to crack-addicted mothers is rising steeply. The infant mortality rate in poor black areas is twice that for the rest of Manhattan.

Public debate and political discussion of these issues always seem to end in argument about "solutions," or in mutually agreed-upon despair that nothing can be done for "these people."

And there's no denying that the problems are overwhelming. Visit "these people" on their home turf, however, and an entirely different human truth emerges. Meet ghetto children who are growing roses and cabbages in a cathedral garden, talk to a Head Start teacher, spend a day with a nurse-midwife, and the problems are no longer seen in their headlined isolation. They are all part of a continuum. While

■

222

frantic, last-minute "programs" created in answer to a crisis almost never help, intelligent and coherent long-term plans – drawing on the expertise of the front-line workers, not on politically catchy spur-of-the-moment ideas – could change everything. Decent housing, accessible jobs, adequate infant nutrition, small and compassionate nurseries and schools, social supports for young mothers – none of this is mysterious.

Because I was interested in the lives of children, I came to meet some of the extraordinary people who work with them, and to understand the enormous human wealth of New York: the teachers, nurses, midwives, planners, public-agency lawyers and activists, social workers and civil servants, and the volunteers, white, black, and Hispanic. Their dogged commitment, despite their depressing firsthand knowledge of the difficulties facing them and their clients, is the vital element of New York that is never mentioned in trendy novels.

One day soon after I moved to New York, I met a wealthy woman who devoted her entire time and energy to furthering the cause of midwifery and women's health. Filled with optimistic enthusiasm, she urged me to take the subway to the Bronx ("No problem!") and visit a remarkable experiment in alternative maternity care – a hospital where the poorest women in the city were receiving the most advanced and enlightened kind of services.

Not long after, I did visit the maternity ward of the North Central Bronx Hospital. Therese Dondero, the nurse-midwife who headed the maternity ward, a warmly intelligent and attractive woman, spent much of the day with me, hobbling up and down corridors on a cane. (She died of cancer only a few months later.) She told me about the horrific nutritional levels of the teenage mothers who come to give birth at North Central Bronx. There is a federal food-supplement program for poor pregnant women, but, under Ronald Reagan, it was so starved for funds that it could reach only about one third of those who qualified, Ms Dondero told me. "So . . . we have low-birth-weight babies. Their health, their vigour, their intelligence were all affected. You

■

should just see the difference in the babies whose mothers are able to get the food supplements."

I spent twelve hours watching babies with only half a chance at life coming into the world. I marvelled, not for the last time, that the slums are filled with workers like Ms Dondero who, knowing what odds they face, still commit their entire energy to the job at hand.

"More! More! *Mas! Mas!* Don't stop, don't stop. . . . Give me more, Maribel. *Caramba!* Beautiful." Michelle's voice is as hard and clear as the note on a steel drum. The Puerto Rican teenager on the bed has frightened Bambi eyes and four long, soft braids, slightly mussed after seven hours of labour. She is holding her thighs and pushing hard to get her baby born.

"*Dio*, nobody told me it was going to be like this," she gasps, lying back after the contraction.

Michelle's voice sinks to an infinitely sweet low tone. "That's how all women feel, sweetheart." Her voice, her smile, her touch on Maribel's trembling leg are as radiantly tender as morning light. Maribel beams; she can stand anything, it seems, so long as Michelle is there to interpret it for her.

Michelle is a nurse training for an advanced certificate in midwifery. Throughout this long day, she and Sonya, a senior midwife on the team, will coax, teach, soothe, exhort, and love Maribel into giving a normal, safe, unmedicated birth. At six o'clock in the evening, baby Jonathan finally slips into Sonya's capable brown hands. Maribel has not once asked for pain-killers; not once has she panicked.

This is the North Central Bronx Hospital, a city hospital for the indigent, where nearly all of the more than two thousand births a year are attended to solely by trained midwives. (Obstetricians are there, on call, but are rarely needed.) In the eight years since Therese Dondero, a nurse-midwife, was allowed to organize the obstetrics department along such radical lines – mostly because there was a severe shortage of available medical residents – her midwives have transformed the face of childbirth here.

"I felt that poor women should have the same choices in childbirth that middle-class women have," Ms Dondero told me. The choice, once offered, was seized. The maternity department at North Central Bronx is so successful that it helps to finance the rest of the hospital; it operates at 150 per cent capacity, while maternity wards at nearby traditional hospitals are half empty.

The mostly black and Hispanic welfare mothers and working poor who clamour at the doors are not seeking "a beautiful experience" in childbirth – the usual sneer of traditionalists who oppose natural childbirth. They flock to NCB because they know they can bring mother, sister, aunt, husband, or anyone they need into the labour room. They know the atmosphere is intimate and gentle. Above all, they know that childbirth is safer at NCB, and the babies are healthier.

The figures prove them right. NCB rarely uses drugs, Caesarean sections (only 7 per cent, compared with an average 30 per cent elsewhere), electronic monitoring, anaesthetics, or forceps. Though it serves the most vulnerable population in the city – a daunting 60 per cent of the mothers are high risk – NCB has 25 per cent fewer still births and newborn deaths than other city hospitals, and 7 per cent fewer of the newborns go to intensive care. Furthermore, 60 per cent of the new mothers breast-feed, compared to the one per cent in neighbouring city hospitals.

Judging by the NCB, governments in Canada should promptly legalize midwifery for practice in hospitals, clinics, and birthing centres. And they should take note that Ms Dondero, who knows whereof she speaks, and who is a nurse-midwife herself, thinks that midwives should be trained in a college of midwifery, and not as nurses.

■

"The philosophy is so different . . . midwives are trained to think and act independently," Ms Dondero explained. Her midwives are an impressive example: despite their air of relaxed warmth, they are uncannily swift in a crisis, and they radiate a heartening confidence. Unlike doctors, they are at the bedside throughout the labour – comforting, joking, massaging the back, teaching, responding to the whispered fears or questions of the labouring women.

"I'm scared the baby can't come out. . . . Such a small opening!" Maribel said shyly. "Will it just come right out into the air?" Her mother, her sister, and two midwives were at her bedside to explain and to reassure her.

Though they are often young, unmarried, and appallingly ignorant, NCB patients are able to go through labour calmly. They are not pestered and alarmed by the silly, outmoded procedures of enemas and shaving. They are free to walk around, shower, sip fruit juices. They give birth in the small, gently lit rooms where they have spent their labour. No stirrups, glaring lights, masked doctors, frightening machinery. No frills, either – no chintz curtains or recorded music. This is a poverty operation, but solidly good. The chief obstetrician, Dr. George Kleiner, had a conventional medical approach when he arrived here. "I came, I saw, I was conquered," he jokes now.

Midwifery is a female business. The one doctor who came by during the day I spent there peeked around a curtain, saw that the midwives were too busy to talk to him, and vanished. His brief male presence was disconcerting: most of the women there seem to prefer female support in the labour room. There is a womanly sense of shared experience and bedrock know-how that feels right.

Down the hall from Maribel, a weary twenty-four-year-old with deeply shadowed eyes quietly gave birth to her third child. Whispered hints from the ward aides let me know that this woman's life mirrored all the pain and harshness the Bronx can inflict on its poor. A midwife held the newborn. "Hello, sweet potato," she said tenderly and a little sadly, and handed him to his mother. Money cannot buy, and machines cannot provide, the shared triumph over pain, the knowledge, the delight despite everything, that was in the look they exchanged, mother and midwife.

In a maternity ward, especially one like the NCB, where black, brown, and white women were deeply engaged together in the most elemental of tasks, you sink into a state of mind that is indescribable – unthinkable – in the language of newspapers, television, or pop music. There are simply no uncorrupted words left to use for this passionate commitment to human life and breath. The male vocabulary of power, will, aggression, manipulation, and self-aggrandizement – the language of the news, the streets, the courts, of business and politics – has relegated the experiences of the maternity ward to the margins. Any words one can use to express them are instantly felt as sentimental and therefore dismissable.

But in the small and unadorned rooms where women are giving birth in the middle of one of the most hopelessly poor and violent districts in New York, there is no sentimentality. Everyone, including the mothers, feels the bitter irony of birthing in such a world. But women are the agents here, the centres of will and action; the urgent work is irrevocably their own. Language and feeling are defined by them. There is no shame, no pornographic overtone, no sexual objectification in the heedless animal work of childbirth (the panting, the exposure of nakedness) as there would be anywhere else. Boundaries between the helped and the helpers blur. Skin colour fades into insignificance beside the primacy of femaleness.

This is a real world, too. But its courage, its intimacy, its stripped-to-basics humanity, have no currency in the outside world. Inside the North Central Bronx maternity ward, you can imagine a sane and practical world that would be mobilized to encourage these new babies and their mothers, and to give them basic supports for life. You could imagine using the intimate wisdom gained here to help stop the cycle of poverty-illegitimacy-poverty. But outside, such human simplicities are clearly seen for what they are: impossible.

One recent morning, in the high, handsome committee room of New York's graceful old City Hall, I developed a case of political nausea. Danger: preening politicians at work.

The issue was birth control for teenagers. Every year in New York, fifteen thousand girls younger than seventeen have babies. "Babies having babies" was, in fact, the hot headline issue through much of 1985, before AIDS and crack came into focus. In the fall of 1986, it emerged that the Board of Education had been doing something about the problem. In nine high-school health clinics, mostly in black areas, they'd been giving out condoms and pill prescriptions to sexually active teenagers.

As soon as the program became public knowledge – and despite all the previous moaning and groaning about teenage pregnancy – politicians and church leaders started to howl. Now the contraceptive program has been suspended for six months (how many babies will that add up to?) while the issue is debated.

It's not that all the politicians I heard that day at City Hall were frothing reactionaries. It was the hypocritical quality of the debate that I found sickening. Nor is it a case of black against white: the black council members at this hearing of city council's education committee were as smugly self-inflated as the white. No, it was a case of the puffed-up versus the powerless.

The powerless were Trish, Tracy, Felicia, and Amanda, four teenage black girls (all of them mothers) sitting at the witness table.

"See, I did know about contraceptives," said Tracy, who had her baby at fifteen. "But you couldn't get it without your mother, and I was scared to tell her." Should schools give out contraceptives? Tracy crossed her ankles, laced her fingers together tightly, and sat up straight. "They should, really, I do, I really do think they should."

"We only kids," said Trish, tapping her running shoes nervously beneath her chair. "If they don't help us at school. . . . well, I don't feel too comfortable saying, 'Mommy, I'm having sex.'"

The young mothers took about seven minutes to make their plea. They were listened to with nervous courtesy, the way you might greet your neighbour's pet panther. No questions. Thank you and goodbye.

Then the adult witnesses: the more prominent they were (a rabbi, a medical researcher) the longer and more irrelevantly they talked, and the more unctuously they were courted, flattered, and complimented by the council members – a collection of tub thumpers, pulpit pounders, time-servers, and self-servers to whom only Mark Twain could do proper savage justice.

Time was dribbling away. The hands-on witnesses – the teachers, school nurses, and doctors – cooled their heels.

A Catholic priest was called. Dr. Robert Francoeur teaches biology and human sexuality at Fairleigh Dickinson University. He believes in mandatory sex education from grade three, and in school provision of contraceptives.

"Half the teenagers in this city are sexually active – they are not Romeo and Juliet," he said. "I've taught sexuality to five thousand students, and believe me, I've had white medical students who are sexually experienced who still think you can get pregnant from oral sex or belly-button tickling."

The Reverend Wendell Foster, a black council member, begins to respond. Leisurely, with ministerial flourishes, he expounds on morality, moral decay, and how we all ought to wait for the wedding night.

"This beautiful theme," he says lyrically. He reminisces about his own sexual urges as a youth, and how a little voice told him that the young lady's body was sacred.

An old Queens Democrat mumbles on about the dirty words he knew when he was a kid.

A black woman council member orates about "family values," her pomposity outstripping her vocabulary: "This whole thing frightens me. We have people in our perspective [sic] communities who do have communication with their children. Sex education is not going to reach the conglamerate [sic] of kids who are sexually active. Sex ed. is just taking it away from the parents. Now I warned against this when you took breakfast away from the parents."

Finally, the people who work with the teenage girls get a chance to speak, most notably a gentle-voiced black woman doctor and two black nurses from Boys and Girls High School in Bedford Stuyvesant, where a hundred girls got pregnant last year.

They are too polite, perhaps, to say how destroyed some ghetto parents can be, how unable to offer sex education at home, or how some thirteen-year-old girls can't get parental permission for contraceptives because it's their stepfather who is molesting them. They do point out that only five parents in a school of 3,500 students came to parents' night.

The council members yawn, leave the room, chat among themselves, and chivvy the women to hurry up with their testimony: "We haven't got all morning," they say crossly, having used most of the morning to hear their own voices.

The victims here are the youngsters and their babies. Teenage mothers are poor, and staggeringly unaware of what their future holds. (They will live on welfare; 68 per cent of their babies will grow up in dire poverty; they will never escape.) All recent studies show that thorough sex education helps the girls to understand their right to say no. Withholding contraceptives leads to an annual 57 per

■

cent increase in pregnancies. Obviously, it doesn't impede intercourse.

Adults may vote, but fifteen-year-old mothers don't. So the black politicians on the education committee ignored the plight of the girls and concentrated on polishing their own electoral images.

"Now, my ethnic concern is the survival of the family," said the malapropistic Mary Pinkett, peppering the school nurses with hostile questions, then strolling outside when they tried to answer.

The teenagers were no longer there to hear their representatives. They were back in the ghetto with their babies.

Eventually, the health clinics were restored (though they were no longer allowed to distribute condoms). But the debate about their family-planning role had given me a glimpse into the repugnantly self-serving and negligent political structure that is so indifferent to the fate of the city's children. No governmental initiative in the ghetto, it seems, is ever undertaken with the simple clarity of those who actually work there. It is always short-term, political, expedient, and doomed to failure. There is a gulf of experience, language, and motive between those who sit in council chambers and seek to advance themselves, and those who labour in maternity wards, health clinics, and schools, where they are trying to keep mothers and children alive, sheltered, and purposeful.

Those children who survive end up in the public schools of New York, and it was in these green-painted hallways and battered classrooms that I experienced some of the most heart-breaking and also some of the most inspiringly hopeful moments of my three years in New York.

By mid-1987, I had visited enough New York schools to realize that the once-proud public system, incubator for so much immigrant genius, had hit rock-bottom. For me, the question was: what led to this appalling chaos and failure?

And could Canadian schools ever face the same disasters? It seems preposterous; but in fact, the larger Canadian cities – especially Toronto – perilously duplicate the conditions that led to New York's spectacular schooling collapse.

As rents and land values skyrocketed, manufacturing (and its reliable supply of blue-collar jobs) simply evaporated from New York, in the steepest industrial decline experienced by any American city. With financial and information services booming, New York hardly bothered to notice. But soon, company headquarters, too, with all their entry-level office jobs, decided to flee New York's high costs. By now, only two kinds of jobs are generally available: white-collar work in the rapidly expanding financial industry, which demands high levels of skill and training, and minimum-wage service jobs, which can't support a family and which are widely and correctly perceived as a dead end.

For children growing up in poverty, a high-school diploma that won't get you anywhere but McDonald's is a cynical joke. Without hope of rewarding work, students do not bother to attend school. And without a literate local work force to fill entry-level jobs, more and more corporations are tempted to move away. (In 1987, New York Telephone, looking for workers who could speak English and file names alphabetically, tested sixty thousand applicants – and found three thousand qualified.)

Toronto has ominous similarities to New York in all these destructive ways: extortionist rents and land values, a concentration of money-industry jobs, a drastic ebb of manufacturing, a growing poverty-stricken population disaffected from the schools, a cost of living high enough to discourage the in-migration of new, energetic teachers, and an ethos of ambitious greed that is tempting the middle class to desert the public system in favour of the "excellence" they perceive in élitist private schools.

Once the middle class has left, with its money and its clout, politicians have no further interest in the public-school system; it can be left to decay. Children, after all, are only voters in escrow; poverty children, as that hearing at New

York City Hall showed so clearly, don't count even that much.

In 1987, as New York briefly turned its alarmed attention to the ruined school system because of a public search for a new schools chancellor, I seized the opportunity to try to describe for Canadian readers the plight of Manhattan schools.

... The clincher for most New Yorkers has been, ironically, not the despair of schoolchildren, but the flight of corporations from New York, many of them citing the hopelessness of hiring competent entry-level staff. The media have been lashing out day after day at the system's failures. Anywhere from 30 to 50 per cent of high-school students drop out; a third of the graduates are functionally illiterate; truancy is endemic; six thousand homeless children in squalid welfare hotels do not attend school at all. More than half of all teenage mothers quit school – and one-third of black teenage girls get pregnant.

The school buildings (half of them more than fifty years old) are dismally run down. As schools struggle to feed and clothe their pupils, more than a third of whom are from welfare families, many can't even supply pencils and paper. Dirty, ramshackle, and vast, most schools are hatefully bleak environments.

Newspapers speak openly of organized crime involvement in school lunch programs, bus companies, and construction projects. The school custodians, who have a disgraceful sweetheart contract with the Board of Education, act as school landlords, demanding extortionate fees for use of the school building by community groups (thus discouraging parent participation), and refusing to fix broken toilets and windows beyond an arbitrary quota. The custodians are not accountable to anyone in the school system. Rumours of corruption are rife; their president was mysteriously murdered this year. Last time the board tried to challenge the janitors' hege-

■

mony, they went on strike, poured hot lead in the school locks, and dismantled boilers. Concerned citizens who try to oppose the custodians at school board meetings have been beaten up in the board's parking lot. No one, not even at the highest level of authority, dared be quoted in this column on the subject of custodians.

How did things get so bad?

The rot began in the mid-seventies, when New York was nearly bankrupt and school budgets were hacked to smithereens. Fifteen thousand teachers were laid off. Those who were left were completely demoralized. The middle class (mostly white, but most middle-class blacks, too) fled to private schools, leaving a school population that is 80 per cent minority, mostly poor and disorganized. With no strong, vocal constituency to support the schools, the politicians and bureaucrats were left to do their self-serving worst. Money is no longer the chief problem: a rudderless bureaucracy and criminally indifferent governments must take the blame.

With a million students in a thousand crumbling buildings, there are still few librarians or libraries in elementary schools, few school nurses, and only one guidance counsellor for every thousand students. Under then governor Nelson Rockefeller, hasty and expedient "reforms" in the late 1960s handed over control of the primary schools to thirty-two elected community school boards. All observers now admit that many community boards are riddled with corruption, patronage, and ignorance. Special interest groups, including school officials and local politicos, sit on the boards and wield undue influence. Only a grotesquely low 5 per cent of the electorate bothers to vote in school board elections. It's a perfect example of how a grass roots idea inspired by democratic, egalitarian, and humane impulses can be completely subverted by an entrenched political structure inimical to any but its own interests.

The New York Board of Education, which is directly responsible for the high schools and for special education, is accountable to no one: the seven members are political appointees of the borough presidents and of uninterested, blustering Mayor Ed Koch. Nobody has a good word to say for this powerful board. Even some of its members (who earn $36,000 a year for their part-time job, and who have personal assistants and secretaries) think the board should be disbanded or radically altered.

A massive and universally hated bureaucracy exerts a paralysing hold over the system. After Rockefeller's "decentralization," the bureaucracy actually multiplied, expanding from one full office building to six. The headquarters is unofficially known as the Leaning Tower of Jell-O . . .

In the winter of 1989, the thoroughly corrupt system began to unravel. A black school principal in the Bronx was arrested while buying crack in the street. In the investigation that followed, the rottenness of the Bronx community board was dragged into the light. Three board members and a former superintendent were arrested on charges of theft. The rest of the board members were suspended. So great is the control of the local political machine, and so powerless the electorate, that the suspended members were re-elected only a few months later.

Crookedness, not lack of public funding, was the problem. Investigators found $13,000 worth of postage stamps stuffed in a drawer, and a warehouse full of uninventoried school supplies. While the children in this school district, one of the poorest and most hopeless in the city, had watched helplessly as their inter-school sports were eliminated for want of funds, the school board had eight full-time employees whose sole job, as part of a "media-team," was to photograph and videotape the board members as they attended official functions.

The community boards grew out of the racial ferment of the 1960s. Black communities rose up in anger at the Democratic machine and at the mostly Jewish teachers' union, which had a firm grip on the schools, and demanded control. When the white politicians caved in, they cynically neglected to build in the protections any public body must have in the corrupt environment of New York politics. As a direct result – though some community boards are more honest than others – the boards were simply gobbled up by local politicians.

In Brooklyn's Williamsburg, for example, where 70 per cent of the public-school children are Hispanic, the board is dominated by people who don't send their children to the local public schools: Hasidim, the Catholic church, the teachers' union, and other mainstays of the local Democractic party. In the past ten years, the board has hired ten white supervisors, one Hispanic, and no blacks.

Enrichment and after-school programs, sports, scholarships, health clinics – anything that might serve the interests of the children – have been treated everywhere as patronage plums and political pay-offs.

I toured one district on the Lower East Side where a vigorous superintendent had much of the basic school program thoroughly under control. (It was clearly not wise to ask how he managed to keep the schools well stocked with supplies, or how he had achieved a productive working arrangement with the custodians.) One of the district's employees drove me from school to school in his beat-up car; we ate falafel as we drove, and he treated me to a typically candid New York-style interview. "That high school," he said, as we drove past a battered concrete fortress, "had a broken furnace and absolutely no heat for two winters in a row. Plenty of rats, though." As we pulled up to a grim primary school – I'll call it School A – I spotted a flamboyantly painted Checker cab parked in the principal's spot. "Oh, yeah, the principal, that's his car," said the school official with a shrug. "He's a real dick, this guy. He's a lawyer, mostly spends his time away from school doing real-estate deals."

New to New York then, I looked astonished. The official answered my unasked question. "He's a nephew of one of the

Hasids on the community board. He doesn't bother us, we just ignore him." Sure enough, when the principal oozed out to meet us, exuding hospitality, he was unable to tell me how many pupils he had, what special programs were in effect, or what the racial composition of his student body was.

The vice principal, an energetic and bright-eyed woman who actually runs the school, deftly extricated us from his presence – just as he was pointing to a galaxy of pictures of himself on his office wall – and took me to see the school.

Peeling green paint, echoingly empty corridors, armed security guards at the door, chain-link fencing closing in the stair wells so no one can jump or be pushed over the banisters – the setting is as hostile as it is possible to imagine. But even here, there are teachers and children who can jump-start the visitor's languishing optimism.

The teachers here have been galvanized by a new "mastery" program, initiated by the local superintendent. The program strikes me as expensively packaged jargon for what we would expect in any well-run elementary school in a crisis neighbourhood: monthly "reality therapy" sessions for the teachers, projects in which different grades work together, time for teachers to talk together, structured goals for each lesson. Teachers constantly evaluate what each pupil has learned. No one fails; a teacher keeps teaching – in groups of six students – until each student has mastered the lesson.

To an observer, this plan seems to work ("Our teachers are up and out of their chairs!" enthuses my guide) because both teachers and students are given individual encouragement and support and a chance to work co-operatively with their peers. Elementary, you'd think – but a radical leap from so many public schools here in which teachers have quite clearly given up.

In another school – call it School B – where the entire effort of the staff is to keep control, I walked down eerily silent hallways past the open doors of deathly silent classrooms while the principal boasted to me of his school's "discipline." I glanced through one open classroom door and saw the teacher leaning back in her chair, chewing gum and read-

■

ing a comic book, while the eight-year-olds scritched their pencils dolefully, filling out mimeographed worksheets. Aware suddenly of our passing presence, the teacher looked up from her comic book and barked, "Too much noise here!" at the totally silent class. The principal beamed.

In School A, on the contrary – despite its patronage principal and ugly physical plant – classrooms hummed with energy. In a grade four "enrichment" class for bright students, where all the students, typically, are black and Hispanic, the teacher bubbled over with enthusiasm. The walls are ablaze with "abstract art" produced after a Museum of Modern Art visit. On the blackboard, the names of Voltaire and Jonathan Swift are scrawled. "We were just discussing satire," the teacher, Stephanie Pollatsek, explains. The children in the class, she tells me, are voracious readers, currently racing through Kipling's "Rikki-Tikki-Tavi."

In a school system where 40 per cent of high-school graduates are illiterate, this is a stunning level of intellectual achievement. One teacher here told me that a major problem in the district is to find parents who will get involved in the school. "Quite a few of our children are living with grandparents, friends, or other relatives because both their parents have died of AIDS."

To see the odds this district is fighting, consider School B, which plays host to 173 homeless children every day, feeding them breakfast, lunch, and dinner. The other four hundred students are almost as poor: all of them qualify for free lunches, and the local families are so marginal and move so frequently that, according to the principal, the school has "a 100 per cent pupil turnover every year." The principal told me that the breakfast plan was begun after he noticed that the children were beside themselves on Monday morning – crying, fighting, falling asleep. He finally learned that they were simply starving; most hadn't had a real meal all weekend.

At this level of stress and poverty, there are no "mastery" plans. A major goal for the kindergarten children is to teach them their names, phone numbers, and addresses in the first term.

■

The principal gestured out the window to the street, which resembled downtown Beirut. "Alphabet City," he explained. "Drug dealers on every corner. No one out there but drug dealers, drug buyers, and undercover cops. Your children and mine couldn't walk down the block here and get out alive. But the kids here are tough; they know how to survive."

His assurance disturbed me. This is the school that prides itself on its silence and discipline. To me, these cowed and miserable youngsters seemed not "disciplined" or "survivors," but simply crushed into apathy.

Uptown, in Harlem, a very different school – Central Park East – has drawn enormous attention recently, especially since its pioneering founder and principal, Deborah Meier, won a MacArthur Foundation "genius" award of several hundred thousand dollars in recognition of her efforts.

Ms Meier's alternative high school believes in basics: learning to think. That can be done only in small classes. In high schools of five thousand students, the norm for New York, schooling consists mostly of herd control; daily, 20 per cent of the students are truant, and the administration permanently loses track of thousands every year.

At Central Park East, 145 students occupy separate quarters in a huge old high school, and no one gets lost. The atmosphere is intimate, intense, and collegial. Each student belongs to an "advisory group" of fifteen, which meets daily with a teacher-adviser to discuss ethical questions, school work, or problems.

The day I spent there, the whole school was involved in an ongoing study of political power, a theme that cut across the English, history, and humanities classes and zeroed in on the shifts in power caused by the French and American revolutions. Half the day is spent on humanities, with some classes running to two hours, and half the day on science and mathematics. No driver education, no home economics. Students who want athletics or a second language learn before or after school.

■

Whisking down the hall – she deliberately has no office and no desk – principal Debby Meier commandeered me to come chat with her advisory group about being a writer. I dreaded it: students rarely have any questions to ask of a writer besides "Where do you get your ideas?" and "How much do you make?" But this group of young teenagers was different. With a few subtly planted questions, Meier soon had them discussing practice and perseverance: how often did I rewrite? How did I know when to stop rewriting? Wasn't all that work *boring*? A young musician in the group leaped to answer that question himself. Vividly, his eyes alight, he described working at the piano for two, three, or even four hours, without noticing the passing of time. The others stared at him, astonished. Then, gradually, others found parallels in their own lives, consciously realizing for the first time the pleasure of absorption in a voluntarily chosen task. One spoke of skiing, another of basketball. Despite their rebellious wisecracks, I could see that it was beginning to dawn on them that learning, too, could be its own reward.

With mostly minority students, mostly lower or working class, Central Park East is driving forward its own revolution: humane education with rigorous intellectual content.

The secret at School A in District 1, and at Central Park East, is that committed teachers working with each other to develop their own curricula, in manageably small schools, can transform nightmarish battlegrounds into energetic centres of hope and learning. By 1989, Central Park East had 325 students, and not a single one dropped out during the 1988–1989 school year.

Dotted all over the city, alternative or "magnet" schools are one vigorous response of teachers and parents to the crazy system for which they work. Not only do they hammer out a plan of education that is responsive to their own student bodies' needs, rather than to political or media pressure, but they quietly redress one of the system's most worrying features – its *de facto* segregation.

■

Recent estimates show that by the year 2000, New York's public schools will be filled entirely with racial minorities. Even now, it's a shock to a visitor to see whole schools populated only by poor black or Hispanic children. Schools like Central Park East, or magnet public schools that specialize in science, the arts, enrichment, or languages, counter that unwholesome lopsidedness by attracting a healthy balance of the privileged and the deprived, the black and the white.

It's not a perfect answer. For one thing, the most disorganized poor are unlikely to make the effort to find such schools for their children; some ghetto principals complain bitterly that they are left with "the dregs" after magnet schools siphon off the most promising youngsters. But a magnet school exists even for those who are left behind: one pioneering principal insists on searching out students who are so disruptive that they are rejected by everyone else.

Seeing the alternative schools emphasized for me once again the strange dichotomy between the visionaries who work on the front lines, and the incompetents and crooks who often hold the levers of system-wide power.

That's not unique to New York. In every jurisdiction in Canada one can find politicians and school board trustees who, without having come near a living, breathing child in years, are ready to hand down instant solutions to the dilemmas of schooling in a complex society. "More three Rs!" "More discipline!" "Longer school year!" So long as the proposed solution is sufficiently sweeping, mechanical, and inflexible, it will have its passionate adherents. In New York, this propensity to simple-minded nostrums is exacerbated by sheer numbers and by pressure from the media. Public demands for a quick fix led the entire school system down a ruinous path: the path of standardized testing.

American schools are test crazy.

From the moment kindergarten begins until high school ends, American students are peppered with city, state, and national tests, tests of life experience, skill, competency, "mastery," and general knowledge.

New York's recently appointed schools chancellor, Richard Green [now deceased], immediately announced that he would begin testing all kindergarten kids and holding back those who didn't pass. Test mania has dominated American schools at least since the early 1960s. No one escapes. For the most rarefied toddler in Cerutti frocks and the most ragged tenement dweller, even the pre-school years are darkened by looming tests that will slot them for life. And doctors now are suggesting (in a study financed by the American Academy of Pediatricians) that the drug propanolol may be the answer for students with extreme anxiety about SATs, the universal Scholastic Aptitude Test.

"Yep, we have the MATs, DRPs, PEPs, CTPs, TOBEs, BINLs, Regents, SATs . . . you want more?" said a public school superintendent. He was nonplussed when I asked how he felt about the tests. "We have to have them," he explained. "The *New York Times* prints the school reading scores every year." A school that scores low is publicly reviled; superintendents or entire school boards may be dismissed; parent and teacher morale plummets. But, I persisted, do the tests help children learn? "Are you kidding?" he snorted. "The kids get physically sick, and the teachers are down the hall puking."

The tests, in fact, determine the curriculum. Nowhere is this more damaging than in the precious art of reading. For the first four or five years of school, many children never read a good book. Instead, they work their way through stilted basal readers, modern clones of the detestable *Dick and Jane*. They plough through endless language work books and drill sheets that hammer home phonics gobbledegook about "blends," "long *as*" and the names of consonants. They circle endless multiple choice answers about what's wrong with deliberately faulty sentences; they fill in thousands of blanks in words and paragraphs. The work is broken down into these absurd fragments so that the children can be tested at every stage. It's exactly like factory assembly-line work.

And, as the Canadian educator Frank Smith points out in his lucid, passionate book *Insult to Intelligence*, none of this has anything to do with how people really learn to read. The craze for packaged learning, drills, and tests, he writes, stems from the bureaucratic urge to control and quantify.

Check it out, as I did. I earn my living with words, but I'm baffled by the tortured syntax and essentially meaningless drills of typical grade three and four language work books. As for the ubiquitous multiple choice tests, what literate adult hasn't been stumped by one of these nightmarish quizzes in which three or four answers, depending on the subtlety of your interpretation, might all be equally correct?

Last fall, I wrote about how my teenage daughter, Jenny, a mathematical illiterate, had shot ahead in math through the innovative, supportive teaching at her United Nations school. But I had reckoned without senior year and the looming SATs. Suddenly, math class became a two-month competitive drill for the tests. Jenny lost all sense of the meaning of numbers; "math anxiety" surged back; she permanently dropped math.

The tests defraud the students in other ways, too. Recently, a watch-dog group in West Virginia did a study of nationally standardized tests. Every single state, it revealed, was being told by the test company that its students scored "above average." In other words, "average" has no meaning – and neither do the tests.

You really have to question the learning capacities of the politicians and administrators who run the schools. Despite mountains of evidence, they haven't yet twigged to the fact that it's the constant testing that is helping to destroy teaching, learning, and literacy.

By now, it's estimated that forty million Americans, including one-third or more of all high-school graduates, are illiterate. The news gets worse every year. The response is usually, "More tests!" Universities and colleges demand them to simplify their entrance procedures. Politicians insist on them to prove that they're doing something. Parents demand them because they're anxious. Corporations demand them because they want quantified evidence of a trained work force. In the words of the chairman of Xerox, schools are now providing "product [students] with a 50 per cent defect rate."

Now Canadians are demanding them. With a chill of dismay, I read last year that even the great scholar Northrop Frye has reluctantly concluded that high schools should return to standardized tests. Soon, as our children limp and labour through work books and drill sheets and grow farther and farther away from reading real books, we, too, will boast a 30 per cent illiteracy rate.

It's ironic. Standardized tests grew out of democratic schooling. Equal education for all, with quality control – that is, tests – built in to make sure everyone was up to snuff. But we've come full circle. A currently famous get-tough high-school principal in New Jersey summarily expelled sixty impoverished students because they were bringing down the school's test scores.

If school systems poured even half the money they spend on tests and their attendant paperwork into creating smaller, more intimate schools where teachers could know their students, we'd never need another DRP, BINL, or SAT.

Gradually, the educational winds are shifting. Standardization, towards which Canadians are now moving like lemmings, has proven so catastrophic in the United States that the latest trend is towards "school-centred decision making." In other words, the hierarchically imposed solutions don't, and can't, work in such a diverse population. Instead, many American school districts are encouraging parents, principals, and teachers to work together to streamline curricula and approaches that work best for their children.

■

The very best teachers have always been subversive; in order to respond in serious ways to their students' real needs, they have to ignore some of the more insane rules and regulations of the bureaucracy. In New York, where wave after wave of top-down instant solutions have been imposed by politicians and enforced by the swollen bureaucracy, a teacher who really followed the rules would do nothing but fill in forms. (Teachers in New York have to punch time-clocks, like factory hands, and fill in lengthy requisitions for minor repairs that will never be done.)

Debby Meier, the rumpled, intelligent, harassed, passionately committed principal of Central Park East, works her way around the rules to create a school where youngsters learn. In another Harlem public school, I met a teacher who works within the system but has added one vital ingredient that makes all the difference.

Nicole Gill, age nine, is hopping from one foot to the other (partly from excitement and partly because her pink party shoes are too tight) and telling me that *The Little House on the Prairie* is her favourite book.

Montrees Williams, twelve, whose spiffy frilled ankle socks match her white dress, says shyly, but with an air of imparting a precious secret, that she is up to page twenty-five in *Charlotte's Web*. I ask Byron Hurst, eleven, if he likes to read, and he corrects me quietly but firmly: "I *love* to read."

Five little boys from a lower grade have their heads together, laughing wildly over Beverly Cleary's *The Mouse on the Motorcycle* and reading snatches out loud.

Meanwhile, Tara Dickerson, eleven, who wants to be an obstetrician even though she doesn't specially like science – "I expect that as I grow older I'll learn to appreciate the scientific arts" – is explaining to me the special allure of fiction: "Reading can give you more aspects to life. You can experience wild imagination, you can be anything you want to be, even on another planet."

■

Of course, if you lived here, where Tara does, another planet might look pretty good to you, too. This is a public school in Harlem, where low reading scores are a constant political scandal; where nearly all the children are black, poor, and living in single-parent families; where school budgets are so tight that teachers buy pencils and lined paper out of their own pockets; where schools routinely have to clothe as well as feed many of their pupils, and where a sign on the principal's door here at P.S. 92 warns ominously, "Nobody said teaching is easy."

The magical difference at P.S. 92 is Beth Pettit, who has taught here for seventeen years. She may not seem like anyone's idea of a fairy godmother: a large woman with china-blue eyes, a red rose in her lapel to match the red gift-tie rope on her pony-tail, and a voice permanently pitched at a level to keep generations of tough kids in line. But with the simple idea of giving kids their own books and by communicating her own love of reading, Ms Pettit has transformed hundreds of lives. "Would you believe we've sent more than two hundred kids to private schools, on scholarship?" she roars happily at me.

I believe it. Ms Pettit's energy and devotion are prodigious. In 1970, a parent showed her a flyer about Reading Is Fundamental. RIF, a national non-profit organization, arranges publishers' discounts so that participating teachers and parents can buy good fiction cheaply. Then the books are given, free and with lots of hoopla, games, carnivals, and prizes, to schoolchildren.

Ms Pettit raced around raising money – once she scrounged 453 kilograms of aluminum soft-drink cans to sell to a recycler – and soon her RIF projects branched luxuriantly to include a gifted class on Saturdays and a full-time summer program that draws 150 children from all over the city. "You just have to see it – all these kids sitting out there on the pavement in the heat, listening to stories read aloud. Their favourites? Fairy tales. And *Tikki Tikki Tembo*, where they can all join in. Yes, the very first child I ever had in the RIF program has graduated from Duke University and is working for a publisher."

It should be crashingly obvious: what motivates kids to love reading is, first of all, the daily contact with an adult who shares her own delight in good books. Just as crucial is the chance to choose, hear, own, read, and talk about exciting stories. These two essentials make everything else irrelevant. The painful irony is that in some school districts, while parents and teachers wage ideological wars over reading scores and teaching techniques, the children's interest in reading is being quietly murdered by mind-numbing primers, not to mention the fatal example of adults who don't feel or communicate a passion for reading.

The children of P.S. 92, heaven knows, may have nothing else in the way of privileges, but they have the basics: Beth Pettit's generously shared enthusiasm (she reads aloud every day) and the thrill of ownership.

Three times a year, the students troop in to a special room to browse through tables laden with shiny new paperbacks. From kindergarten through grade six, each student amasses a personal home library of twenty-eight volumes. Total cost: a mere two thousand dollars a year – the federal government matches the money Ms Pettit raises. I was there on Distribution Day, when class after class poured into the room, many of the youngsters in their best clothes in honour of the occasion.

"Oooh, I want both of these," agonized one girl.

"I'll swap wit' you if you get a good one."

"Get this, *Black Beauty*, man, it'll make you cry!"

"Did your sister read this? What did she say about it?"

"Hey, listen to this good part . . . the boy Keith is friends with the mouse . . ."

"Why don't you get a book you can read?" one diminutive boy scolded another. "Instead of just that old puzzle book."

Book talk. Genuine, spontaneous book talk, child to child. Given the heady freedom of choice, they exercise it seriously, poring over the jacket blurbs. Anything with "black" in the title is snapped up – *Black Beauty*, *The Black Stallion* – and detective, mystery, and adventure stories are feverishly popular.

No wonder that this year alone, in Ms Pettit's grade four and five classes (where "every one of them has been held back at least a year and their ages are nine to thirteen") some of the kids have leap-frogged two years ahead in reading ability.

Montrees sidles up to me a few minutes later with an embarrassed private whisper: "Can you put in the newspaper that our teacher is fantastic?"

Out in the hall, an amazing sight: on their way back to their classrooms before lunch, the kids have stopped, hunkered down on the floor, and started reading their books.

Uh-huh, Montrees. The teacher is fantastic.

By the summer of 1989, Beth Pettit had 325 children in the summer program at neighbouring St. Aloysius Church; she got a grant to hire as helpers fifteen dedicated college students – all of them black and Hispanic youngsters who have come up through her classes. The RIF scheme is still going strong. Tara Dickerson is in a junior high for the gifted; Montrees is working with Beth for the summer. The crack problem in the neighbourhood got so bad last year that P.S. 92 had to map out a "safe route" for the children to follow to school, but this year, police, responding to pressure from the community, have cleaned things up a lot. The kids are still reading and listening to stories.

It's dangerous to sentimentalize individual efforts: though one magnificent teacher can touch hundreds of lives, New York schools are processing millions (many of them straight to permanent unemployment and crime), and change has to be forged in every district, school by school, before anyone will be entitled to rest on her laurels. It's also folly to think that school alone can change everything. Children so

■

bereft of the simplest comforts of daily life – children who may have to wake their mother from a drug trance before they can be fed, or who come to school both hungry and beaten – may be unreachable by anyone. And, of course, those who aren't in school can't be reached. Aside from the homeless, there are hundreds, possibly thousands, of immigrant children who stay home from school to work in sweatshops. The drug trade has imported so much violence into the schools – a couple of thousand assaults are registered every year – that many youngsters may stay home from fear. Even children from relatively stable homes may be unfitted for learning by their constant immersion in television.

Still, some schools, some classes, some teachers shine out like lonely lighthouses in a system darkened by graft and neglect.

Here comes Brenda, one of 250 kindergarten miracles at P.S. 192 in crime-riddled Washington Heights. It's Brenda's turn to read her class a story today. Purple hair-bobbles bobbing and eyes sparkling, Brenda leaps to choose *The Gingerbread Man* from a well-stuffed book-case. "The boy opeded the oven," she begins, putting her own spin on the word "opened," as her teacher, Al Gordon, holds the book up so everyone can see the pictures.

Pink and purple hair bobbles like Brenda's are a hot number in Mr. Gordon's kindergarten. Nearly every little girl, neatly brushed and combed, has them – except for one moppet who wears two perkily defiant bows made of torn strips of bed sheets. Those bows speak volumes. "Poor," they say, "but not down and out."

Poverty is endemic here. Last year, the city called P.S. 192 "the worst school in the worst district in the worst crack area" in Manhattan. Reading scores were so appalling that the whole local school board was fired.

This year, most of these kindergarten kids will be joyously literate by the end of the year.

■

And this in spite of the fact that 92 per cent of the children are Dominican immigrants whose parents are illiterate; 96 per cent live below the poverty line; and the few black children, like Brenda, come from a notorious welfare hotel where four children recently died in a fire.

The difference is an innovative program called Open Sesame, developed by the American Reading Council. Out with the mind-numbing work books and stilted "basal readers." In with books, real books by good authors, and a school-wide devotion to the pleasures of language.

Brenda, for example. She is telling the story from memory, watching the pictures and picking out occasional words she can recognize. The class is raptly attentive.

"Run, run, as fast as you can, you can't catch me, I'm the gingerbread man!" they chime in happily. Brenda is really leaning into the story now. Unconsciously, she shoves her hands down the back of her purple pants to rest on her minuscule tush. She gets to the exciting part: the runaway gingerbread man meets a bear. "A *bear!*" exclaims Brenda, opening her eyes wide and drawing out the word dramatically. When it's time for the chorus, she whips around and cues the class with a pointed finger.

Now the ill-fated gingerbread man meets a fox. "And the fox said, 'Come a little closer!'" Brenda reads, making her voice wheedle and beckoning with a crooked finger. By now, her whole small body expresses delight and anticipation. In a minute, the fox will eat up the gingerbread man. Brenda relishes the climax. She beams at the last picture, which shows the fox with a comically distended belly.

"And Mr. Fox," she concludes enthusiastically, "had a baby!"

Even though Al Gordon has to fight back a smile and explain that a "he" fox can't have a baby, everyone is happy and satisfied. Brenda dances back to her place in the circle, grinning and rubbing three kids' heads in joyful salute as she passes.

Brenda thinks of herself as a reader. Books are packages of pleasure to her; stories are an exciting part of her life. Next year in grade one, when she can already read some of her favourite books fluently, she will begin to learn spelling by choosing "key words" – words that are important to her – and having the teacher write them down. Children in grades two and three here can readily spell words like "microphone" and "helicopter" from their personal collection of key words.

Julia Palmer, a distinguished grey-haired woman with a New England accent, who heads the American Reading Council and pioneered this Open Sesame program, marches me briskly to a grade three classroom and shows me, wordlessly, some of the children's key word booklets. She knows that I know of the welfare hotel fire and will not miss the poignant impact of key words like "children" and "brown" and "fire."

The hallway and classroom walls here are crowded with vivacious and sometimes startlingly poetic stories dictated by these young language spinners. Words are printed and pinned up everywhere. Every class begins every day with silent reading of real books.

When the teacher is called out of Brenda's kindergarten class, I'm hastily recruited to read aloud. The kids choose the classic *Goodnight Moon* – on the very day when its eighty-year-old illustrator, Clement Hurd, dies in California. Good night, Clement, but not goodbye. Your pictures are still alive here in P.S. 192, reflected in the enchanted eyes of even the toughest, most rackety little boys, who are chorusing the words aloud as I read.

"Since this program started," Al Gordon tells me later, "books are as exciting to them as TV cartoons. We drop everything and read at least three or four times in a morning."

In Canada, many schools are already doing the same thing and calling it the "whole language" approach. Spelling and the mechanics of literacy are woven in after the children have already learned to feel at home and happy with the printed word.

■

In the United States, where basal readers and elaborate packaged reading programs are a billion-dollar business, something so simple and right as reading real books is still seen as revolutionary.

I choose the word advisedly: approaches to education are highly political. Right-wing politicians have, for a decade, favoured "back to basics," a sort of educational fundamentalism. Now, U.S. educators realize they are facing a literacy crisis. Even the Rand Corporation recently declared that "three *R*s" curricula and standardized testing have produced "a bureaucratic hell." Its conclusion: kids learn best when teachers can develop their own curricula to suit individual children and local conditions.

It can take a long time for new approaches to work their way through already entrenched systems. Even though all of P.S. 192 has been galvanized by the Open Sesame program – and the parents come happily to the warmly welcoming little "parents' library" to drink coffee and borrow children's books in English and Spanish, some of them learning to read for the first time in order to share with their children – even despite all this astonishing change, there are still the standardized tests to deal with.

"All this," says Julia Palmer, waving a hand at a class full of kids chanting a story out loud, "all this has to stop in grade two. We have to drop it all and begin to drill for the standardized reading test."

But the pendulum is about to swing back. Real books and real reading – not "reading skills" – have been rediscovered. Bright-eyed Brenda, I'm happy to say, is on the cutting edge.

If anything, my personal journeys through the city's public schools reaffirmed my awe at the spirited dedication of the best New Yorkers. Faced with the daunting odds they face every day, year after year, the injustices inflicted by corrupt politicians and the hopelessness of ghetto life, I myself might have succumbed to weary cynicism. But people as radically different as Irish working-class Beth Pettit, patrician Julia Palmer, and intellectual Debby Meier – people of substance, conviction, and amazing drive – and the lively, vulnerable children they teach and inspire, are the stuff and fibre of the New York I love.

CHAPTER 8

■

A Canadian in New York

In Bradley's, a dark, noisy, sophisticated piano bar, I'm squashed into the crowd, trying to hear my favourite jazz, but eavesdropping willy-nilly on what I think of as a typical American conversation.

She: "Well, actually I'm divorced . . . but I don't take a cent from my ex. I do very well, I mean, I make a *large* salary."

He: "Oh, so do I; I'm doing very well. Very, very well. I make a *lot* of money."

My friend and I, secret Canadians, exchange satirical glances. How *American* to boast about money.

She: "So, what are you doing for the summer? Got a share in the Hamptons?"

He: "Actually, I'm just back from doing a little yachting in my home town."

She (pouncing): "Where's that?"

He: "Oh, a great little place. Owen Sound, heard of it?"

He tossed this off with such a breezily modest nonchalance that for a moment it snapped with white-flannel nautical elegance . . . Bar Harbour, Newport, Kennebunkport.

It's easy for Canadians to "pass." I don't know if our Ontario swain convinced his lady that Owen Sound was a snazzy New England resort town, but Americans know so little about us that he may well have succeeded. Once they're informed that they're talking to a Canadian, Americans insist they hear us saying "oot," "aboot," and "hoos" for "out," "about," and "house." This is exaggerated but has a kernel of truth. Clench-jawed Canadians close off the diphthong; Americans, more relaxed (or slack), simply jettison it, ("aht, abaht") the way they ditched the written "u" in "labour." Aside from this minimal quirk, they can perceive no difference in us. Indeed, since all the differences are historical and attitudinal, they are invisible; we Canadians, like the invasion of the pod people, make perfect spies of the American scene.

I grew wary about revealing my Canadian identity to affable strangers; quite often, it would lead me into one of those conversations at cross purposes that end with cranky feelings on both sides.

"Canadian! Well, that's fine, that's the same thing as being American." This is offered with the jovial, coaxing condescension of an uncle offering a Popsicle to a shy toddler. The intentions are entirely friendly.

"Uh, no, not exactly . . . we *are* a separate country, quite different, really." Honour, with a *u*, compels me to this nit-picking.

"Oh. I see. So you're anti-American. Oh, no, don't apologize, they're all like that: we give everyone money and they all just love to knock us."

Americans as wounded innocents, big, generous teddy bears, buzzed by ungrateful mosquitoes. A more elegant version of this ethnocentrism surfaced in the *New York Times*, where I was startled to read in the entertainment section one day that Canadian folk music provides "an interesting regional variation" in the American mainstream. This kindly assumption that we are a region of Greater U.S.A. (and an interesting variation, at that) is so widespread, and so benevolently expressed, that one contradicts it only at the risk of seeming tiresomely schismatic or hostile. It's almost impossible for Americans, brought up in an atmosphere of relentless boosterism, to conceive that we may like or even admire them and still want to remain our own separate selves.

Of course, among my anti-Reagan American acquaintances, I enjoyed a certain cachet, having the good sense to be a citizen of a country with medicare, the National Film Board, and a less bellicose foreign policy. But for the most part, I had difficulty convincing people that our wish to retain our Canadian identity had nothing to do with anti-Americanism – so evident did it seem to Americans, being the biggest and the best, that everyone except the most relentless enemy would want to *be* them.

■

When Adrienne Clarkson came to New York in the winter of 1988 to speak to the Americas Society on "the perversity of being Canadian," I was eager to hear how she handled this delicate and maddening question.

... Adrienne seemed the perfect Canadian for the job: soft of voice, steely of mind, a child of the Chinese diaspora, educated in Canada, France, and New York, a broadcaster, publisher, novelist, and, for five years, Ontario's dynamic agent-general in Paris.

"We know what Canadian culture is, in our strange and unexpressed land, but find ourselves unable to tell others," Ms Clarkson admitted to the lunch-time crowd of publishers and journalists at the Americas Society. Nevertheless, she tried her best, gently describing how our frozen north and vast empty spaces, together with our loyalist legacy of parliamentary democracy, have shaped us, and led us to work out a fine balance of public and private enterprise – an equilibrium that Ms Clarkson sees as threatened by the free trade deal. "We want to be your partners, not lackeys who get over-dependent and hostile. You'll like us better that way," she said soothingly.

This tactful reassurance is essential when speaking at the Americas Society, a private, non-profit institution housed (by the munificent Rockefellers) in a lavish palace on Park Avenue. Here prominent Canadians lecture to American business people who have just begun to worry (delicious irony) about Canadian investment in the American economy. Think of the Reichmanns, who own the largest single chunk of Manhattan, of Garth Drabinsky's massive Cineplex invasion, of Robert Campeau's takeover of Bloomingdale's.

Adrienne was there, however, not to boast about rich men's conquests, but to explain why so many Canadians oppose the free trade deal. For non-corporate Canadians, the deal seems to threaten our cultural autonomy, wiping out the subsidies that support our magazines, books, art, theatre, public broadcasting, and film board.

I myself have tried to explain this Canadian fixation about autonomy to Americans and found that the most sympathetic response I can expect is a discussion–closing pat on the head: "Of course, of course, we understand these Canadian . . . er . . . sensitivities."

After Clarkson's speech, Lansing Lamont, former *Time* magazine correspondent in Ottawa and Washington and now director of the Society's Canadian Affairs program, expounded on the communications gap. "There are two quite different mind-sets, all right. Neither group quite grasps what the other is all about. Canadians say, 'We have to protect our small bit of turf,' and Americans say, 'It's a free world, and anyway, it's all business, so what's the big squeak?'"

[When Adrienne Clarkson spoke, many Canadians were still squeaking desperately against climbing into that elephantine American marriage bed. More than a year has passed; the marriage is consummated, and now it is indeed all business.]

It was a funny, friendly, and pointed speech. But, as my father used to say, go bang your head against the wall. That night, at a festive dinner hosted by Canadian Consul-General Bob Johnstone and his wife, Popsy, a lively conversation about British, Canadian, and American characteristics was stopped short by the puzzled wife of an important American publisher. "I don't get it," she said, wrinkling her brow and waving her spoon to halt the discussion. "You keep talking about Canadians. Aren't you all Americans, too?"

Perched in Manhattan, I was constantly buffeted by little contradictory winds. American boldness and freedom of expression exhilarated me; it was like gulping oxygen after a lifetime of constricted breathing. But it was maddening to see how narrowly the American press used this freedom, and how slavishly the biggest, most powerful papers echoed the world-view of their government.

I should be used to the shock of U.S. centripetal thinking by now, but I have this Canadian quirk. I keep expecting the U.S. press to recognize the independent existence of other nations.

A foolish weakness. To read the U.S. newspapers is to realize, after all, that everything in the world revolves helplessly around the vortex of U.S. interests, and anything that does not, does not exist.

Just the other day, I was quietly blackening my fingers with the *Times* [this was not, as some indignant readers thought, a slur on the paper, but a comment on its messy, stain-everything ink] over a morning cup of coffee when my eyes lit on a seemingly routine front-page news story. "Jamaican Leader, a U.S. Ally, Hard-Pressed by Leftist Foe," read the headline. The Leftist Foe in question is not, as you might think, some ravening guerrilla chief, but Michael Manley, former prime minister of Jamaica and now leader of the opposition Social Democratic Party. [Manley was elected prime minister again in 1988.]

The story's first paragraph reads this way: "President Reagan's closest ally in the Caribbean, Prime Minister Edward P.G. Seaga, is in serious political trouble, and an old rival, who has embraced Cuba and criticized United States policy in Central America, is striving to replace him."

Note that this is the *New York Times*, the glory of the U.S. press, and that we are not discussing here an editorial or think piece but a straightforward news story.

Note that the most important thing about Mr. Seaga is not that he is Jamaica's prime minister, but that he is Mr. Reagan's closest ally. And that Michael Manley's name does not even rate a mention at the top of the story, his mere identity being eclipsed by the electrifying news that he has "embraced" Cuba and that he has criticized U.S. policy in Central America – as who has not?

But it gets more lurid. The leftist foe is "striving" to replace Mr. Seaga – not in a bloody uprising, as you might be led to think, but in a democratic election. The "flamboyant" Mr. Manley, it says here, had "wrecked" the Jamaican economy when he was "Socialist" prime minister. He "relinquished" his office after a campaign in which "800 Jamaicans were killed" – we are not told by whom – and if he wins the next election, it will be "a defeat for the Reagan administration."

Every word is loaded to give you a negative, distorted view of a dangerous enemy. But it was that defeat-for-Reagan line that had me transfixed. Babies, they say, think the world exists only for their tiny, omnipotent selves; they think it's their cry that summons the mother into existence. It is hard to credit, though, how relentlessly Americans and their media seem to believe, entirely unself-consciously, that the world is their hustings and that every vote cast is cast for or against them personally.

"A defeat for Reagan." Amazing. Get lost, you two million Jamaicans; you may have thought this island was your home, but it's just an annex to the O.K. Corral.

Foreign diplomats fume about "bias" in the U.S. foreign coverage, but it is really more like blindness. The more the media deal in narrow, for-us-or-agin'-us judgements, the less able they are to interpret reality. (Canada just does not exist in U.S. newspapers, except when our sense of national identity irritates them. This week, the *Times* devoted a lengthy story to the call by the Caplan-Sauvageau Task Force on Broadcasting for more Canadian content.)

The insistence on a narrowly partisan view of events leads to some shocking reporting. Those "800 dead," for example: the implication is that Mr. Manley, that hard-pressing leftist foe, must have been responsible. But according to *Globe and Mail* news coverage of those violent 1980 elections, "about 450" were killed by uncon-

∎

trollable armed gangs *on both sides*. And Mr. Manley, despite the *Times*, had no monopoly on flamboyance: both leaders appear to have graduated from the Running Dog of Imperialism school of political rhetoric. Mr. Seaga warned direly that Mr. Manley, if he lost, might call in the Cuban army; Mr. Manley accused Mr. Seaga of being in the pay of the CIA.

Even more revealing is the way the two regimes are judged by the *Times*. Mr. Manley is said to have wrecked the economy – no mention, mind you, that the wreckage was helped along by depressed bauxite markets, the hostility of the International Monetary Fund, and the cut-off of aid from the United States. Since Mr. Seaga became prime minister, the economy has been truly devastated, with thousands laid off, hospitals and schools closed, and a falling standard of living.

How does the *Times* describe this? Mildly. Mr. Seaga, it says, has "been unable to overcome a 50 per cent loss of income from bauxite." And this despite the fact that Mr. Seaga has reaped more lavish aid from the United States for his Reaganomics regime than almost any other country in the world.

In fact, though you would never know it from the *Times*, Reagan officials, according to close observers of the Jamaican scene, are deeply embarrassed by the dramatic failure of Seaga's economic policies. Even the Jamaican businessmen, whose Private Sector Organization backed Mr. Seaga, are said to be quietly relieved at the prospect of Mr. Manley's return to power, especially now that he has toned down his naïve enthusiasm about Cuba. Over the past two years, furthermore, Mr. Manley has had frequent and cordial consultations with U.S. officials at the very highest State Department level.

It is the old irony: the Americans overreact to political opponents abroad. Then, when they want to change direction, they find their hysterical propaganda has gone too far to let them retreat. Blinkered journalism, docilely repeating the party line, is part of the problem.

■

Canadian journalists working in the United States are often provoked into giving silent thanks for our little-guy status. It helps us to keep the rest of the world in saner focus, and to remember that we are not the centre of the universe.

Encouraged by the enthusiastic response to this column from Canadian readers and reporters, I decided to pay closer attention to television news for a follow-up column. It happened to be the week, in September, 1986, when an American reporter, Nicholas Daniloff, was arrested in Moscow as a spy, just before a scheduled United States-Russia summit. To save the summit meeting, the Americans were forced to initiate frantic manoeuvres to free Daniloff; a trade of prisoners was quickly arranged. Meanwhile, official Washington engaged in its usual little-boy antics. Doddering Reagan proved that his macho ascendancy was much more important to him than was Daniloff or the peace talks; the word went out instantly that America didn't care about the summit anyway ("just a meeting, not really a summit after all"), and besides, the United States "won" the stand-off. What startled me was how slavishly the fourth estate echoed and reinforced the government's imbecilic posturing.

One little word – "blink" – bobbed around all last week on U.S. television news. Just like a fishing float, it served as a small, vivid clue to what goes on beneath the surface of U.S. political coverage.

It was President Ronald Reagan, with his reliance on tough-guy movie clichés, who first used the expression. "They blinked," he said, explaining the Soviets' willingness to release U.S. reporter Nicholas Daniloff. This meant, apparently, that in the boxing bout between two macho powers, one chickened out.

Instantly, the idea of "blinking" became both the context and the language of every television news broadcast that I watched in a three-day siege of channel hopping. As the story of the Daniloff-Zakharov-Orlov exchange unfolded, every news anchor and reporter zeroed in unquestioningly on what seemed to them the key importance of the event: who blinked? Each of them used the word as his own, not as a quotation from the president or even as a symbol of Reagan's one-dimensional approach.

When the swap was finally completed, the *Times* summed up on Wednesday with a front-page headline, "Keeping the Score," that echoed TV's infantile preoccupations. "First of all, who won and who lost?" asked the *Times* story. The president himself couldn't have come up with a more fatuously athletic view of foreign policy.

"The problem with American media," quipped a CBC newsperson based in New York, "is that it's voluntary *Tass.* "

Parroting the official State Department line, TV newscasters deliver a bright-eyed, blow-dried, mindless chauvinism that would be hilarious – if its impact weren't so pervasive.

They unanimously assumed, for example, Mr. Daniloff's innocence, and Mr. Zakharov's guilt. Many repeated the government's assertion that Mr. Daniloff's release was proof that he was not a spy. But when Mr. Zakharov was released by the United States, nobody seemed to take that as proof that he, too, was innocent.

Why did the United States back off its initial refusal to trade? Why had Mr. Reagan become so urgent about a summit? No one asked. Very few even mentioned the word "summit" until the trade was completed and a hasty retreat had to be made from the "blink" scenario.

Then, of course, news announcers worried whether Mr. Reagan had appeared "weak" or, incredibly, they supported George Shultz's straight-faced claim that there was no connection between the releases of Daniloff and Zakharov.

There's a strange mixture of haste and vacuity in the interminable three hours of TV news every evening between five and eight o'clock. On Monday, when the results of the negotiations were still unclear, every channel filled its news time with reporters endlessly repeating that there was "nothing to report." One, desperate for a "win-lose" scoop, even babbled that "George Shultz played tennis today but we don't know the score." Trivial details – the exact time of a "no comment" comment, the name of the in-flight movie Mr. Daniloff watched as he flew home – were relayed as important facts. We saw countless shots of Mr. Shultz, Mr. Reagan, and Soviet Foreign Minister Eduard Shevardnadze walking in and out of buildings and refusing to comment, while on-the-spot reporters breathlessly told us how many other news crews were hanging around with "nothing to report."

All this "nothing" left precious little time for analysis. Even later, experts were limited to meaningless ten-second clips – "They must want a summit very bad" – so that we could be shown more replays of Daniloff-at-the-airport scenes.

Americans don't seem comfortable with rapid-fire speech, despite their long practice at breakneck reporting. In the space of twenty-four hours, I heard newscasters uttering such pithy phrases as "guilty on all accounts," "the striff and strain of negotiations," "the State Department is shedding nothing but darkness," "Trebelink concentration camp," "irregegularities," and, best of all, the apparently intentional, "We sent an oblank message to the Soviets." O'blank? Oblanque?

Why all the haste? To make time for commercials, of course. And for interviews with celebrities – almost always focused admiringly on the vast sums earned by authors, gymnasts, or other athletes.

Verbal blunders, though, and the growing tendency to "infotainment," are the least of U.S. television's shortcomings. Much more serious is the drastic reversal of the media's self-definition since the Watergate era. Today, media people identify themselves so closely with the administration that, during televised White House press

■

266

conferences, they sound like government officials: "Mr. President, what are we going to do about . . ."

The most (though not very) independent voice I heard was that of ABC's Peter Jennings, a Canadian, who smiled proudly in announcing that he would continue to call it a "summit" despite the president's preference for the term "meeting." (In such tiny increments is measured a newscaster's autonomy.)

"The attitude here is that anyone who casts doubt on what the administration says is on dangerous ground," commented Keith Morrison, the Canadian anchorman for KNBC news in Los Angeles. "No one asks questions. The media adapt reality to make it into a palatable fiction, colouring events with pejorative language (for example, news from Nicaragua) to make it more listenable or watchable."

Mr. Morrison thinks that shallow coverage comes from a generation of producers who have grown up with TV and see it solely in terms of giving people what they want. "The mandate is only to make money. Most are not the least bit interested in issues. I haven't met anyone who is consumed by a desire either to inflame or to inform."

How I longed for the crisp, impartial tones of Canadian TV. Surely our networks, public and private, would have scrutinized the government's motives. Some literate analyst would have probed a bit; there wouldn't have been the same overwhelming uniformity of views. Well, you don't know what you've got till you don't have it. I used to groan about the vapid maunderings of Canadian TV reporters filling time at political conventions, or about the artificial confrontations staged by the *Journal*. Distance – and American TV – have sharpened my appreciation. By now, I'm convinced that it's our dear old CBC that keeps us sane, sceptical, and Canadian.

Fate (and the Tories) punished me for momentarily giving in to archetypal Canadian smugness. Not even waiting until the

Americans asked, the Canadian government has rushed about, like a bride flinging off her wedding dress, wildly tearing apart our regional and cultural subsidies. Via Rail vanishes into the distance; the magazines bite the dust; the CBC, $140 million torn from its budget, prepares to go down into the embrace of corporate advertisers.

What makes us Canadian, anyway? In a world where we know things only through the media – books, newspapers, magazines, television, and radio – it is our media that keep us conscious – not just of our history and of each other (how many of us have spent time in the Arctic, or in distant provinces?), but also of the shared, unspoken assumptions that flow from and sustain our system of government and our web of values.

Without Canadian media – and they can't exist without public support – we will soon be an interesting regional variation of the American mainstream. All-commercial television news, geared to reflect corporate views without offending and to whisk us painlessly and thoughtlessly on to the next commercial, will feed us the same line of propaganda that has led Americans to years of folly in Central America.

Canadians tend to venerate the *New York Times* as a superb newspaper of record; the glamour and power of New York cling to it – though, as Joseph C. Goulden points out in his book *Fit to Print*, the *Times* carries so little coverage of real New York politics that when the powerful and corrupt municipal politician Donald Manes tried to kill himself, the *Times* had to explain to its readers who he was.

The *Times* is also vigorously ideological, particularly in its foreign coverage. Only by living in New York and reading it daily (something I had looked forward to as a special privilege) did I begin to develop the uneasy awareness that something was askew about *Times* coverage of important events.

The most blatant example of propagandist news surfaced in the *New York Times* in the winter of 1988. James LeMoyne, a journalist described by another paper, the *New York Observer*, as a "pro-contra propagandist," had a story from

■

268

San Salvador in the *Times*. The story, which carried LeMoyne's byline, seemed like an even-handed account of political violence leading up to El Salvador's elections. LeMoyne described a dozen recent and well-documented cases of torture and murder of civilians by right-wing death squads linked to the army. Then, just to even things up, he devoted the bulk of the article to threats of violence by left-wing "Marxist guerillas." And he described, as though he had been there and interviewed witnesses, how the guerrillas murdered two villagers who had registered to vote. As a warning to others not to vote, LeMoyne said, the guerrillas executed the men and stuffed the voters' registration cards in the corpses' mouths.

Alternative papers in New York immediately refuted the story, citing El Salvadoran sources who claimed the "Marxist" killings were invented by the military. The *Times* itself almost immediately received information throwing doubt on the truth of the episode; apparently, the account of the murders first surfaced in a right-wing newspaper in El Salvador, which quoted the military as its source.

It took the *Times*, the paper of record and of enormous influence, almost seven months to print a retraction admitting that the story was false.

Leaving aside such egregious examples, the *Times* regularly did its bit for official disinformation. The Sandinistas were routinely described as Communists and their activities cast in the most sinister light, while the scurvy band of mercenaries known as the contras were distinguished by the *Times* with the name of "rebels."

Going forth from the very centre of Manhattan, bearing the name of New York into the farthest corners of the world, the *Times* is peculiarly un–New York in its determinedly neo-conservative world view. For New York is still a bastion of liberal Democrats and oppositionists of every stripe; it is here (and not just because of the presence of the United Nations) that underdogs, rebels, and radicals, from Bishop Tutu to Daniel Ortega, can be assured of a tumultuous welcome and an outpouring of empathetic fellow feeling.

■

It was not in Washington, but in New York, that thousands came to mourn the pointless slaughter of a young American at the hands of the American-armed contras.

"Ben Linder. *Presente!*" says the man on the podium. It is the Nicaraguan way of saluting someone who has fallen in the war, and insisting that his or her spirit still lives.

Ben Linder, of course, is not materially present, because he is dead and buried, and this is his memorial service, at the Stephen Wise Free Synagogue on the Upper West Side.

Mr. Linder, a slight, bespectacled, twenty-seven-year-old engineer from Seattle, was killed in a contra raid on April 28 [1987] as he worked at a hydroelectric project in the rough, remote hills of northern Nicaragua. As he lay wounded in the field, a contra shot him point-blank in the head.

"I once drove Ben in my jeep up to El Cua, where he was working, and he showed me this tiny Swiss generator, made in 1955, that he was trying to fix," said George Moore, a speaker at the memorial service. "He was trying to bring light to about two thousand farmhouses . . ."

The Iran-contra hearings go on and on in Washington, but the deeper puzzle of all the deaths inflicted on Nicaragua remains unsolved. To destroy a small, poverty-stricken country, the United States has been willing to lie, cheat, beg, steal, murder, arm its enemies, subvert and bully its allies, corrupt its foreign policy, and traduce its democracy. All this for Nicaragua – when no blood-soaked Latin tyrant (and there have been plenty of them) ever evoked more than the mildest U.S. rebuke.

The sheer, mad disproportion of the Reaganite attack is wearying. One feels hopeless against such rabid perseverance. Almost 70 per cent of Americans are consistently opposed to aid for the contras, but even this has no effect on Washington.

At Mr. Linder's memorial service, the old stalwarts of the Vietnam protest years – Rev. William Sloane Coffin, Episcopal Bishop Paul Moore, Rabbi Balfour Brickner – spoke first, and their rhetoric, too, seemed tired and stale. A grey-haired folkie sang, too glibly; there was prolonged, sentimental applause for some white-haired veterans of the Abraham Lincoln Brigade.

Then everything changed. Mr. Linder's young friends rose, one by one, to pay tribute to him. They had fresh faces, shiny hair, and no rhetoric at all. Amy King, a friend of Ben's older sister, remembered "Little Ben . . . It was a family joke that he was the perennial kid brother. I could never believe that he was more than thirteen. We joked: 'You mean, the Nicaraguan people need a thirteen-year-old engineer?' Now I have to catch up to him." She was trying hard, she said, to learn from Ben's parents. They, in this terrible moment, wanted Americans to remember the thousands of Nicaraguan dead, and to keep the death of their American son in some kind of perspective.

Alison Quam, who was Ben's girl-friend for seven years, looking very young and slender in a grey dress, talked about a letter he sent her from Nicaragua four years ago, to be opened only in case of emergency.

"Last week," said Ms Quam, her voice wavering, "I opened the letter."

She read us bits of it: "Keep on walking, Alison . . . live your life energetically and joyfully."

This part of the service was almost unbearable, because now Ben Linder was a real person – a young man who did clown tricks for village children, who seemed to have a radiantly calm, unpretentious spirit, who was happy to be working with an unsullied purpose for thirteen dollars a month. He knew he was on a contra "death list," and was afraid, but quietly determined to keep on.

"He was good friends with my two-year-old son," said Alice Christov, who was an ABC radio reporter in Nicaragua. "I thought they would always be friends." Ms

■

Christov talked about the contras, and how she had seen babies and mothers they murdered. "I say to my fellow journalists, you can be a good journalist and tell the truth, even when your own country is in the wrong."

The dispirited detachment that had hung over me earlier began to lift. It was almost possible to believe, listening to these fresh voices, that the United States could change, and the undercurrent had already begun to shift. Later, Mr. Linder's friend George Moore told me: "I believe that the opposition is growing, in church movements and on campuses, and that within two years the people's resistance to the war will change from a passive to an active one."

By the time the service ended, a current of enraged grief ran through the crowd. And when the last singer said, quietly but resonantly, "Ben Linder. *Presente!*" mine were not the only eyes that stung with tears.

I came home, still shaken by the young man's death, and found my husband watching the TV news. The blonde, handsome, angry face of Florida Representative Connie Mack filled the screen. "You asked for it," he was yelling in cold-steel tones. The camera moved to the shocked faces of Mr. Linder's parents, who had gone to the subcommittee on foreign affairs to talk about how the contras had shot their son in the head as he lay on the ground. "You come here to blame your country, the president, and the people who are fighting for freedom," the Republican congressman ranted. He accused them of "politicizing" their grief.

The contras are terrorists – bumbling, corrupt, but crudely vicious. They rob, rape, and murder Nicaraguan peasants. Their Washington sponsors seem like lunatics, or worse. I turned off the television and went to bed. A question danced before me in the dark.

What has Canada said publicly to the United States about this crazy war?

The answer came at me in the dark. Canada has maintained a cowardly public silence. Canada has said nothing. Canada is complicit.

If American rat-pack journalism got me down, the irrepress-
ible wit and courage of American dissenters were endlessly
refreshing. When I first arrived in New York, President
Reagan's attorney general, Edwin Meese, was mounting a
full-scale legal attack on affirmative action. Affirmative
action plans had been widely entrenched in the United States
since the late 1960s, and they had made a stunning impact in
opening doors to blacks and women. To my surprise, the
staunchest opposition to the Reagan attack was coming from
the National Association of Manufacturers. After ten years of
enforced compliance, the country's biggest industries were
happy with the results, claiming that they had a more productive, more contented and diverse work-force.

I started to call corporate spokesmen to verify this surprising report. In Canada, phone calls like these are certain to
end in dull evasions – corporate verbiage designed to muffle
opinion. On the one hand, this, on the other hand, that.

I reached William McEwen, chairman of the Resources
and Equal Opportunity Committee of the manufacturers'
association, which represented 13,500 U.S. companies and
85 per cent of America's manufacturing jobs. I told him that
Canadian industry was furiously opposed to mandatory
affirmative action and was insisting that government make
any such plan purely voluntary.

"There's no such thing as voluntary compliance with
affirmative action laws," said Mr. McEwen promptly, in his
rolling Southern voice. "If voluntary compliance worked,
Moses would have come down from the mountain with the
Ten Guidelines."

I thought I had died and gone to journalists' heaven.
Every company official I spoke to gave me immediate, vigorous, and colourful answers.

American self-confidence may seem obnoxious to out-
siders, especially when it's in the service of aggressive foreign
policy or Neanderthal domestic goals. But we tend to forget
that the American opposition has the same buoyant sense of
entitlement. Brawling, boisterous, or impassioned, Americans fight their political battles with a degree of forthright-

ness and humour that seems almost inconceivable in Canada.

I was brought up in an era when the universal Canadian dictum seemed to be, "If you don't have anything nice to say, don't say anything." Critics and opponents of the mainstream were seen as *ill-mannered*. (William Kilbourn, York University historian, tells a joke he claims was circulating in New York in 1988: Why does a Canadian cross the road? Answer: to get to the middle.) Defiant gestures were – and still are – severely frowned upon. Recently, a Toronto lawyer, Susan Eng, was appointed to the police commission, and declined to swear fealty to the Queen when taking her oath of office. One of the most enlightened and able columnists in the *Globe and Mail* attacked her in the harshest possible terms – for what strikes me as a relatively mild gesture of nationalist sentiment.

Americans have a thoroughly different approach to dissent. After sixties radical Abbie Hoffman committed suicide in the spring of 1989, a *Village Voice* writer reminisced about Hoffman's prolific invention of funny and dramatic protests against the Vietnam war. Hoffman, she reported, had once said that true liberty was the freedom "to cry 'Theatre!' in a crowded fire."

New Yorkers are indefatigable when it comes to crying theatre. Time and again, my New York friends jostled me to look at things in a new light. When the Baby M case – in which surrogate mother Mary Beth Whitehead changed her mind about handing over her baby and was taken to court by the couple who had hired her – became the biggest news story in the city, I dallied for several weeks, unable to penetrate the rights and wrongs of the case. I am a critic-at-large by profession, with strong opinions, but I'm also a Canadian. Before I reach a conclusion, I often find myself mentally deferring to authority, doubting my own instincts, deciding I must be mistaken. I wanted to empathize with Mary Beth Whitehead in the Baby M case. But public opinion was so unanimous, so vociferous. . . . I found myself thinking, "But if the *judge* says. . . . If *all* the media agree. . . ."

■

Esther Broner called me to point out the misogynist bias of the news stories. Phyllis Chesler, already overburdened with work, organized a demonstration outside Noel Keane's Manhattan clinic. (Keane, a lawyer, had set up a lucrative surrogate brokerage.) There, I met and interviewed dozens of knowledgeable and articulate protestors; Phyllis plied me with documents, transcripts, articles. I went home and began to read the newspaper accounts of the case with a more critical eye. By the time the judgement was handed down, I was ready.

Everyone knew that Mary Beth Whitehead, a perfectly good mother, was going to lose – the courtroom bias and public fury against her were obvious – but the harshness of the decision that stripped her of all her maternal rights was extraordinary. The natural claim of motherhood has been dismissed as though she were a robot. Judge Harvey Sorkow has made it official now: middle-class self-control and material advantages, rather than mother love, are "in the baby's best interests."

Mrs. Whitehead was publicly pilloried for breaking her contract, as though contracts are sacred and not broken every day by businessmen and baseball players. And this contract – $10,000 in exchange for a baby – seems to flout the anti-slavery laws, not to mention the laws against payment for adoption. And what is so contemptible about a woman who refuses the money and risks everything to keep the baby she has nurtured and breast-fed for four and a half months?

Like many another woman with no education and no money, Mrs. Whitehead willingly signed an agreement that made her a virtual slave. William Stern had the right to control her body. He demanded that she have amniocentesis, and she did, over her doctor's objections. He also had the right to demand that she have an abortion if the baby were less than perfect. All the risk was hers: if she miscarried in the first four months, she would receive no fee at all – and only $1,000 if she miscarried later. If she were damaged, or if she died, he was free and clear. He wasn't even obliged to take the baby. The contract was for the payment of $10,000 only if, and when, he accepted delivery of a flawless, custom-bred baby. If that's not trafficking in human beings, what is?

Yet, in court, Judge Sorkow refused to hear testimony about the contract being in conflict with public policy. He insisted on evidence being limited to "the best interests of the baby," and then refused to hear Mrs. Whitehead's experts in mother-infant bonding, or on the effects of separation on the baby. How impartial was he? Long before the trial, he gave the Sterns an *ex parte* order for custody of the five-week-old infant, without the Whiteheads' knowledge or presence at the hearing.

Judge Sorkow was palpably impatient and hard-line with Mrs. Whitehead's lawyer during the trial, but allowed wide and sometimes shocking latitude to the Sterns' sleek, high-powered counsel, even letting him grill Mrs. Whitehead on the irrelevant misdeeds of her relatives.

It felt like a Salem witch trial: attention blazed narrowly on Mrs. Whitehead's faults, her unfitness, her low-class taste, while the groomed and thin-lipped Sterns slipped quietly in and out of court, unharassed and unquestioned. "Experts" testified, asininely, that Mary Beth Whitehead played pat-a-cake the wrong way, and that she was pathologically narcissistic for dyeing her prematurely white hair black.

I think Mrs. Whitehead was "gaslighted." Mr. Stern, listening to her anguish on the long-distance phone, coolly taped her as she was goaded, by his frozen impassivity and unresponsiveness, to more and more frantic and silly threats. She sounded crazy, but any devoted mother of a newborn can imagine making crazy threats if armed sheriffs came to take that baby away forever.

And what about the Sterns, those culturally ambitious, affluent ($90,000 a year) people? Their fitness to parent was never closely scrutinized, though this was in effect a custody trial. Here's a couple that never tried to conceive and never approached an adoption agency. Betsy Stern is fertile, but the Sterns concealed this fact from Mrs. Whitehead. New York hospitals are spilling over with abandoned babies, but Mr. Stern thought a baby of another race would make him "feel different."

Mrs. Whitehead was labelled "hysterical"; no one said the same of Mr. Stern, who screamed in court that his wife "might die" if she tried to have a baby. (Medical witnesses said that her "extremely mild" multiple sclerosis might improve during pregnancy. In any case, Dr. Stern, a pediatrician, never even consulted a physician about this supposed affliction until the court case was under way.)

Other remote-control fathers have quietly gone away when a surrogate mother changed her mind. Not Mr. Stern. He sent police to take the five-week-old infant from its mother, and slapped a lien on the impoverished Whiteheads' property.

What kind of man would make a pitch for public sympathy on the grounds that his relatives died in the Holocaust? I'll answer that. The same man who would marry a Methodist, impregnate a Catholic, pledge to raise the child Unitarian, and then lay claim to the child on the basis of carrying on his heritage.

There was enormous public sympathy with the Sterns. People admire successful professionals. Dr. Lee Salk, himself the victor in a bitter custody battle, called Mrs. Whitehead a "surrogate uterus." Such language is common in the surrogate business. As Gena Corea documents in her brilliant book, *The Mother Machine*, surrogate mothers are called "hatcheries," "vehicles," "incubators," "receptacles" – anything but humans with deep, wrenching, engulfing feelings they may not have dreamed of when they signed the preconception agreement.

Surrogates are poor women who rent their bodies to rich women who cannot, or will not, undergo pregnancy. It is ludicrous to talk of the women's rights to use their bodies as they please when they are, like prostitutes, so clearly without social and economic choices. We do not, after all, permit the sale of body organs.

Fertility is declining in our radiated, drugged, overmedicated age; now it's a scarce resource that prosperous men can buy. How chillingly reality mimics Margaret Atwood's novel *The Handmaid's Tale*, as the powerful scientific, legal, and medical establishments rush to support commercial baby farming.

This week, surrogate entrepreneur Noel Keane crowed about the judge's validation of "a man's right to procreate." A repugnant phrase, since it implies that a man's right to purchase and use the body of a woman and to appropriate her "product" should override a woman's human right to refuse.

Legal experts, on the other hand, almost unanimously condemned the ruling. One called Judge Sorkow "the little itty-bitty judge from Hackensack" and derided Sorkow's ruling that such inhumane contracts are legal. Others called on legislatures to make surrogate contracts unenforceable.

Jill Krementz, an author and an adoptive mother, commented to me: "The Sterns won't always have the judge with them. One day that child will be the judge; she'll look at what they did to her mother, who loved and fought to keep her, and she'll ruin their lives."

As it turned out, the Sterns may be spared that retribution. One year after the court case, Chief Justice Robert Wilentz of the New Jersey Supreme Court overturned Judge Sorkow's decision, restored Mary Beth Whitehead's maternal rights, ordered visitation rights for her, and outlawed surrogacy contracts in New Jersey. Such contracts, he said, agree in advance, for payment, which parent is to have custody, without any regard for the child's well-being. This "violates the policy of this state that the rights of the natural parents are equal . . . the father's right no greater than the mother's." Some contracts, he wrote, are not only not binding, but not legal: poverty will drive some people to agree to work in unsafe conditions, for example, but that doesn't make the contract lawful.

Point by point, Wilentz validated the feminist analysis of the case. He "could not conceive of any other case where a perfectly fit mother was expected to surrender her newly born infant, perhaps forever, and was then told she was a bad mother because she did not."

Wilentz excoriated Sorkow's harshness towards Mrs. Whitehead in the courtroom, and was particularly wry about the limits of Bill Stern's so-called right to procreate. "The custody, care, companionship and nurturing that follow birth are not parts of the right to procreation."

He reaffirmed that custody should be determined by the best interests of the child, pointing out that a child's happiness does not necessarily depend on money, and stressing that there are "values that society deems more important than granting to wealth whatever it can buy." Surrogacy, he said, was "no scientific miracle" but simply a new use of artificial insemination, and one whose "unregulated use can bring suffering to all involved."

The vigour with which New York feminists had protested the Baby M trial, long before its final outcome was clear, was a bracing example to me. It was not the only time I was to find myself chivvied along to fresh analyses by my New York friends. However liberated I thought I was before, however much an instinctive dissenter from accepted wisdoms, I frequently found myself hidebound compared to the daring intellectual forays of the people I met, listened to, and read in Manhattan. A history of sharp, articulate criticism, argument, dissent, and bold modernism made them far more ready than I to think the previously unthought.

■

Their attitudes to Israel were a case in point. Most of my friends had powerful ties to Israel; some had been born there, others had lived there for years; some had children serving in the Israeli army; most had an unshakable lifelong commitment to the survival of the state, and a long, arduous history of active support. Yet, from the first, they astonished me by their outspoken anger and anguish about the Israeli government's actions – and this was well before the intifada.

As a Canadian Jew of World War Two vintage, I had a lifetime habit of defensiveness, wariness, and closing the ranks against the hostility of more powerful groups. Closed ranks, I began to see in New York, too often meant closed minds.

I had grown up in Toronto in an era of open anti-Semitism; even when I was a child, I would read the newspaper and my heart would jump with alarm at any capital J in a news story, then settle back to its regular rhythm only when I saw that the word was "June" or "Jewellery." Public school, with its flags, its anthems, its pictures of the royal family and Tom Thomson's pine tree – public school represented Canada to me, and the full authority of the adult world. And for a Jewish child in a Gentile neighbourhood, public school was a gauntlet of thorns. The principal, some of the teachers, and many of the pupils were vociferously and demonstratively anti–Semitic. I learned a permanent wary distrust and sense of separation. When, as a young teenager, I discovered Labour Zionism, I discovered a philosophy that thrillingly promised dignity, cultural survival, enlightened statehood, and, above all, safety.

Even when Israel elected the right-wing Menachem Begin and sent its troops into Lebanon, even when I had to censure those actions severely in my own mind, I was stubbornly opposed to open criticism of our beleaguered state. To keep the faith, I had to blind myself to the just claims of Palestinians; luckily for my moral double standard, they made it easy for me with forty years of boycott, rejectionism, bloody-handed terror, and vicious public rhetoric. Israel's critics, too often ignorant of, or indifferent to, the painful history that lay behind

Israel's new belligerence, did not move me. Didn't I know those voices all too well from the school yard, accusing me every Christmas and Easter of killing Jesus?

In New York, the largest Jewish city in the world, my defensiveness melted away. Shocked at first by my friends' blithe openness, their reckless disregard of what "they" might think or how enemies might rejoice, I was nevertheless pushed and pulled to consider a new way of being loyal to Israel. Though the process was as painful and protracted as peeling off my outer layer of skin, I began to force myself to examine every preconception I had held dear. Reading history with new critical alertness, watching the escalatingly horrific news, I cried with anger and agony as I confronted, for the first time, sharp truths about my own much-battered people. I braced myself to put aside my bitterness at those critics of Israel who were motivated by prejudice: their motives were irrelevant. I dismissed, finally, my fury that Arabs have never been pressed to denounce forty years of Arab terrorism. Blame, hatred, and defensiveness could never help save lives, restore decency, and preserve Israel: only the truth, justice, and sanely pragmatic policies, so far as I could understand them, should matter.

I attended parlour meetings where visitors from Israel – articulate, intense military leaders, writers, and philosophers – begged us North Americans to take a stand against the occupation of the West Bank. Despite a lifetime of Canadian Jewish conditioning, of being taught to keep my head down and not make waves, I went on Canadian radio (*Morningside*) to talk about how difficult it was for Jews to criticize Israel. Finally, I marched, I signed petitions. And I did something crazy; I cried "Theatre!" in a crowded fire.

Well, it probably wasn't the proudest day in Canadian diplomacy (spouse division), but it sure as heck was satisfying.

I'd been hacking away at my computer all day; late in the afternoon, I went to the bedroom window to take a breather. The sidewalk facing our apartment was black and blue: black with a mob of three or four hundred Hasidim in their uniform black, ankle-length coats and black hats; blue with a thin line of shirt-sleeved New York police hemming them in.

Evidently, the Hasidim were there to demonstrate against Shimon Peres, foreign minister of Israel, who was in town to put a proposal for an international peace conference before the United Nations. Mr. Peres usually stays in the hotel next door to our apartment building.

Up to my window came the deep roar of the demonstrators, the hee-haw of police sirens as more and more cars wailed up, the good-natured admonitions of the police ("Back up, there; back up!").

Every now and then stray Hasidim wriggled past the barricades and into the traffic, poking handfuls of leaflets into car windows. Police officers would lope after them and herd them back; the street was white and yellow with spilled leaflets.

Gradually, the mob's roar took shape in my ears.

"Peres Hitler! Peres Nazi!"

I didn't believe it. I shoved the window higher, blocked the escaping cat with my elbow, and leaned out. Maybe they were saying, "Peres Nasty"?

No, I had heard right.

And suddenly I just couldn't stand it any more. All the world's unreasoning hatred went bubbling into my ears like the poison that killed Hamlet's father. The roaring Hasidim blurred into the all-male Iranian mob outside the Saudi Arabian Embassy last week, screaming, "Death to America! Destroy Israel!" behind another patient line of blue. And the Iranians blurred into the pointy-headed Klan, screaming against a brotherhood march down south last spring, and they blurred, too, into the phalanx of T-shirted young men I saw in Greenwich Village, carrying baseball bats and chanting, "We hate fags! We hate fags!"

■

All those Righteous Ones, with their certainties and their hatreds and their gross perversions of decent speech. To hear this horde of religious fanatics – Jews screaming "Nazi" at another Jew – was the ultimate profanity, the inexcusable debasement of the memory of the Holocaust.

I plunked the cat on the floor, slammed the window, and marched out of the apartment and into the elevator with such a militant air that the doorman took one look at me, burst out laughing, and said, "Going to throw rotten eggs?"

Not quite. But I strode across the block to the thick wall of black coats and said, to the first one I came to, "Did you call Peres a Nazi?" A smirk creased his white, fish-belly face. "Yes," he said with infantile satisfaction.

"Disgusting!" I snapped. "A disgusting disgrace to the Jewish people."

His face registered pure shock. Adrenalin racing, I waded farther into the mob, addressing my remarks to individual faces. "You call Peres a Nazi? Feh! A disgrace!"

"Wash your mouth out, you little smart alec!" I said to one startled pip-squeak. I was playing the quintessential Jewish mama of folklore and relishing every moment of it, especially my sudden realization that these big mouths were unnerved.

Now it got funny. Ripples ran through the furthest reaches of the crowd. They turned from the barricades along the street and began to yell at me, a long, mooing, wordless howl.

I planted my feet firmly in their midst, stuck my arms akimbo, and roared with as much force as I could combine with dignity, "*Shalom achshav!*" ("Peace now!" – the slogan and the name of Israel's largest peace group). The more they mooed at me, the more I shouted, "Peace now!"

It was gloriously surprising: a wall of stunned Hasidim circled me centrifugally, their eyes goggling between their jiggling side locks. Shock and fear registered on their pale, sweating faces. They seemed flabbergasted to have ventured so far outside their customary self-imposed ghetto and to have someone bellow back at them.

Objectively, I admit, it must have been a hilarious sight, this round, curly, female person standing very four-square in their midst and yelling triumphantly at them, one by one, "Hah! Peace!"

The circle around me began to buckle from the sheer weight of the bodies pressing in behind; scrawny Hasidim were bouncing off each other, arms flying, and, written on their faces, a paralysing conflict between a naked desire to kill and an awareness of certain pertinent biblical prohibitions.

Okay, I admit it, I was being as crazy as they were, yelling "Peace!" at every fixated extremist mob and cult in the world, all the maniacs who want to kill Turks or Jews or unbelievers or whoever doesn't agree with their tunnel-vision dogma.

But it felt wonderful. Just as they were beginning to surge against me, eyes panicky and mouths stretched with howling "Shame! Boo-oo!" a solid blue arm reached through the crush and circled through mine.

"This way, ma'am," said a voice as quietly firm and respectful as a headwaiter at Le Cirque.

I strolled serenely away, my police escort discreetly vanishing, the black sea parting on either side of me and then crashing back together (painfully, I hope) in my wake.

Maybe I wouldn't have done something quite so nutty in my home town, where ancient rules of conduct cling like cobwebby inhibitions. And I sure wouldn't have done it in Tehran or Jerusalem, where fanatics have the numerical ascendancy to act as violently as they feel. But New York is the perfect place to be a foreigner, and of all the absurd acts one may commit in a lifetime, shouting down a fundamentalist mob is surely the most pleasing that will ever come my way.

■

The freedom I felt to wade into that black-coated crowd was a token of my inward liberation from fixed opinion and hardened intellectual habits. That attitude – "This is New York, honey!" – of tough defiance and aggressive challenge had become a part of me, too.

At a more serious and deeper level, changing the way I thought and spoke about Israel, though difficult, was like living a new life and creating myself afresh, without the sad, bitter, deadening baggage of the past. All this moral and intellectual movement – so rare a gift in middle age, so exhilarating after the first pain abated – I owed to the critical liveliness of New York and the spiritual vigour of the people I came to know there.

Jane Jacobs wrote, "A city's very wholeness in bringing together people with communities of interest is one of its greatest assets, possibly the greatest." Marshall Berman, writing of New York as the quintessential capital of modernism, spoke of its "public dialogue which, since ancient Athens and Jerusalem, has been the city's most authentic reason for being." And Thomas Bender praised the modern metropolis for enabling "conversation in public"; New York itself, he said "has been and is itself a many-voiced conversation of unparalleled complexity . . . What holds people and ideas together, what brings them into contact in a way that does not happen elsewhere, is simply the glamour and excitement of it all."

In New York I found my community of interest; I joined that public dialogue for which I thirsted, and was stimulated and affirmed, every day, by that many-voiced conversation.

No wonder that, when I was back in Toronto, and sat down to write this book, I was leadenly stalled for week after week, until one night I began impulsively to describe the bustling streets and their beloved chaos, which, to me, signalled a whole way of being and thinking, a way of being alive to the world, to the past, and to change, that had been a revelation to me. I wrote a few pages and then burst into tears, allowing myself for the first time to admit and to mourn the end of the happiest sojourn of my life.

■

Before I left Manhattan, I had let the *Globe* know that I was leaving them, too: there didn't seem any point to writing a column if I couldn't write about New York. Saying good-bye to my readers and to my adopted city, I tried to sum up the terribly tangled complex of feelings inspired by that most fascinating of cities.

Sylvester Stallone walked past the front door of our apartment building last week, giving the doormen something to talk about.

"So, what do you think of the Rambo movies?" I asked, searching for a politely neutral response.

The doorman frowned. "Well," he said at last, "they're good movies; they don't hurt America none."

Knee-jerk chauvinism is one thing I'm not going to miss about New York when we move back to Toronto. What Canadian, after all, when asked for an opinion about a pop-trash movie, would first consider Canada's image?

That Americans are hyper-patriotic is a cliché, but until you live in the midst of mindless boosterism, you can't really appreciate how ridiculous it can be. I was present, for example, when a family court judge in New Jersey bullied and patronized the wife in a divorce case. She happened to be a Canadian Inuk. When her lawyer objected to the judge's near-racism, His Honour started screaming in court, full volume: "I'm an American! I love this country! It's the greatest . . ." His rant had nothing to do with the case; it was just his automatic response to any and all challenges.

A taxi driver, commenting on an admittedly stupid proposal for a cabbies' dress code, said, "This is America! I can do whatever I want."

The idea of limitless personal freedom, however illu-sory, is linked in American children's minds with their country's greatness. They grow up with the idea that "America" is the biggest, the best, the most powerful, the

■

country where naturally everyone in the world would want to live. It takes a strenuous effort of mind for an American to think that the French or Chinese or Canadians may actually prefer to be who they are.

The flip side of this conceit, at least here in New York, is an extraordinary warmth and generosity. Strangers talk to you on the elevator; friendships blossom in a day; live here a week and you belong. Contrary to ill-informed stereotypes, ordinary New Yorkers "get involved" – with lost, sick, or unfortunate strangers – to a degree I've never seen in my native Toronto.

And it would be hard to match New York's cultural ambition, or the population density, which supports close to a hundred universities and colleges, plus uncountable hundreds of theatres, galleries, and museums.

Toronto, despite its recent pretensions – mostly based on real-estate development – was never an intellectual hothouse. When twentieth-century ideas were shattering past certainties, we were snugly insular. Waves of immigrants, carrying the excitements of modernism with them, washed up on this shore, not Canada's. When World War Two brought European intellectuals and artists to North America, Canada thought that "none is too many."

And it's the remnants, the last backwash, of that intellectual intensity that give New York its special flavour. All the new novels about New York are sourly oblivious of what to me is the most real New York – the energetic, worldly, culturally alert middle class that provides a tolerant audience for all the avant-garde scribbling, thinking, painting, acting, dancing, and music-making that goes on here.

My heart leapt with a glad sense of being at home the very first week I was in Manhattan. I'd been scouring Toronto for a new novel by Lore Segal. Almost no one had heard of it; those who had hadn't yet seen a copy. I walked into the first bookstore I saw in New York, asked for the book, and the clerk said with friendly scorn, "Aw,

■

you and five hundred others! Sold out; come back in a week." Five hundred others! I felt like a new member of a commonwealth of readers.

No matter what your passion, you can indulge it here. The Big Onion: layers and layers of cultural life. Our family discovered a crackling black gospel musical, *Mama I Want To Sing!*, in a theatre on the edge of Harlem. We were the only whites in the audience that night, but never mind: we were swept up in a surge of musical high spirits and good fellowship that still makes us grin at the memory. And we were probably the only straight people one night at a performance of *Hamlette*, a hilarious, moving, thoroughly riveting transvestite performance of Shakespeare. It played in a seedy dump on the Lower East Side in a neighbourhood so grim you had to ring the buzzer to be admitted. It made Shakespeare so immediate and new that it brought tears to our eyes.

It's been glorious to be part of all that. But parting is only partly sweet sorrow: day by day, New York also displays more symptoms of the American diseases – crazy politics, violence, corruption, homelessness, social injustice, educational inequality, runaway real-estate speculation – that has victimized thousands and driven artists and workers into exile.

Among the things Americans don't have: real political choices; medicare; Smarties; HP Sauce; the CBC; Nancy White. And soon, I can't help feeling, they won't have much of New York left, either.

Symbols of the new crassitocracy are visible from my bedroom window. Five giant condos, all hideous and all tumescently out of scale, march across the skyline where there were none a scant few years ago. I used to see roof gardens, nineteenth-century copper roof ornaments, wooden water tanks, river, and bridges. Now, brassy towers impose their arrogant bulk and gloomy shadows across the view.

New York as an imperial capital still exerts a magnetic pull on many Canadians, a fascinated mingling of loath-

■

ing and love. I began this column three years ago when I moved here; what luck to be able to combine my delight in exploring the city with my job as a columnist. It's been, as the kids say, a slice. Now that I'm going home, it seems an appropriate time to move on to other tasks, and to say thank you, readers, and goodbye.

A Brief Guide to the Guides
■

There can never be too many guidebooks; I feast on them before I visit a new place, and they reliably reward me with a lively fund of anecdotes to enrich my perspective, a deepened understanding of what I'm seeing.

My years in New York were the first time, though, that I had a chance to live in a place I'd read about, use the guidebooks over an extended period of time, compare one with another, and weigh them against my own experience and discoveries.

In a sense, the novelists and poets are the best guides; New York would have been more one-dimensional for me without Walt Whitman, Herman Melville, Henry James, Edith Wharton, James Merrill, Frank O'Hara, Henry Roth (*Call It Sleep*), Kate Simon (especially *Bronx Primitive*), Elizabeth Bishop, Marianne Moore, E.B. White, Grace Paley (including her book of poems, *Leaning Forward*), and a dozen others.

Of course, I went a little mad in my devotions. Rummaging through the shelves of the New York Bound, a treasure-house of rare and out-of-print works about New York, I found books to charm the heart of the fanatic. I was sorely tempted to buy the original water-stained log-books, written in fading copperplate, of a ship that berthed in New York harbour. I did yield, happily, to Ashcan artist John Sloan's diaries (*New York Scene*), in which he tells of setting up a studio on 14th Street in the early 1900s, and then discovering that carpenters working in the flat next door had bored a hole in the wall in the fond fantasy that they could spy on his nude models (he didn't have any). Also at New York Bound, I pounced on *Come One! Come All!*, Don Freeman's light-hearted and sparkling memoir, complete with drawings, of his early years in New York. He had come from California hoping to work as a jazz trumpeter, and wound up

■

making a living as a newspaper theatre illustrator while creating his own lovable prints and paintings of New York life. The book is long out of print, but if you ever find a copy, you'll have one of the sunniest and most endearing accounts of Bohemian New York in the time of Fiorello LaGuardia.

The owner of New York Bound, which is now in Rockefeller Centre, is Barbara Cohen, who edited, with Seymour Chwast and Steven Heller, a delectable large-sized paperback anthology called *New York Observed: Artists and Writers Look at the City*.

Practical guidebooks to New York can fill several shelves; I'll mention here only those I found myself using and reusing. I began with the magnificent *WPA Guide to New York*, a massive paperback handsomely reproduced just as it first appeared in 1939. Subtitled "A Comprehensive Guide to the Five Boroughs of the Metropolis," this is the work of the Federal Writers' Project, a depression-era public-employment scheme for out-of-work writers, many of them later to be famous.

Sympathetic, populist and optimistic in tone, urbanely conversational, occasionally wry, and historically informed in style, the *WPA Guide* is still the best overall introduction to the city. Its many black-and-white photographs marvellously evoke the feel of that "last age of innocence," as its companion volume, *New York Panorama*, nostalgically calls it. *Panorama*, too, which consists of essays by the same group of talented writers (about New York art, music, language, Harlem, publishing, theatre, jazz), is a glowing example of urban appreciation. These books are emphatically not just nostalgia items; every time I discovered a new and interesting place in New York, I would find myself leafing through the two WPA books to see if it was mentioned. I frequently gained a historical perspective, learned long-since-neglected bits of city lore, and felt enriched by the sense of continuity in ideas as well as sights.

European visitors to New York can almost always be spotted standing in the middle of the sidewalk and consulting their green Michelin guides. The Michelin for New York is characteristically thorough, but I found it too stodgy in tone and almost oblivious to the jittery pulse of the streets and the allure of the eccentric. The Fodor's 1989 guide is the more satisfying of the traditionally organized tourist guides, more sprightly in style, and, because it includes shopping, restaurants, and hotels, more utilitarian. Penguin has a new (1989) guide to the city, which strives for hipness; though it is not nearly as thorough as the Fodor's, it is certainly more discriminating, more upscale and slightly off-beat in its recommended shops and restaurants. I would use it as an extra.

But the all-round winner, for me – the liveliest, most useful, convenient, and thorough – is *New York City Access* by Richard Saul Wurman. A tall paperback that will fit in a purse, *Access* gives you street-by-street, almost building-by-building information for each neighbourhood – restaurants, shops, architecture, parks, history, each with relevant details like prices, hours, and phone numbers. Each type of entry is colour coded. If you find yourself in the East Village, for example, and glance at the relevant section, say, on page 96, you will find: red entries for restaurants and clubs like the World, Cave Canem and Two Boots (an Italian-Cajun restaurant with see-through plastic bar); black entries for neighbouring historical sights – the New York Marble Cemetery tucked away down an alley, the City Lore folk-lore centre, the Anthology Film Archives in the Second Avenue Courthouse building; green entries for the stupendous Tower Records and a specialty toy shop. Any single page of *Access* could keep you busy, interested, amused, informed, fed, and watered for a whole day.

Access also features terrific snippets of local slang; celebrities' favourite hang-outs; excellent subway and neighbourhood maps; seating plans of theatres; charming sketches; useful phone numbers; tips on transportation; lists of the best walking tour organizations.

Walking tours are undoubtedly the best way for newcomers to learn the byways and hidden stories of New York, and the city abounds in colourful, dedicated tour guides, some of whose specialties are: ghosts, birds, deli, gospel singing, artists' studios. Consult the Manhattan yellow pages or check out the Municipal Art Society and the 92nd Street Y (at 92nd and Lexington) for good selections of specialized tours.

Many business districts in Manhattan print their own colourful, informative brochures; at my local library, the Donnell branch on 53rd Street, I picked up a terrific little map of the street, and similar leaflets are available in many locations. Central Park has an information booth with free maps and informative pamphlets, and even vest-pocket parks sometimes supply interesting brochures at the refreshment kiosk.

You can also concoct your own deeply pleasurable walking tours from books like Gerard R. Wolfe's *New York, Walking Tours of Architecture and History*. Wolfe is not only wonderfully knowledgeable but also deliciously anecdotal. As he guides you around lower Manhattan, for example, he brings alive the adventurers, thieves, dreamers, and daredevils who populated these streets a hundred years ago, while drawing your attention to the little alleys, windows, roofs, or restaurants that are enduring evidence of earlier days. I used Wolfe's book to plan a walking tour of Brooklyn Heights and Cobble Hill that is one of my fondest New York memories.

For the avid sightseer, there is no more complete and essential guide to New York architecture than the *AIA Guide to New York City* by Elliot Willensky and Norval White (for the New York Chapter of the American Institute of Architects). It was out of print but much recommended the whole time I lived in New York; by the time it was updated and reissued, I was back in Toronto. I read it anyway, delighting in its block-by-block analysis and history of the streetscape. It's not as leisurely and chatty as Wolfe, but it does have a sprinkling of amusing anecdotes to lighten the architecturally thorough text. Be warned: indispensable it may be, but far too heavy for any but the most intrepid to carry around.

If you have a long time to spend in New York, or already know its more popular sights, David Yeadon's *New York's Nooks and Crannies; Unusual Walking Tours in All Five Boroughs* is charming and useful. He not only guides you to completely out-of-the-way places like City Island (a time-warp fishing, oystering, and yachting village on an island in the Bronx), but also shares insider tips on downtown New York – don't eat in the tiny Chinese restaurants on Division Street on Monday; that's the chef's day off.

To get around the city, use the wide range of transportation maps available, and don't rely on the friendly but often wrong advice of strangers. Any subway token booth will give you a free map of the subway and bus system; the drawback is that it is awkward to unfold and to use without revealing yourself as a lost lamb. (An important protection against pickpockets and muggers is *not* to hang around distractedly consulting a map on subway platforms or street corners.)

For daily use, I swore by neat little *StreetWise* plastic maps, available for the transit system or for each neighbourhood and widely sold in tobacconists or bookshops. *StreetWise* maps are small enough to hold in the palm of your hand, durable and clear.

If I were unfamiliar with New York and had business to transact there, however, I would depend on *Flashmaps Instant Guide*, a small, business-like paperback with detailed maps for getting into, around, and out of the city by car, bus, and subway; listings of hotels, theatres, and restaurants, by district, with phone numbers; museum and gallery information; and address-finding charts. It is brisk, no-nonsense, and thoroughly useful.

Guidebooks, of course, no matter how frantically they update themselves, can't point you towards the latest in performance art, experimental music and theatre, special film series, or off-off-Broadway productions. Most visitors to New York are very well served by the listings and reviews in the *New Yorker* and the *Village Voice*.

The most frequent (and tricky) request of visitors to Manhattan is for a recommended restaurant and food guide. That's difficult; it depends so much on individual taste. Seymour Britchkey's *Restaurant Guide* was fun for his often hilarious and bitchkey descriptions of a restaurant's style and clientele; Mimi Sheraton's taste (*Favourite New York Restau-*

■

rants) was closest to mine – though not, of course, infallibly – and therefore most pleasing. She's particularly good at recommending specific dishes ... advice worth following when you are spending fifty or sixty dollars a person. *Gault and Millaut* was useless to me – a sort of yuppie foreigner's guide to the sleekest and most pretentious of New York. They loved what I loathed.

In practice, the guide I used most was *Zagat New York City Restaurant Survey*. Slim, terse, practical, this annually updated book depends on the write-in opinions of volunteer restaurant scouts; anyone who eats out a lot can be a Zagat critic. The result is surprisingly reliable. People who eat out, it seems, as compared to the more precious and rarefied restaurant critics, value the things that matter to me, too: how the food tastes, how comfortable the restaurant is, when it's open, how much it costs.

When I knew I was going to be out exploring on foot all day in an unfamiliar neighbourhood, I often slipped *Passport To New York Restaurants*, by John Mariani and Peter Meltzer, into my pocket. It's smaller and thinner than a pack of American cigarettes, and offers compact, useful information, street by street, on hundreds of restaurants. Just the thing to consult when it's lunch-time and you're wandering in SoHo, TriBeCa (TRIangle, BElow CAnal), or SOFI (SOuth of the FlatIron).

My favourite food book of all is *The Food Lovers' Guide to the Real New York* by Myra Alperson and Mark Clifford, a guide to small ethnic food stores, restaurants, and markets in all five boroughs, complete with folksy photographs and excellent directions on getting there. I often followed their suggestions (to Little Italy in the Bronx, to Italian caffès on the Lower East Side, to Greek bakeries and Italian sausage factories in Hell's Kitchen, and to Arab food in Brooklyn) and was never disappointed.

Inveterate shoppers can extend their range by consulting a shopping guide. *The Village Voice Guide to Manhattan's Hottest Shopping Neighbourhoods* is a particularly dangerous stimulant to consumer madness. I've tracked down incredible bargains with a guide to the Lower East Side and consulted a number of guides to "kids' New York" for young visitors. Then there

■

are highly specialized travel books – for Jewish sightseers and kosher eaters, for example. The most engaging and useful of these is *The Rough Guide to New York* by Martin Dunford and Jack Holland, which has a cheerfully low-budget, counter-culture slant and plentiful references to gay and lesbian resources. In its dissident tone and its politically frank and sophisticated brief history of the city, this is a quintessentially New York guide.

Find all these books, and more, at Doubleday on Fifth. For another excellent (and more serious) collection of guide-books, don't miss the Urban Centre Bookstore in the beautiful historic Villard Houses at Madison Avenue and 51st Street. Members of the Municipal Art Society, an important urban preservationist group, get a discount.

No matter which art form is your particular passion – opera, jazz, chamber music, dance, film, sculpture, abstract painting or figurative, novels, or poetry – pursuing it in New York, through specialized performances, bookstores, libraries, and archives, will be rewarding in itself, and will also pull you deeper into the life of the city in a way no guidebook ever can. My husband and I, for example, developed a passion for the Ashcan School while we lived in New York. Their prints were chosen to illustrate this book, in part because their affectionate tribute to the city's energy and diversity remains as fresh and pertinent today as it ever was. And, as figurative artists, the Ashcan group and their later descendants – as well as those who are loosely linked to them in feeling, if not in style, like Raphael Soyer and Jacob Laurence – bring the earlier city alive before our eyes.

Tracking down their works led us into a tantilizing network of galleries, public and private, used bookstores, and print shops. There we met equally besotted *aficionados* whose knowledge, and enthusiastic willingness to share it with neophytes, drew us deeper into a web of connection with the animating ideas of the city and its past. The Ashcan artists, turn-of-the-century painters who defied stuffy academic convention in order to depict the robust lives of ordinary people (and Bohemians) in New York, favoured the medium of lithographs because they were democratically accessible. To me, the Ashcan painters represent New York's best qualities, now almost eclipsed: tolerance, humour, vitality, indignation and political protest, an enthusiasm for simple pleasures and amusements, scorn for the pretensions of wealth, and democratic egalitarianism.

The Ashcan label now loosely applies to John Sloan's followers and later realists. Look for the works of Sloan, Reginald Marsh, George Bellows, Stuart Davis (better known as a brilliant modernist, but an early student of Sloan, too), Howard Cook, Mabel Dwight, Peggy Bacon and Glenn O. Coleman, as well as Martin Lewis, Minna Citron, and Don Freeman; they will lead you on to many others for whom New York was an inspiration.

The Whitney has the largest collection of Ashcan artists in New York, though few are on regular display. But you can find their works at the following private galleries: Kraushaar, Sylvan Cole, Associated American Artists, Harbour, and Sragow. (Private galleries in New York are not intimidating; they welcome lookers and explorers as well as buyers.)

New York is inexhaustible, and so are the books that will unfold its secrets to you. I'll mention only two more that I loved. First, Jerome Charyn's *Metropolis, New York as Myth, Marketplace and Magic Land*, a racy, sharp, wise-guy insider's look at Manhattan by an abrasively bright immigrant's son. I especially relished the portraits of little-known fascinating and important people, like Douglas Leigh, the lighting engineer who invented the smoking Camels billboard, made Fred Astaire dance across an electric sign, and came back in the 1970s to bathe the skyscrapers in coloured lights . . . or Roxy, the slum kid who built a palace on Broadway and gave his name to a thousand movie houses.

And then there's Marshall Berman's *All That's Solid Melts into Air*, a vigorous, heartfelt, intellectually stirring work of cultural history about the meaning of modernity. The whole book is movingly suffused with Berman's loving, angry homage to the infinitely mesmerizing world capital of modernism, New York.

■

End Notes

■

CHAPTER I

Page 20: "rumoured to have been based on a mason's seive."
Bernard Rudofsky, *Streets for People*, Van Nostrand Reinhold,
1982.

page 20: William H. Whyte, *City, Rediscovering the Centre*,
Doubleday, 1988.

page 21: Senegalese pedlars. In 1987, Donald Trump
demanded that the city sweep the pavement of Fifth Avenue
clean of pedlars. The city complied; the pedlars relocated to
Madison Avenue. The new rich insist on cosmetic changes,
but maybe this tendency is not so new. On the Major Deegan
Expressway, as you head north out of the city through the
Bronx, you could see gaily coloured curtains painted by the
city onto the blank windows of abandoned apartment buildings. This loony hypocrisy was rescinded in 1989.

page 28: By summer of 1989, the mustard "spritzers" (they
had a name by now) had spread to Fifth Avenue, where they
tried their scam on a New York woman who had won several
marathons. They were foiled.

page 30: "Maybe the preponderance of blacks and Hispanics
. . ." Alan H. Levine, a civil-rights lawyer who represented
some 42nd Street movie owners in a suit against Times
Square developers, made this claim in the *New York Times*,
Saturday, March 19, 1988.

page 33: "The Spoils of the Park," a pamphlet, privately
printed in 1882, and reproduced in *Landscape into Cityscape*,
edited by Albert Fein, Van Nostrand Reinhold, 1981.

page 37: Roller skaters in Central Park. Mimi Kramer, drama
critic of the *New Yorker*, remarked in the May 15, 1989 issue

■

that it is "against city dweller rules" to comment on the park roller skaters, street musicians, Zabar's [a spectacular food store] or other "colourful" sights, because to comment on them is to sentimentalize them. Luckily for uncool outlanders, we don't have to live by such stringently hip codes of conduct.

page 38: According to New York City police, quoted in *New York Newsday* on April 21, 1989, after the rape, "Central Park is by far the lowest crime precinct in New York City." There were only two murders in the park in 1988, and only two reported rapes from January to April, 1989.

page 43: Operation GreenThumb is run by the city's Department of General Services; phone them for more information.

CHAPTER 2

page 56: New York audiences hooted with knowing delight at the scene in the movie *Crossing Delancey* in which single women, on the way home after work, avoid each others' eyes as they circle the steam table at a Korean deli, filling plastic boxes for a lonely take-out dinner.

page 59: Frederick Law Olmsted, quoted by Thomas Bender, in *New York Intellect*, Alfred A. Knopf, 1987.

page 83: Beach Pneumatic subway, described by Stan Fischler, *Uptown, Downtown: A Trip through Time on New York's Subways*, Hawthorn/Dutton, 1976.

CHAPTER 3

page 87: "cataclysmic money." Jane Jacobs, *The Death and Life of Great American Cities*, Vintage, 1961.

page 89: The quotations from Tom Wolfe in this chapter are drawn from Toby Thompson, "The Evolution of Dandy Tom," *Vanity Fair*, October 1987.

page 88: "Homeboy" is a New York term for a black youth who exaggerates ghetto characteristics in a highly stylized way: flopping Adidas, chunky gold jewellery, radio constantly tuned to rap music, swaggeringly springy walk.

Among ghetto youths, it's also a term of endearment: "Yo, my man, my homeboy!"

page 97: Vreeland is quoted by Debora Silverman in *Selling Culture*, Pantheon, 1986. I lived in the same apartment building as the reclusive Vreeland, but never saw her.

page 99: Julie Baumgold, "Dancing on the Lip of the Volcano," *New York*, November 30, 1987.

page 112: Eleanor Holmes Norton, "Restoring the Traditional Black Family," *New York Times Magazine*, June 3, 1985.

CHAPTER 4

page 120: "the upwardly mobile black population." It's important to note that this is the view of an outsider. An incisively different view of "the glass ceiling" that bars middle-class professional blacks from the highest rungs of the ladder is presented by David Jones in *Dissent* magazine's special issue on New York, Fall, 1987. Jones makes the point that talented black students on scholarship at prep schools and Ivy League universities feel they have earned special privilege as part of the "meritocracy." But their success in the middle-class effectively prevents them from establishing solidarity with or providing political leadership for less privileged blacks. Thus, when they finally are brought up short by invisible barriers to professional advancement, they may be personally devastated, lacking a racial and political perspective.

page 128: Douglas Martin, in the *New York Times*, on April 25, 1988, reported that at festivities staged by the New York State Rifle and Pistol Clubs, a Queens anti-crime organization called the Good Samaritans gave Goetz a plaque that honoured him for "wasting four vicious criminals and humiliating a gutless District Attorney." A smiling Goetz said, "The judge should have sentenced me to a testimonial dinner or a ticker tape parade."

page 129: Donald Trump's ad appeared in all four daily papers on May 1, 1989.

page 130: Al Sharpton. See William Bastone, Joe Conason, Jack Newfield, and Tom Robbins, "The Hustler," in the *Village Voice*, February 2, 1988, and Playthell Benjamin, "Jive At Five: How Big Al and the Bully Boys Bogarted the Movement," in the *Village Voice*, July 19, 1988.

page 134: Don Terry, "During Week of an Infamous Rape, 28 Other Victims Suffer in New York," *New York Times*, May 29, 1989.

page 135: Nina Bernstein, "A Child's Garden of Curses," *New York Newsday*, April 6, 1988.

page 142: On June 23, 1989, the *New York Times* published a poll that showed that 61 per cent of New Yorkers think race relations are generally bad. A resounding 60 per cent of whites and 51 per cent of blacks thought a mayor could do a lot to improve race relations.

CHAPTER 5

page 149: Grace Paley's books are *The Little Disturbances of Man*, Doubleday, 1958 and Penguin, 1985; *Enormous Changes at the Last Minute*, Penguin, 1975; *Later the Same Day*, Penguin, 1986; and a collection of poems, *Leaning Forward*, Granite Press, 1985.

CHAPTER 6

page 183: Though New Yorkers seem to have given up on achieving change through the political system, they are extremely active on a local level through what they call "community boards" – neighbourhood activist groups. Hundreds of such community groups monitor development in their areas, agitate for low-income housing, and deal with city agencies on a quasi-official basis. The Lotus Garden, described in Chapter One, owes its existence to fierce lobbying of the developer by local activists. Major developments and irresponsible city schemes are often halted, at least temporarily, by these characteristically vocal and alert community groups.

page 187: Vince ("Fish") Cafaro, quoted in the *New York Times*, April 30, 1987.

page 188: Father Louis Gigante. See William Bastone, "God's Bailbondsman," *Village Voice*, June 20, 1989.

page 188: Fake Vermont birth certificates. See *New York Times*, December 4, 1987.

page 189: Corrupt Children's Aid. See *New York Times*, March 14, 1988.

page 189: Vito Castellano. See William Bastone, "The Armory Advantage," *Village Voice*, June 14, 1988.

page 197: Jack Newfield and Wayne Barrett, *City for Sale, Ed Koch and the Betrayal of New York*, Harper and Row, 1988.

page 199: After it was made known publicly that Roy Cohn, who had consistently denied his homosexuality, had died of AIDS, his dear friend William F. Buckley, Jr., changed his mind about the necessity of forcibly tattooing all AIDS carriers. Cohn was correctly described by John Hess as "one of the most repulsive figures of our times" (*New York Observer*, April 25, 1988).

page 202: Roger Starr, quoted in the *New York Observer*, October 3, 1988.

page 205: Harry Macklowe, in an article by Charles Bagli in the *New York Observer*, May 30, 1988.

CHAPTER 7

page 235: Bronx school board corruption. See the *New York Times*, January 27, 1989, and May 21, 1989.

page 236: Williamsburg school board. Lynnell Hancock, "Race and Power," *Village Voice*, April 25, 1989.

page 238: Bruce Lambert wrote, "In this generation in New York City alone, experts estimate that 50,000 to 100,000 children will lose at least one parent to AIDS or have already done so." His article appeared on page one of the *New York*

■

Times on July 17, 1989. Since most cases of heterosexually transmitted AIDS are occurring in the black and Hispanic communities, this means an agonizing new burden for New York's minority children. The number of children in foster care has doubled in the past two years, due to crack and AIDS.

CHAPTER 8

page 268: *Fit to Print*, Lyle Stuart Inc., 1988.

page 268: James LeMoyne, *New York Times*, February 29, 1988.

page 285: Jane Jacobs, *The Death and Life of Great American Cities*, Vintage, 1961.

page 285: Marshall Berman, *All That Is Solid Melts into Air*, Penguin, 1988.

page 285: Thomas Bender, *New York Intellect*, Alfred A. Knopf, 1987.

page 287: "None is too many" was the phrase used by Canada's director of immigration to describe how many Jews fleeing Hitler's Europe would be allowed into Canada. Irving Abella and Harold Troper documented the era and made the phrase into a grim symbol of Canada's official anti-Semitism. See *None Is Too Many*, Lester and Orpen Dennys, 1982.

List of Illustrations

■

COVER: "New York Night" (lithograph), 1931, by Howard Cook.

CHAPTER ONE: "In Central Park" (lithograph), WPA period, by Mabel Dwight.

CHAPTER TWO: "Bookstalls" (wood engraving), 1931, by Howard Cook.

CHAPTER THREE: "The Passing Show" (lithograph), 1941, by Don Freeman.

CHAPTER FOUR: "A Breadline, New York" (wood engraving), 1935, by Clare Leighton.

CHAPTER FIVE: "Greetings from the House of Weyhe 1929" (wood engraving), 1929, by Howard Cook.

CHAPTER SIX: "Harbour Skyline" (soft-ground and aquatint), 1930, by Howard Cook.

CHAPTER SEVEN: "School's Out" (lithograph), 1936, by Don Freeman.

CHAPTER EIGHT: "Times Square Sector" (etching), 1930, by Howard Cook.

"In Central Park," "Harbour Skyline," "Greetings from the House of Weyhe 1929," and "School's Out" are from the Print Collection, Miriam and Ira D. Wallach Division of Arts, Prints and Photographs, the New York Public Library; Astor, Lenox and Tilden Foundations.

"New York Night" ("City Night"), "Bookstalls," and "Times Square Sector" are from the Philadelphia Museum of Art; given by Carl Zigrosscr.

"The Passing Show" and "A Breadline, New York" are from a private collection.